ENVIRONMENTAL CONFLICT RESOLUTION

Edited by
Christopher Napier

CAMERON MAY
LONDON

Copyright © Cameron May 1998
Reprinted 2000

Published 1998 by Cameron May Ltd. 69-71 Bondway, London SW8
1SQ. Tel: +44 (0)171 582 7567 Fax: +44 (0)171 793 8353
E-Mail: nickmay@cameronmay.com
World Wide Web: http://www.cameronmay.com

ISBN 1 874698 66 X

Printed by T J I Digital

University (

Subject to statu:
via you

http://voya

Exeter 1
Exmouth
Plymouth

ENVIRONMENTAL
CONFLICT
RESOLUTION

CONTENTS

About the Authors..9

Foreword...13

Chapter I
ENVIRONMENTAL CONFLICT RESOLUTION: THE AMERICAN EXPERIENCE

1. **Introduction**..16
2. **History**
    2.1   Early Experiments
    2.2   Financial Support
    2.3   Seminal Publications
    2.4   Government Experiments in Negotiated Rule Making
3. **Recent Trends**
4. **The Theory of Environmental Mediation**
5. **Special Difficulties Involved in Resolving Environmental Disputes**
    5.1   Identifying the Stakeholders
    5.2   Internal Discipline
    5.3   The Necessity of Government Approval
    5.4   Multiplicity and Complexity of Issues
    5.5   Bounding the Agreement: the Difficulty in Defining Terms
    5.6   The Economic Problem: Assigning Market Values to the Environment
    5.7   Conflicting Claims to Public Interest Representation
    5.8   Implementation
6. **What Practitioners Agree On**
7. **Holding the Mediator Accountable**
8. **The Strengths and Weaknesses of Mediation in Resolving Environmental Disputes**
    8.1   Strengths
    8.2   Perceived Weaknesses and Some Rebuttals
9. **The Transferability of Environmental Dispute Resolution (EDR) Theory as Practised in the United States: What can be Learned from the American Experience?**
10. **Obstacles to the Development of Indigenous Theory**
    10.1 Neutrality
    10.2 Transparency
    10.3 Commitment
    10.4 The Role of (and Belief in) Science

10.5   The Role and Responsibility of Government

Chapter II
ENVIRONMENTAL CONFLICT RESOLUTION IN GERMANY

1.   **Introduction**..60
2.   **The Politico-administrative and Legal Context**
      2.1   Development of Environmental Policy in Germany: a Brief
      Overview
      2.2   Policy Style and Legal Climate
      2.3   Changing Conditions for the Context for Environmental
             Cooperation
3.   **The Development of Environmental Dispute Resolution (EDR)**
      3.1   A Difficult Starting Point
      3.2   Overview
      3.3   Regulatory Action and Standard-setting
      3.3.1 Enforcement and Informal Administrative Activity
      3.3.2 Norm and Standard-setting Processes (Reg Neg)
             (1) Standard-setting
             (2) Technical Standard-setting
      3.4   Alternative Dispute Resolution (ADR) in Other Areas
4.   **The Mediation Procedure in the District of Neuss**
      4.1   Introduction
      4.2   Background Information on the District of Neuss
      4.3   Background to the Neuss Mediation Procedure
      4.4   Chronology of the Mediation Procedure
      4.5   How the Procedure Stands and Overview of the Results
      4.6   Results of Research into the Neuss Procedure
      4.7   Participants= Assessment of the Procedure
      4.8   Gravitational Force of Conventional Political Processes
      4.9   Conclusion
5.   **Experiences with EDR: Results, Problems and Advantages**
      5.1   A General Balance
      5.2   Problems
      5.3   Lawyers and EDR
      5.4   A Brief Résumé

Part III
ENVIRONMENTAL CONSENSUS-BUILDING AND CONFLICT
RESOLUTION IN THE UK

1   **Introduction**..115

2 **Reasons for the Emergence of Collaborative Processes in the UK**
    2.1   Problems with Current Procedures
    2.2   High-profile Environmental Conflicts
    2.3   Growing Awareness of Alternative Dispute Resolution (ADR)
    2.4   Developments in Community Participation
3 **Experiences with Collaborative Processes**
    3.1   Developments over the Last Five Years
    3.2   Current Uses of Collaborative Processes and Areas for Growth
            3.2.1   Local level
            3.2.2   National level
            3.2.3   European level
            3.2.4   Dialogues Initiated by Business
            3.2.5   Dialogues Initiated by National Government
            3.2.6   Dialogues Initiated by Local Government
            3.2.7   Mediation Inititated by Lawyers
            3.2.8   Investment in the Future and Prevention of Conflict
            3.2.9   Effects of the Regulatory Framework on Consensus-building Efforts
    3.3   Characteristics of Situations that are Appropriate for Consensus-building
    3.4   Benefits of Consensus-building
    3.5   Challenges Facing the Development of Collaborative Processes in the UK
4 **Practice of Collaborative Problem-solving in the UK**
    4.1   Stages of the Process
    4.2   The Facilitator
    4.3   Skills and Techniques
5 **Conclusions: Development Continues**

ChapterIV
THE PRACTICE OF COOPERATIVE ENVIRONMENTAL CONFLICT RESOLUTIONIN DEVELOPING COUNTRIES

1.   **Introduction**..168
2.   **Environmental Dispute Resolution (EDR): Contexts and Definitions**
3.   **A Continuum of EDR Approaches and Procedures**
    3.1   Command Decision-making
    3.2   Consultative Decision-making
    3.3   Co-operative Decision-making and Dispute Resolution

4.   **History and Applications of EDR in the Developing World**
5.   **Motivators and Perceived Advantages for Using EDR**
6.   **The Development of Practice and Institutional Arrangements for EDR**
     6.1   Domestic NGOs and Universities
     6.2   International Professional Conflict Management Practitioners and Firms
     6.3   International Non-Governmental and Governmental Development Agencies and Foundations
     6.4   Domestic Governmental Organisations
7.   **Some Institutional Models of EDR Programmes and Service Providers**
8.   **Possible Activities and Roles in Institutional Development**
9.   **Arenas of Applications: Appropriate Issues for EDR**
10. **Development of EDR Service Providers and Professionals**
11. **Further Development of EDR: Issues, Obstacles, Opportunities and Trends**
     11.1   Developing Culturally Appropriate Dispute Resolution Approaches and Procedures
     11.2   The Problem of Resolving Disputes in a Weak or Under-defined Legal/Regulatory Environment
     11.3   Resistance by Potential Parties
     11.4   Lack of Resource on the Part of Government Agencies and Public Interest Groups
12. **Conclusion**

Chapter V
THE PRACTICE OF MEDIATION IN COMMERCIAL
ENVIRONMENTAL DISPUTES

Introduction..197
1.   When are Mediation Techniques suitable?
2.   The Mediation Agreement
3.   The Pre-mediation Procedure
4.   The Mediation Process
5.   Failure to Agree
6.   The Settlement Agreement
7.   Case Study
8.   Conclusion

Appendices..209
Index..277

ABOUT THE AUTHORS

CHRISTOPHER NAPIER

Christopher Napier is a partner of Clifford Chance, the international law firm. He is based in London and specialises in the resolution of conflicts concerning environmental and health & safety matters, using mediation and facilitation, arbitration and litigation. After serving fourteen years as a Seaman Officer in the Royal Navy, mainly in submarines, he trained as a solicitor, qualifying in 1979, and became a partner of Clifford Chance in 1983.

Mr Napier was a founder partner of the Clifford Chance European Environment Group and has worked within it since 1989. He is a well-known expert in environmental law and dispute resolution. He has managed a number of high-profile and complex environmental cases in the higher Courts in England, and the resolution of environmental disputes using mediation. He is qualified to facilitate for the resolution of environmental conflict by process of consensus-building and stakeholder dialogue.

Christopher Napier speaks regularly at conferences and is the author of numerous papers and articles on environmental and health & safety matters. He is a member of the UK Environmental Law Association, of the Law Society of England & Wales, and of the International Bar Association.

PROFESSOR LAWRENCE SUSSKIND

Professor Lawrence Susskind is the Ford Professor of Urban and Environmental Planning at the Massachusetts Institute of Technology, and the first Executive Director of the Program on Negotiation at Harvard Law School, a consortium for the improvement of theory and practice in the field of dispute resolution.

Professor Susskind is one of the United States' most experienced public and environmental dispute mediators and an international figure in the dispute resolution field. He has served as court-appointed special master, trainer, and a mediator for neighbourhood, municipal, state and national agencies and organisations in North America, Europe and the Far East.

Professor Susskind is President of the Consensus Building Institute (CBI: see above). CBI facilitated the Workshop on Climate Change that brought together representatives from twenty-three nations and environmental organisations to consult on issues to be resolved at the Kyoto Conference, and the Policy Dialogue on Trade and the Environment that brought senior GATT/WTO officials together with international leaders of environmental organisations.

He is the publishers of Consensus, a quarterly newspaper distributed by the Public Disputes Network, and is author or co-author of nine books, including Dealing with an Angry Public, Reinventing Congress for the 21st Century, Environmental Diplomacy: Negotiating More Effective Global Agreements and Breaking the Impasse: Consensual Approaches to Resolving Public Disputes.

JOSHUA SECUNDA

Joshua Secunda is a Senior Enforcement Counsel for the Resource, Conservation and Recovery Act (RCRA) at the US Environmental Protection Agency's New England Region (EPA). He has served as the Regional enforcement lead for hazardous waste clean-up and permit matters under RCRA. In addition, he participates on the development of national enforcement policies and in the drafting of national enforcement guidances for EPA. He has also served as Legal Co-ordinator for Project XL, EPA's experimental program to encourage the development of innovative industrial technologies that are environmentally "friendly", as well as economically attractive.

Mr Secunda is a Senior Associate at the Consensus Building Institute (CBI), a not-for-profit organisation that provides mediation and dispute system design services to public and private clients worldwide. In this capacity, he has assisted in the facilitation of the Ocean Resources Roundtable involving multiple state and federal agencies, the hazardous waste remediation and redevelopment of the Massachusetts Military Reservation on Cape Cod in Massachusetts, and the international global warming workshop in Schlangenbad, Germany, during which representatives from twenty-three nations and environmental organisations came together to confer on their countries' varying positions to be presented at the Kyoto Conference.

He is a graduate of Tufts University (BA cum laude), the Boston College School of Law (JD), the Vermont Law School (Master's in Environmental Law and Public Policy, magna cum laude) and Harvard University's Kennedy School of Government (Master's in Public Administration). He is the co-author, with Professor Susskind, of The Risks and the Advantages of Agency Discretion: Evidence from EPA's Project XL.

DR HELMUT WEIDNER

Dr Helmut Weidner is a political scientist and Senior Researcher at the Social Science Research Centre Berlin. His main field of research is international comparison of environmental policies and politics. He is co-director of the research group on environmental mediation and completed a seminar on Advanced Conflict Resolution at the Banff Centre for Management in Canada. Dr Weidner's recent publications include National Environmental Policies: A Comparative

Study of Capacity Building, Springer: Berlin, New York 1997 (coedited with Martin Jänicke); Successful Environmental Policy: A Critical Evaluation of 24 Cases, Edition sigma, Berlin 1995 (coedited with Martin Jänicke); Basiselemente einer erfolgreichen Umweltpolitik, Edition sigma, Berlin 1996.

HALLY INGRAM
Hally Ingram is the Manager of The Environment Councils mediation and facilitation services, which she was instrumental in setting up in the UK over five years ago. She has practised as a community mediator and environmental facilitator and has extensive experience in the design of participatory processes. In 1996 she was awarded a Winston Churchill Fellowship to research how collaborative processes are used to resolve disputes and make decisions in environmental and public policy in the US. Hally has managed many participatory projects relating to the environment and sustainable development at the local, national and international levels. Recent examples include stakeholder workshops about the Camisea Gas Project in Peru, consulting communities about the development of local plans, such as housing allocation, and enabling different interest groups to explore the implications of genetically modified organisms.

ROBIN L JUNI
Robin Juni is an attorney in the international law firm of Jones, Day, Reavis & Pogue, and an adjunct professor at The George Washington University Law School in Washington, D.C. Much of the research for her section of this work was completed while Ms. Juni held an Atlantic Fellowship in Public Policy at the Oxford Centre for Socio-Legal Studies in 1996-97.

DR CHRISTOPHER W. MOORE
Dr Christopher W. Moore is a Partner of CDR Associates, a collaborative decision-making and conflict management firm based in the United States. He is an internationally known mediator and facilitator, a dispute systems designer and a trainer in environmental and public dispute resolution. He has worked in the field of conflict management in twenty-one countries in Africa, Asia, the Middle East, Latin America, and Pacific regions.

Dr Moore has successfully resolved disputes in the US over air emissions policies, regulation of mining activities, dam and hydropower development and operations, protection of threatened or endangered species, growth management and land use issues. Some of his international environmental projects include: consultations with the Indonesian Ministry of the Environment to establish a nation-wide water pollution dispute resolution system; work with the Turkish and Polish Ministries of the Environment, Russian regional environmental agencies and corporate and non-governmental organisations in these countries to introduce environmental conflict management procedures into institutional decision-making structures; and design and implementation of international negotiation training seminars for the Palestinian National Negotiating Team participating in multi-lateral Middle East peace talks on water and the environment.

Other public dispute projects include: consultation and training for the Organization of American States to develop negotiation procedures for use by the government and popular organisations to implement peace accords that ended a 36-year long civil war; consultation with the National Peace Committee and National Peace Accord Structures in South Africa to establish regional and local peace committees to address and resolve potentially violent political conflicts; development and establishment of municipal Multicultural Cooperation Committees in a number of Bulgarian cities, to prevent and address conflicts between ethnic Bulgarians, Turks and Rom; and mediation design and training for judges and staff of the Haitian and Sri Lankan Ministries of Justice to establish nation-wide mediation services to resolve civil disputes. Dr Moore is the author of numerous articles and books including The Mediation Process: Practical Strategies for Resolving Conflict (Jossey-Bass, Ca.: Second Edition, 1996), and was formerly a Vice President of the Society of Professionals in Dispute Resolution (SPIDR).

Foreword

In recent times environmental issues have come increasingly to be seen as real issues. Multiple factors have contributed to the pressures and strains on the environment, including competition for resources at cheap prices, growth in population, urbanisation and vehicle use, declining water supply and quality, emissions from industrial plants, production of ever greater quantities of waste, and decline in biodiversity. In differing degrees of severity, these issues apply to every region of the world.

Whilst the long-term objective of many is for the environment to be favoured over commercial and short-term interests, this is by no means true of all; and the poverty and competition which would result from a real halt to commercial development would probably be more destructive to the environment than continuing the present trend of development. The overall balance which needs to be struck is "sustainable development", but this concept is difficult to apply to specific situations and to development projects in the face of local competing interests and views. The result is environmental conflict between the various interests.

The cost of installing new process technology and remediating contaminated land has ensured that environmental matters are now an intrinsic part of commercial life, whether in the running of an industrial installation, the purchase of land, a merger or acquisition, or a finance transaction. One consequence is that environmental conflict now arises in the commercial context, between buyers and sellers, lenders and borrowers, operators of industrial plants and their regulators and neighbours, and in many other commercial concerns.

The formal land-use planning and litigation mechanisms traditionally used for resolving these types of environmental conflict can be costly, and are designed around an intended outcome of one participant as the winner and the other participants as losers. In some cases these mechanisms remain the appropriate or only way of resolving the conflict, but in others a better resolution of the competing interests can be found by seeking a different solution, and one which carries a high degree of consensus amongst the participants and other interested parties, a so-called "win-win" result. Such consensual solutions very often result in benefits for the environment and sustainable development, and greater long-term commitment from the interested parties. In some countries the traditional formal mechanisms hardly exist in practical terms, or cannot be relied on, and so other mechanisms must be found to resolve environmental conflict.

It is in this context that mediation and facilitation techniques are becoming commonly used in the United States, Europe and developing countries as a way of reaching consensual solutions to environmental conflict and disputes. These techniques are finding increasing support and interest within government, local government, regulators, business, legal systems and courts, and the public. In the context of new projects, their flexibility allows all interested parties to become involved in the environmental debate, and to contribute their views in a manner and at a cost appropriate to their interest and resources. In commercial disputes the use of these techniques opens the way to a solution which is good for all those involved. In countries where formal dispute resolution mechanisms are unreliable, these techniques offer a method of resolving environmental conflict.

"Environmental Conflict Resolution" is believed to be the first publication to give a comprehensive and worldwide review of the history and current practice of environmental conflict resolution. Experienced and distinguished practitioners describe the mediation and facilitation techniques used and how they have developed in the United States, Germany, the United Kingdom and the developing countries. The application today of facilitation techniques to achieve resolution of environmental conflict, and the practice of mediation to reolve commercial environmental disputes, are discussed. There is analysis of the success of the results and comparison with the more traditional methods of dispute resolution. Actual cases are always invaluable in bringing discussion to life, and many are discussed here.

Encouraging assessments are given of prospects for the future for these techniques in the arena of environmental conflict. I have no doubt from my own involvement with environmental dispute resolution over the last ten years that these assessments will prove well founded.

It follows that "Environmental Conflict Resolution" will be of value to all those, within national and local government, industry, commerce, academia, and the legal, accountancy and consultancy professions, who face and deal with conflict in the environmental arena.

I would like to express my thanks to all the authors for their hard work, to Suzanne Clabon and Barbara Ford for assisting me in the editorial work, and to Cameron May for the idea.

Christopher Napier, Clifford Chance

CHAPTER I
ENVIRONMENTAL CONFLICT RESOLUTION:
THE AMERICAN EXPERIENCE

ENVIRONMENTAL CONFLICT RESOLUTION: THE AMERICAN EXPERIENCE

Professor Lawrence E. Susskind and Joshua Secunda

1. Introduction

Environmental Dispute Resolution (EDR) consists of a variety of techniques and strategies aimed at resolving disagreements among stakeholders in a range of public disputes which involve environmental quality or natural resource management.

These techniques have been tried for almost two decades in the United States and seem to produce good results. That is, they appear to be more effective at producing outcomes that are more satisfying to the parties, leaving them in a better position to deal with their differences in the future as well as with the difficulties of policy implementation. Experience with public dispute resolution in the US indicates that consensual approaches to handling conflict can yield outcomes that are fairer, more efficient, wiser and more stable than traditional methods, at least some of the time. Moreover, it is arguable that consensual approaches are consistently better than conventional approaches in generating public confidence in government and empowering citizens to take greater responsibility for meeting the needs of all segments of society.

There is some debate about this, since systematic analysis of EDR is quite difficult. Nevertheless, on the presumption that the results merit attention, this chapter aims to: (1) describe the practice and summarise the theory of EDR as it has evolved in the US, (2) analyse its strengths and weaknesses from a variety of perspectives, and (3) suggest ways in which these ideas might be helpful in other countries.

2. History

The 1970s was the decade of the environment in the US. This ten-year period saw passage of the National Environmental Policy Act in 1969, the Resource Conservation and Recovery Act (RCRA) in 1970, the Clean Air Act amendments and the establishment of the United States Environmental Protection Agency. In 1972 alone, the Federal Water Pollution Control Act, the Federal Environmental Pesticide Control Act, the Ocean Dumping Act and the Coastal Zone Management Act were all enacted.

That same decade also saw the birth of the alternate dispute resolution (ADR) movement. At the beginning of the 1970s, American citizens enmeshed in heated environmental public policy disputes had few meaningful options, other than litigation pursuant to one or more of the above statutes. It did not matter whether disputants were members of a citizens group fighting the actions of a government agency, angry neighbours confronting each other, or officials unable to agree on important policy decisions. All had limited choices when traditional legislative and administrative options for settling disagreements did not work. The vast majority carried their disputes to court. Others opted for protracted political confrontations involving demonstrations, contentious public hearings or angry media volleys. Meanwhile court dockets overloaded, litigation dragged on and the machinery of government stalled. Gridlock appeared to be epidemic in the public policy arena.

From the mid-1970s, this began to change. A growing number of Americans began experimenting with creative new approaches to dealing with conflict. In the private sector, attention focused on ways of resolving disagreements between private firms and individuals without resorting to expensive litigation. Such dispute resolution techniques as the mini-trial, private judging and mediation were seen in greater number. In the public sector - and at the intersection of private-public disputes - interest grew in processes such as facilitation and mediation to help disputing parties move beyond impasse to settlement. A few individuals also began to use consensus building techniques as a means of harmonising conflicting interests and building agreement before full-scale public disputes crystallised.

Early efforts to resolve public disputes drew their inspiration from several sources, including industrial relations, social psychology and small group dynamics, and international relations. However, the industrial relations arena had the greatest influence. The institutionalisation of procedures for settling disputes between labour and management provided a framework for understanding the sources of public conflict and the dynamics of public disputes. It also provided evidence of the helpful role that mediation might play in the resolution of environmental disputes.

2.1 Early Experiments[1]

Meaningful experiments with dispute resolution in the public sector commenced in the late 1970s. Each experiment broke ground in a different way. However, they all reflected a shared belief that conventional methods for managing conflict in the public sector were unsatisfactory: they sapped financial resources, took an unreasonably long time to produce agreement, and did little or nothing to improve relationships among disputing parties. In an effort to find better ways of coping with important disagreements in society, these early experimenters crafted new approaches to resolving and avoiding disputes. Their work represented the first stirrings of an emerging field.[2]

Environmental disputes provided one of the first arenas in which individual practitioners (i.e. mediators) began exploring the applicability to public conflicts of dispute resolution techniques and processes. Mediation was tested as a means of avoiding the protracted court battles produced when parties warred with each other over actual or potential environmental degradation.[3] The potential of environmental mediation, designed to bring people face-to-face to educate each other about their real interests and search for mutual gains, attracted the attention of practitioners.[4]

The first significant environmental dispute to be mediated was a long-running controversy over the proposed location of a flood control dam on the Snoqualmie River in the State of Washington.[5] The project's proponents were pitted against environmental stakeholders concerned about the survival of the river's ecosystem, farmers concerned about cutbacks in water available for irrigation, and citizen representatives concerned about the uncontrolled suburban sprawl a dam might trigger. Two of the first environmental mediators, Gerald Cormick and Jane McCarthy, acted in the absence of precedent in 1974 when they initiated and then facilitated a dialogue among the opposing parties. In doing so, Cormick formulated a working definition of environmental mediation as "...a voluntary process in which those involved in a dispute jointly explore and reconcile their differences. The mediator has no authority to impose a settlement. His or her strength lies in the ability to assist the parties in resolving their own differences. The mediated dispute is settled when the parties themselves reach what they consider to be a workable solution"[6]

After a year's work with the mediators, an agreement was forged around plans for the construction of the dam, additional flood control initiatives, recommended land use controls and a basin-wide coordinating council.[7]

Early proponents of environmental dispute resolution claimed that informal bargaining techniques would make it easier to tailor settlements to the special circumstances of each case. Such tailored settlements, free from the more restricted procedures imposed by formal institutions (i.e., the court system), could turn distributive win-lose confrontations into integrative, joint problem-solving opportunities, within which the parties could search for mutually beneficial solutions. The credibility of interest-based negotiation theory was buttressed by the Grayrocks Dam controversy, which began in 1973 and ended in 1979.

This dispute contained all the elements of a classic development vs. the environment confrontation.

The Missouri Basin Power Project (MBPP) proposed construction of a $1.6 billion coal-fired power plant on the Laramie River near Wheatland, Wyoming. To supply essential cooling water for the plant, the MBPP proposed to build a dam and reservoir on the Laramie River. The likely diminution of streamflow created a dispute with Nebraskan farmers and ranchers over water rights in this agriculture-dominated economy. Further, environmentalists charged that the dam would jeopardise the endangered Whooping Crane by adversely affect its habitat along the North Platte River in neighboring Nebraska.

Both environmentalists and state officials wanted to prevent the Grayrocks project from siphoning too much water from the North Platte. Thus, they joined forces in a federal court suit against the US Army Corps of Engineers and the Rural Electrification Administration, alleging that they had issued permits and loan guarantees for the project without having adequately considered its environmental impacts.

It appeared that the parties would be enmeshed in a lengthy legal battle. The developers of the project were anxious to complete it on schedule. After a series of negotiating sessions involving all the concerned parties (state and federal agencies, environmental organisations and the developer - ten stakeholders in all), an agreement was reached allowing the project to go ahead while furnishing guarantees to the environmentalists and Nebraska officials that water flows in the North Platte would remain at acceptable levels. Among other provisions, the parties agreed to establish a trust for the purpose of funding activities to protect and maintain the Whooping Cranes critical habitat. This tailored settlement established maximum limits on water consumed by the project, specified minimum flows to be maintained in the North Platte and established a monitoring system to confirm that the flows specified in the settlement were being met.

The National Coal Policy Project set still another precedent for environmental dispute resolution in the 1970s: the first effort to convene business and environmental leaders in an attempt to reach consensus on national policy.[8] This ground-breaking experiment, organised under the auspices of the Georgetown University Center for Strategic and International Studies, involved up to 105 participants confronting over 200 separate issues. Working through nine task-force groups, the participants addressed more than two hundred specific issues, reaching agreement on nearly 90 percent of them.[9] Few of the project's results were actually implemented and some non-participating NGOs strongly criticised the outcome. "Nevertheless, as in the Snoqualmie case, the most significant contribution of the National Coal Policy Project may have been the precedent it set, demonstrating that there might be less confrontational and more cooperative ways to deal with controversial environmental issues."[10]

A mediators involvement in resolving the Storm King Mountain dispute provided even more evidence that potentially expensive, lengthy environmental disputes might be better solved through mediation, rather than litigation.[11] This controversy involved environmentalists, the Consolidated Edison power company and other utilities, and state and federal regulators. The dispute began in 1963 over a proposed pump-storage power station at scenic Storm King Mountain in the Hudson River highlands, forty miles north of New York City. Environmentalists opposed the plant on various grounds, particularly the alleged threat which the plant posed to the habitat of the striped bass (a valuable game fish). Seventeen years of litigation followed, involving three environmental groups, four public agencies and five utility companies. Estimated combined costs to the parties totalled over $6 million in legal fees and other court costs.[12]

In April, 1979, a former administrator of the US Environmental Protection Agency was invited to mediate the dispute. In December, 1980, the parties formally signed an out-of-court settlement. Plans for the station were abandoned and some environmental restrictions on other generating plants on the Hudson River were relaxed. "The combined costs of the mediator's time and expenses and the fees of the attorneys and technical people involved in the negotiations, must have been only a tiny fraction of the costs of the previous litigation - and an even smaller fraction of the total costs of the projects involved."[13]

2.2 Financial Support

As difficult as it is to imagine a field of public conflict resolution without the example of labour-management mediation, it is even harder to believe that the field might have developed as it did without the active interest and support of several highly influential grantmaking foundations. During the 1970s, and even into the early 1980s, most dispute resolution services were offered at low or no cost to the disputants by foundation-sponsored, non-profit private or university-based institutions...Foundation support removed the major issue of who would pay for the mediator's services, with its attending complications for the mediator's neutrality."[14]

The various programmatic interests that these foundations funded in the 1960s and 1970s significantly influenced the development of the field.

The Ford Foundation funded initial attempts to apply the mediation techniques developed in labour-management contract disputes to the public arena.[15] It also funded the first experiments in environmental dispute resolution, including the Snoqualmie dam controversy. The Foundation provided general support for the Institute for Environmental Studies at the University of Washington in Seattle and the Office of Environmental Mediation at the University of Wisconsin. It co-founded the National Institute of Dispute Resolution (NIDR). In 1987, the Ford Foundation endowed the Fund for Research in Dispute Resolution (FRDR), one of the first sustained sources of research support dedicated to dispute resolution.[16]

The William A. and Flora Hewlett Foundation approached the dispute resolution field from a different angle, funding theory building efforts in the conflict resolution field.[17] In the words of a Hewlett Foundation official:

"...our principal interest was in learning more about different processes and in building theory. Mediation and arbitration were fairly well understood...We were more interested in processes that mediators used before formal mediation begins, processes that could be used before a dispute crystallised, and processes that didn't necessarily need professionals to implement them but that lent themselves to implementation by ordinary people."[18]

In pursuing these goals, the Foundation supported the 1982 Florisant, Colorado meeting on environmental dispute resolution (perhaps the first gathering of EDR professionals); the 1992 Charlottesville Symposium (The Cutting Edge) for senior environmental dispute resolution practitioners with the most experience in the field; the development of umbrella institutions (the Society for Professionals in Dispute Resolution (SPIDR), National Institute for Dispute Resolution (NIDR)), practitioner organizations (CDR Associates, Conflict Clinic, Justice Center of Atlanta), and theory building institutions (e.g. the Institute for Conflict Analysis and Resolution at George Mason University and the Program on Negotiation at Harvard University).[19]

As conflict resolution gained credibility as a constructive alternative to litigation, the field grew less dependent on foundation support and became more market-oriented. Groups of professional practitioners like the Center for Dispute Resolution (Boulder, Colorado), the Mediation Institute (Seattle, Washington), and ENDISPUTE, Inc. (Boston and Washington) were able to survive and grow. Their early efforts to communicate with each other and to foster an informal network led to the establishment of the Public/Environmental Dispute Resolution Section of SPIDR in 1985.

One of the organizations most responsible for establishing and guiding the direction of the public conflict resolution field has been NIDR. A half-dozen foundations and corporations, some of which had been funding community and environmental dispute resolution programs for more than ten years, joined to form this organization. NIDR's sole mission was supporting growth and innovation in the field. NIDR was officially inaugurated in 1983, with a large block of funds from the Ford Foundation to support researchers and practitioners who wanted to analyze the progress of dispute resolution or carry its methodologies into new areas. One of NIDR's most significant contributions in its early years was facilitating and funding the founding of five new state-sponsored offices of mediation in Massachusetts, New Jersey, Hawaii, Wisconsin and Minnesota (all of which focused heavily on EDR).[20]

At the same time, the growing public interest in mediation, consensus building and other innovative processes for managing disagreement produced a demand for training in an emerging set of conflict management skills. In just a few years, courses, workshops, and seminars mushroomed across the country. In academic settings, students and professors worked together to create new programs specifically geared towards training a cadre of public dispute resolution professionals.[21] The Program on Negotiation at Harvard Law School, as well as similar university-based programs in Virginia, Georgia, Hawaii, New Jersey and Minnesota provided teaching materials and additional impetus to these academic efforts.

2.3 Seminal Publications

Finally, several authors worked to create the published basis of dispute resolution theory, producing books that described efforts to apply mediation and consensus building, and offering a new body of empirical analysis to demonstrate the value of these experiments.[22] The desire among researchers and practitioners to have regular access to the wealth of information about new developments in the field led to the creation of newsletters like Consensus, published by the Public Disputes Network at the Program on Negotiation. By documenting diverse examples of new projects and programs, offering detailed profiles of organizations specializing in public dispute resolution, and presenting a comprehensive listings of organizations and solo practitioners in all regions of the United States, Consensus helped to foster an active and informed demand for dispute resolution services.

2.4 Governmental Experiments in Negotiated Rule Making

At the federal level, a new approach to dealing with contentious agency rule making was being developed. For decades, the process of writing regulations had been losing credibility among government officials, businesses, citizen activists and critics of administrative law. These groups were frustrated by the lengthy delays, high costs and frequent litigation that arose during the conventional process of drafting regulations pursuant to new legislation.

Compounding this problem was the lack of legitimacy surrounding many regulations - particularly those involving complex scientific and technical tradeoffs - after they were formulated. Federal agencies had been granted broad discretionary powers by the courts. Participation of groups most likely to be affected by agency decisions consisted of the right to submit formal statements to the rule-making "record" on which the agency was required to ground its decisions. This formal, trial-like process did not allow stakeholders a means of providing input into policy choices and technical judgments that agencies inevitably made as they developed controversial regulations. As a result, stakeholders almost invariably resorted to challenging these regulations in court.[23] In the early 1980s, mounting dissatisfaction with federal rule making propelled the Administrative Conference of the United States (ACUS) to recommend that agencies try new procedures based on the principles of negotiation.[24] The Conference envisioned a process by which a new rule would be developed through direct negotiation and collaborative fact finding among all parties likely to be affected by its promulgation. This approach aimed to reduce the time, cost and acrimony associated with conventional rule making by taking account of conflicting interests throughout the development of a rule's specific provisions. In pursuing this goal, advocates of negotiated rule making sought to create avenues for groups to participate at every step of regulatory decision making. Thus, negotiated rule making held out the promise of producing rules with greater legitimacy in the eyes of the public, thereby eliminating the endless cycles of litigation that bogged down agency action. Negotiated rule-making earned growing legitimacy and acceptance as greater numbers of people became familiar with the value of involving representatives of the public in agency decision making.

The Environmental Protection Agency (EPA) was one of the first agencies to experiment with the negotiated rule making process. In early 1984, the Agency announced that it would use the process to develop a rule governing noncompliance penalties for classes of heavy duty vehicles or engines that exceeded allowable air quality emissions levels. After four months of negotiation and joint fact-finding facilitated by a neutral conflict resolution expert, the participating stakeholders reached consensus. Following on the heels of this successful demonstration, the EPA again used negotiated rule making to develop standards governing the procedures for registering new pesticides.[25]

Other agencies soon followed suit and in the latter part of the 1980s, many agencies began implementing collaborative decision making processes. Most significantly, Congress enacted the Negotiated Rulemaking Act in 1990 to legitimise this alternative approach to regulatory decision making.[26] By 1995, more than a dozen agencies in the United States and Canada had used negotiated rulemaking procedures successfully.[27]

Numerous governmental units at the state and local level rapidly followed suit. Public utilities commissions worked with citizen groups, businesses and other agencies to negotiate new utility rates, or draft plans to moderate rate shock when utility bills were expected to skyrocket. In some states, legislatures have enacted statutes that require builders of hazardous waste sites to enter into assisted negotiations with communities that are under consideration as potential facility hosts.[28] Connecticut used consensus building to formulate a fair share allocation of affordable housing responsibilities.[29]

Facilitated negotiation has also been employed by city governments. One municipality brought together members of the City Council with representatives of neighborhood groups and scientists to explore a technical controversy over the risks posed by a proposed trash-to-energy plant. Other city and local governments have used mediation programs to supplement adjudicatory processes for managing zoning disputes.[30]

3. Recent Trends

The activity that characterised the mid-1980s transformed dispute resolution and consensus building in the public sector. Consequently, the arenas where public dispute resolution were first introduced also underwent dramatic change. These changes coalesced into major trends that are still unfolding today. By reflecting on how each of the early strands of public dispute resolution was shaped by developments in the field, we may be able to shed some light on where current trends are headed.

Some centers dedicated to offering community dispute resolution services responded to the growing legitimacy and public interest in mediation by broadening the scope of their objectives. Initially, these centers were conceived as mechanisms for alleviating pressure on the court system by providing an alternative forum where minor misdemeanor cases and civil suits could be settled by trained volunteers. However, a few dispute resolution centers boldly entered new territory. They expanded their activities to include highly visible and controversial policy disputes and consensus building processes aimed at forging agreement among multiple parties on major issues of public policy. While these centers have continued to focus most of their efforts on the kinds of interpersonal disputes typically arising between neighbors or among several community members, they have also embraced opportunities to use their negotiation and facilitation skills to enhance community participation in environmentally complex decision-making processes.

For instance, the early success of the Justice Center of Atlanta in settling small scale disputes led a court to recommend its services for resolving a protracted battle over a proposed four lane highway in the metropolitan Atlanta area. With the assistance of an out-of-state facilitator, the Center convened a dialogue among representatives of the City of Atlanta, the State of Georgia, and twenty four neighborhood coalitions to develop a consensus on the fate of the proposed $27 million project.[31] Similarly, the Neighborhood Justice Center of Honolulu began by offering Hawaiian communities trained volunteer mediators to settle disputes between family members, neighbors, tenants and landlords, and consumers and merchants. After several years, the Center expanded its scope to include a Conflict Management Program, which utilised highly trained volunteers to help government agencies, community groups and private developers build agreement on contentious policy decisions. In one case, the Center helped build agreement on the siting of a controversial geothermal energy plant.

Organizations and individuals applying mediation to environmental disputes also broadened their mission. While these practitioners had originally focused on applying mediation skills to site-specific environmental disputes, their widespread recognition soon produced requests to facilitate negotiations involving increasingly complex and geographically far-reaching environmental conflicts, such as the adoption of regional and statewide growth management policies. The Environmental Institute at the University of Virginia initiated the Chesapeake Bay Roundtable, credited with forging a consensus that led to passage of the Chesapeake Bay Preservation Act by the Virginia Assembly. They also convened a consensus-building process to study and build agreement on a set of coordinated measures to protect surface water quality in Virginia watersheds.[32]

Increasingly, these practitioners ensured the sustainability of their practices by charging fees for their services. Their success led to a dramatic proliferation of new service providers. Many organizations that began with a mission to solve environmental disputes broadened the scope of their efforts to include public dispute resolution more generally. These developments were probably motivated by the tremendous upswing in demand for experienced practitioners.[33]

Today, the institutions and individuals who have made mediation their life's work are now part of a well-established network of professionals, with vehicles for promoting their ideas, sharing information and lessons learned, and disseminating skills and knowledge to others who want to join their ranks.[34] The newsletter "Consensus" is entering its tenth year with over 35,000 subscribers. The four state offices of mediation sponsored by NIDR have multiplied to eighteen, and proposals to add new offices are being developed.[35]

There has also been significant growth in the number and regional diversity of public dispute resolution practitioners.[36] NIDR has estimated that there were 5000 volunteer mediators practicing in 1980; by 1990, there were 15,000. The original 79 community justice centers had grown to 300 in the same decade.[37] Finally, SPIDR's membership grew by 70 percent from 1980 to 1990, and continues to increase substantially each year.[38]

What began as the piecemeal efforts of a few individuals experimenting with new ways to manage conflict has grown into a dynamic field. EDR is now supported by the efforts of a burgeoning group of theorists and highly skilled mediators and facilitators. In short, the practice of environmental mediation in the United States is surprisingly widespread (geographically) and almost entirely unregulated, although some public agencies are moving toward the imposition of minimum qualifications for those who seek to provide services to those agencies, as discussed below.

The growth of the field has been utterly decentralised, leading to the development of a highly diversified view of best practice. Despite the examples offered above, a great deal of environmental mediation activity has gone unreported and unevaluated. This has occurred in part because no agency or organization has responsibility for documentation, and in part because many mediators have been reluctant to have anyone scrutinise their work (either because they felt that evaluators would be too intrusive or because they were afraid to be assessed).

4. The Theory of Environmental Mediation

Almost every effort to protect or enhance environmental quality is perceived as a challenge, at least at the outset, by groups or individuals whose economic self-interest, political beliefs, or values are threatened. Similarly, almost every attempt to promote economic development or technological innovation is viewed as a potential insult to the quality of the natural environment or a threat to the delicate ecological balance upon which we all depend.

Environmental and developmental interests seem locked in a fierce and chronic battle. All parties to environmental disputes claim popular support, aggravating the intransigence of the contending interest groups. As the frequency of environmental disputes has grown, the ability of our social, political and legal institutions to resolve them in a timely, efficient and decisive manner has diminished. Government seems unable to resolve these disputes satisfactorily; in part because government is often a party to them, but primarily because the vitality of US political institutions has been sapped by the fragmentation of political parties into shifting alliances that do not so much govern as react to the pressures of special interest groups and other organized constituencies. This paralysis has placed an enormous burden on our legal system; a burden that the courts may not be able or well suited to handle.

It is in this context that new approaches to resolving environmental disputes have arisen; approaches that offer some means, in addition to traditional legal or political devices, for resolving conflict. Called alternate dispute resolution (ADR), environmental dispute resolution (EDR), conflict avoidance, mediation, or just plain negotiation, these approaches share a critical element: each aims to resolve environmental disputes through out-of-court bargaining, rather than through adversarial legal procedures. All of these approaches seek to manage conflict and to foster voluntary agreements.

5. Special Difficulties Involved in Resolving Environmental Disputes

Practitioners of dispute resolution have described the required conditions that should be present to proceed with mediation or negotiation. They generally agree that it may be appropriate when: 1) the parties have a strong desire to resolve their differences; 2) they are prepared to enter into formal agreements if a settlement is reached; 3) they stand in some relative balance of power; and, 4) when mediation is involved, they can find a neutral party capable of employing dispute resolution techniques and understanding the technical issues underlying the dispute.

These prescriptions are generally helpful. However, they do not speak to all the special difficulties of resolving environmental, as opposed to other types of, disputes. Some of these special problems can be highlighted by contrasting environmental disputes with collective bargaining efforts in the labour relations field, long the model for conflict management in the US.

5.1 Identifying the Stakeholders

If one is to negotiate or mediate effectively, the parties-at-interest (stakeholders) must be at the negotiating table. This presents little problem to a labour mediator; labour-management disputes are almost always bilateral. The identity of the necessary parties (usually two; labour and management) is self-evident, as is the authority of their representatives to speak for their respective sets of interests.

A typical environmental dispute may easily include dozens of stakeholders. If their representatives do not participate in settlement discussions, the negotiation of a stable agreement may be impossible. Consider the proposed construction of a shopping mall in an open field containing a wetland; not an unusual event. Probable stakeholders include various environmental groups (whose agendas may conflict with each other, as well as with that of the developer); several chambers of commerce (some supporting the project, others opposing it due to its potentially negative effect on established local businesses); labour union representatives; public officials controlling zoning, traffic and construction decisions, and; federal and state agencies whose jurisdictions may overlap (i.e., EPA and the Army Corps of Engineers both control wetlands construction decisions; the Department of the Interior and the US Fish and Wildlife Service may become involved if endangered plants and/or animal species are threatened by loss of habitat, etc.). The state may have more stringently protective wetlands and endangered species provisions than provided by the federal government, and is also a necessary party. Finally, citizen groups affected by the development will also demand a role.

In sum, parties to environmental disputes are more numerous and often less obviously identifiable than are the representatives of labour and management. Yet identifying all stakeholders and securing their participation is vital to the success of mediators. There is always the possibility that an agreement will be challenged - and its implementation frustrated - by an individual or group not included in the process. Merely identifying the parties necessary to create an effective working group is a major challenge, to say nothing of facilitating a process that might lead to consensus.

5.2 Internal Discipline

Environmental groups are not as cohesive as labour unions. A nongovernmental organization involved in a settlement effort may fragment internally over a proposed agreement. The mediator may then be faced with new splinter groups attempting to halt implementation of the parent group's bargain. Indeed, this phenomenon may occur within several stakeholder groups, thus creating a plethora of new stakeholders with many new agendas.

5.3 The Necessity of Governmental Approval

Implementation of environmental agreements is often out of the hands of the parties to an agreement. When unions bargain with management, the terms of the settlement are defined by the parties; ratification of the agreement occurs when the principals agree, and members or boards of directors vote. In contrast, environmental settlements are often the responsibility of a government agency. In such cases, the parties to a settlement require agency approval in order to implement their agreement.

If the agency (or agencies) in question has not been a party to the bargaining process (or at least involved as a passive observer), it may determine that it cannot both honor the voluntary settlement and fulfill its statutory mandate. In such cases, public agencies can deny or qualify the necessary permits and licenses or initiate enforcement action, thus frustrating implementation of informally negotiated agreements.

5.4 Multiplicity and Complexity of Issues

Parties to environmental disputes must also consider issues that rarely come up in the context of labour-management disputes; for instance, the possibility of irreversible effects. In labour-management disputes, the concept of irreversible effects is relative (i.e., a disastrous strike or settlement causes a company to leave the state, drive the company to bankruptcy, etc.). But companies can reorganize or be sold, jobs can be absorbed by other businesses; nearly all of these effects can be reversed. On the other hand, an environmental dispute may involve truly irreversible effects: habitat destruction, pollution of potable drinking water, species extinction and negative effects on human health.

In part, this is due to the unique features of ecological systems. In ecological systems, limits are ubiquitous. There are limits to resources; there are also limits to the rate at which the environment can receive wastes and process or store them. Ecosystems are open and linked. Events at one place in the environment may cause repercussions in other places at other times. Thus, the consequences of human action are bound to be unpredictable. Actions massive enough, drastic enough or simply of the right sort may cause irreversible environmental changes.

5.5 Bounding the Agreement: The Difficulty in Defining Terms

Labour disputes share a commonly understood vocabulary, and a common understanding of the dispute's boundaries. Disputants' identities are clear, settlement terms are confined to those parties, and there is little ambiguity as to a settlement's likely impact. The costs of extending a dispute are fairly symmetrical; the costs of a strike are relatively symmetrical, as are the costs of a bad agreement.

Environmental disputes are marked by an inability to make precise or even general determinations of costs, parties and boundaries. The symmetry inherent in labour disputes is almost wholly missing. The costs of environmental disputes are skewed in two ways. For the relatively minor cost of litigation an environmental group can inflict millions of dollars in added interest charges and other costs of delay on a developer. On the other hand, a victorious developer can inflict real (if impossible to quantify in dollars) costs on environmentalists who see the things they value - cleaner air and water, natural uses of land, habitat destruction - endangered. These asymmetries tend to make environmental conflict more intense; conflict costs relatively little to initiate (and escalate) and the costs of defeat are borne almost entirely by the losing party.

Defining issues of time horizons and geographic boundaries are rarely a problem in labour disputes. The length of a contract or length of a work shift is simply another issue to be bargained by the parties. Geographic boundaries would, at most, present an issue of contract interpretation for international business lawyers.

In many environmental disputes, however, issue definition may have profound consequences. Time frame issues can range from determining precisely how long a party will be responsible for remedying any potential negative impacts of a project, to issues that simply cannot be quantified, such as the responsibility the current stakeholders owe to future generations in exercising responsible stewardship over a disputed resource.

As to geographic boundaries, environmental disputes often have none; at best, such boundaries are often ambiguous. The issue of spillover effects is almost always present. For instance, air pollution generated in Eastern Europe adversely affects France, Germany and Great Britain. An agreement to convert an oil-burning power plant to coal in Massachusetts may worsen acid rain fallout elsewhere in the region.[39] An agreement to divert water in the Colorado river may affect the habitat of endangered species, negatively affect agriculture and encourage unwanted development for decades to come.[40] Environmental mediators must often consider the effects of a proposed agreement on parties hundreds of thousands of miles away who are not at the negotiating table.

5.6 The Economic Problem: Assigning Market Values to the Environment

All these complicating factors are exacerbated by the fact that environmental costs and benefits do not translate easily into a common unit of economic analysis. Thus, there is no consensus on how to value particular environmental benefits. The best we can hope for are multiple cost-benefit calculations representing the different vantage points of each interested party. There is, though, no known way for an analyst to amalgamate all the costs of environmental impacts experienced by all the groups affected and determine the correct amount of compensation to be paid. Each group will value a particular impact differently depending, for instance, on its distance from the source of the impact and its socio-economic status.

This lack of shared values makes it difficult to determine what each party to an environmental dispute, is, in fact, willing to accept in the way of a side payment or promise of equivalent environmental value. Yet these are crucial incentives to bargaining.

5.7 Conflicting Claims to Public Interest Representation

All stakeholders attempt to identify their positions with the public interest. This fends off attacks and attracts political support. It also confuses and complicates debate. Once a question is cast in terms of support for the public interest, rather than in terms of balancing or accommodating the interests of various publics, compromise becomes difficult. Indeed, the phenomenon of self-serving statements that their bargaining position represents the public interest is endemic to labour-management disputes.

When analyzing environmental disputes, the public interest problem has two aspects. First, when one side sees itself as the only legitimate representative of the public interest, accommodation becomes difficult. Second, there are real questions as to whether public interest advocates can legitimately be said to represent the public (let alone their own constituency). Often, there is no foolproof way to ensure the agent's loyalty to the individuals whose- interests he claims to represent. This being so, a lawyer may choose to represent his own interests or those of a few active members of that constituency. Then, there is the question of the degree to which the leadership of a stakeholder group or party is responsive to its membership.[41]

5.8 Implementation

Implementation of industrial collective bargaining agreements is rarely a problem. Parties enter a well-understood contractual relationship, with terms that are clear to the parties and to the courts or agencies that interpret or enforce them in future.

Collective bargaining recurs in regular cycles. This makes it difficult for any party to flout an agreement; doing so will only make the next round of bargaining more expensive for both sides. Both sides are aware that if implementation does not occur, the result (work stoppages or other actions) will be costly. There is rarely a question as to whether the parties have the ability to implement the agreement.

This is not the case in environmental disputes. Each environmental agreement tends to be novel. Courts and agencies may interpret them in ways unforeseen by the parties if there are disputes about proper implementation.

6. What Practitioners Agree On

As demonstrated above, the special characteristics of environmental disputes renders the traditional labour-management analogy insufficient. A conflict resolution strategy tailored to the unique demands of environmental disputes has proven to be more successful. Indeed, it is possible to summarise certain theoretical propositions on which most experienced environmental mediators would agree:

I. Almost any multi-party, multi-issue environmental dispute can be mediated as long as questions of fundamental rights do not need to be decided. Whether it is permitted to use a resource in a certain way is a legal matter. Whether the resource *should* be used in a certain way when, legally, other options are also allowed, is an issue which can be mediated. However, if a dispute involves constitutional questions or revolves around definitions of basic rights, consensus may be unattainable; indeed, decisions by consensus may be inappropriate in such cases. Issues which generate conflict over fundamental values, and constitutional and legal rights are not amenable to consensus building.[42]

II. Effective attempts at environmental mediation ought to begin with a conflict assessment. It is vital that there is a pre-mediation phase during which some agency, firm, or official provides credible auspices under which potential parties to a mediation can be canvassed. These private conversations are crucial to getting the right parties to the negotiating table.[43] The purpose of the conflict assessment includes: 1) identification of the various stakeholder groups and their representatives; 2) understanding the concerns of the parties and their interest in working together; 3) the selection of a manageable number of stakeholder representatives; 4) setting procedural groundrules, and; 5) the selection of a neutral party (i.e., facilitator, mediator, etc.) acceptable to all the stakeholders.

III. The mediators goal must be to secure the participation of as many legitimate representatives of stakeholding parties as possible to endorse the mediation effort and to ensure that those who have the power to block the implementation of an agreement participate directly. Such groups, if left out of the process, may fatally oppose an agreement after it has been carefully crafted by all the other parties. This is particularly true in environmental disputes, where consensus-based groups may forget that various federal and state regulatory agencies are, in fact, vital stakeholders.

There are no simple generalisations to be made about the resolution of these problems. Nevertheless, the parties to a public dispute must agree that it is necessary to involve all legitimate stakeholding interests in whatever negotiations are planned. The group must consider whether something should be done to identify and alert people who do not realize that they have a stake in a decision that is about to be made. If a key group is omitted, even unintentionally, the credibility of an ad hoc consensus building effort may be irreparably damaged.

IV. The process of environmental mediation must take place in the sunshine; the process cannot be conducted in secret. Unless the process is transparent, the results are not likely to be credible. This point is particularly critical in encouraging joint fact-finding. The mediator must encourage the collection of information that is believed on all sides. True, decision-makers want to have the best possible information to be certain they are making wise decisions, but the best possible information might not be the most convincing. In fact, it might be counter-productive to share certain information if other stakeholders reject it because of its source. Thus, decision-makers must decide what information others will find compelling. Information gathered, analyzed, modeled, and carefully packaged behind closed doors may have no credibility when it appears, even if it is accurate. The answer is to open the doors wide and pursue fact-finding together. This means gathering data, analyzing data, and drawing conclusions together.[44] Finally, when public officials are involved in the consensus-building process, all open meeting, public notice, and freedom of information requirements must be rigorously met.

V. Building on the above propositions, technical and scientific issues need to be dealt with as part of environmental mediation. It is not appropriate to separate fact finding or technical analysis from the main mediation effort. For mediated agreements to be credible, all stakeholding parties must have confidence that everyone had access to the scientific or technical information they needed to make informed judgments.

As the technical complexity of a dispute increases, the likelihood that suspicion and hostility will interfere with the consensus-building process also increases. Thus, the more technically complex the dispute, the more assistance a mediator may have to find for less scientifically sophisticated stakeholders. Further, the mediator must ensure that funds procured for fact-finding are used for fact-finding, and not to engage partisan advocates or to wage another "battle of the print-out". Unless neutral experts, selected jointly by all parties, are used, technical findings are likely to be less than credible in the eyes of some of the participants.[45]

VI. The product of most environmental negotiations is not a legally binding agreement. Most environmental negotiations produce recommendations that must then be acted upon by bodies with legal authority. However, this rarely undercuts their usefulness. If all the decision-makers are represented during negotiations, the final recommendations (especially those produced by consensus) are almost always accepted by those with formal ratification authority.

VII. The result of environmental mediation in a particular case should not be seen to set precedent. Doing so defeats the advantages inherent in the mediation process, which is designed to be flexible and ad hoc. Logic dictates that different results in similar situations are acceptable. If the parties seek to set a precedent, they should do so in court. Parties must understand that environmental mediation cannot lead in one case to the waiver of laws, regulations, or standards that apply in all similar cases. Successful mediation can, however, provide an agency with the incentive to exercise regulatory discretion (such as delaying a deadline for meeting certain standards).

7. Holding the Mediator Accountable

The growing role mediation now plays in the resolution of environmental disputes has led to debates on whether mediators should be held accountable for their actions. "In other words, how can those affected by the actions of mediators effectively chastise, sue, or fire them?"[46] After all, labour mediators must abide by the rules established by the Federal Mediation and Conciliation Service (FMCS) or the American Arbitration Association (AAA).[47] Failure to do so can lead to loss of accreditation. Labour mediators can be sued if they violate statutes or judicial decisions regarding proper procedure. They can also be discharged by the parties to a dispute, thereby making it harder for incompetent mediators to find work in the future.[48] There are no comparable statutes or judicial decisions that currently apply to environmental mediators.[49] Thus, the moral, legal and economic pressures that ensure the accountability of mediators in other fields do not apply in the environmental arena.

Even if it were clear how environmental mediators could be held accountable, this debate would (and should) continue. The success of most mediation efforts tends to be measured in rather narrow terms. If the parties to a labour dispute are pleased with the agreement they have reached voluntarily and the bargain holds, then the mediator is presumed to have done a good job. In the environmental field, however, broader measures of success are needed, including those that relate to the interests of segments of society only tangentially involved.

If the parties involved in environmental mediation reach an agreement, but fail to maximise the possible joint gains, environmental quality and natural resources may actually be lost.[50] If the key parties involved in an environmental dispute reach an agreement with which they are pleased, but fail to take account of impacts on those not represented directly in the negotiations, public health and safety could be jeopardised. If the key parties to a dispute reach an agreement, but selfishly ignore the interests of future generations, short term agreements could set off environmental time bombs that cannot be defused. Key stakeholders in an environmental dispute may pay only a small price for failing to reach an agreement. However, their failure could impose substantial costs on groups which may be affected indefinitely. Finally, the parties to environmental disputes must be sensitive to the ways in which their agreements effectively set precedents; even informal settlements have a way of becoming binding on others in similar situations.

Guidelines are needed to ensure that environmental mediation efforts are structured properly. Enforcement of such guidelines needs to be institutionalised, and there are at least three procedural approaches to holding environmental mediators accountable. The first involves licensing, certification or registration at the state or federal level; licensed mediators would be expected to adhere to a code of responsibility. A second approach would involve creating environmental mediation offices attached to regulatory agencies or to the attorneys general offices at the federal or state levels. This second approach could be augmented by having administrative law judges require mediation before accepting challenges to the actions of administrative agencies. A third approach would involve enhancing the public's awareness of the risks and opportunities associated with environmental mediation - a well informed public can demand accountability.

It has long been suggested that a code of behavior (as published by the FMCS or by SPIDR) could provide a basis for establishing standards for environmental mediators.[51] However, environmental mediators require standards tailored to their own situation. (The Public/Environmental Section of SPIDR has released a description of best practices that would apply to environmental mediators.) Notwithstanding, many environmental disputes, are still mediated by individuals called upon to intervene because of their positions and not their credentials as mediators. Their success may well depend on their capacity to operate free from the constraints that mediators typically feel.[52]

Environmental mediators, to the extent that they subscribe to the broader view of their responsibilities suggested here, will probably need to possess substantive knowledge about the environmental and regulatory issues at stake. Effective environmental mediation may require teams composed of some individuals with technical backgrounds, some specialised in problem-solving or group dynamics and some with political clout. It would be difficult (and probably inappropriate) to credential such teams.

Finally, a healthy scepticism to the advantages of professionalising environ-mental mediators is probably in order. Other human service movements have discovered the organizational pitfalls that "make every profession, to varying degrees, a conspiracy against the laity."[53] The competitive impulse of some practitioners to set up barriers to entry into the profession (i.e., guilding the profession) should therefore be carefully scrutinised.[54]

The credentials debate becomes less important if environmental mediation is undertaken by independent agencies of government or court-appointed mediators.[55] Legislation could be enacted describing the circumstances and conditions under which mediation should take place. Those regulated and those doing the regulating would jointly select mediators whose names would remain on a standing list or roster. The mediators responsibilities would be spelled out in the legislation. Potential and volunteer mediators could be required to disclose their views concerning the need to protect underrepresented groups, strategies for maximising joint gains, and the importance of considering the precedent-setting nature of mediated agreements.

Courts with responsibility for reviewing the administrative decisions of public agencies might rely more heavily on mediation. Indeed, judges could insist that mediation (or at least joint fact-finding) precede formal challenges to administrative actions. Court appointed mediators would then be accountable to the judges who appointed them as well as to the parties.[56]

In fact, the beginnings of these trends can now be detected in the US and internationally. For instance, EPA's New England Region has now adopted a policy designed to exploit fully the usefulness of mediation to overcome impasse and promote the efficient, consensual resolution of regulatory penalty cases. Specifically, the policy applies to all administrative (Part 22) cases[57], and any other enforcement cases where settlement discussions are at an impasse and the case team believes that mediation may be helpful.[58] In addition to the above presumption, the Agency strongly encourages its attorneys to offer to mediate at the earliest sign that settlement with a small business, municipality, or public agency will not be achieved in an efficient, straightforward way; when a respondent is not represented by counsel; when a respondents counsel appears unfamiliar with environmental enforcement; or when there is a perception that the parties do not understand each other's positions (legal or factual).[59]

A November, 1995 evaluation of the ADR Center of the General Division of Canada's Ontario Court ADR Center spoke positively of the effect of mediation on the litigants and on the cost of litigation.[60] As a result, the Ontario government recently announced that it will make mediation mandatory in all non-family civil cases throughout the Province (including injunction applications) over the next several years.

Finally, section 53A of the Australian Federal Court Act (1976) has been amended to allow the Court to refer proceedings to mediation "with or without the consent of the parties."[61] (Section 53A previously only provided for the referral of proceedings to mediation with the consent of the parties).[62]

Ultimately, the most effective way to hold environmental mediators accountable would be to increase the public's capacity to demand fair and effective behavior on the part of mediators. Of necessity, this strategy is long-term, and could begin with the provision of government funds to ensure the representation of disadvantaged groups with a stake in a mediated dispute. To the extent that certain groups feel that they are not competent to participate in technical aspects of negotiation, funds could be provided to appoint qualified agents to represent them. Representatives of all stakeholding interests ought to be given funds to confer with the people they represent. These are some of the costs associated with creating an informed public.[63]

The community-at-large must keep abreast of the direction of the negotiations, or under-represented groups will be unable to assert their concerns. Although mediation efforts in the labour-management field are conducted in private, this should not be the case with environmental mediation. At least some scheduled sessions should be open to the public and to the news media.[64]

In summary, credentialing should not be insisted upon in the environmental mediation field. The institutionalisation of environmental mediation through formal links to regulatory agencies or the courts is much more likely to produce situations within which the responsibilities of environmental mediators can be defined and monitored appropriately. The process of building an informed public should begin, but the task promises to be very difficult.

Accountability requires that the parties to a dispute as well as members of the community-at-large should be able to hold environmental mediators to their responsibilities. The means of institutionalising the accountability of mediators will only be as effective as the parties to a dispute demand. If the parties fail to see the need for a broad definition of an environmental mediators responsibilities, it will be difficult to ensure accountability on such a basis.[65]

8. The Strengths and Weaknesses of Mediation in Resolving Environmental Disputes

We do not have a systematic evaluation of a large sample of environmental mediation cases. However, there is a great deal of documentation of specific cases and careful reflection on practice by leading practitioners. Therefore, some general statements concerning the pros and cons of EDR, as compared to other dispute resolution mechanisms, are in order.

8.1 Strengths

The anecdotal evidence consistently supports the proposition that EDR produces superior results, particularly when measured in terms of the satisfaction of the parties. This is, in part, due to the essence of the dispute resolution process, which attempts to identify the participants interests and fashion solutions that respond to them. In court-like proceedings, narrow questions or interests are decided within the framework of the law. Most courtroom time is spent ascertaining past facts, not in creating value or brainstorming future possibilities. Verdicts or judges decisions may not address or satisfy any partys interests; indeed, the adjudicatory process may well miss the point of the dispute entirely.

EDR offers better odds that a wise resolution of differences can be fashioned. The EDR process is designed to maximise joint gains for all stakeholders. Court-based adjudication, at least in the United States, is explicitly adversarial; disputes are perceived by the respective advocates as zero sum.

EDR can resolve disputes more efficiently in terms of the time and money expended, and in terms of relationships maintained. Judicial and negotiation processes often use time and money as weapons in a battle of attrition.

EDR's integrative processes can be transformative. Long-term professional relationships can be enhanced, leading to even greater efficiencies in preventing and/or resolving future disputes. This is a significant advantage, since most environmental disputes occur among parties that are likely to be locked into ongoing relationships. Indeed, some practitioners argue that its use promotes the institutionalisation of a particular social ethic that values collaboration as a form of social capital.[66]

8.2 Perceived Weaknesses and Some Rebuttals

It has been noted that EDR (at least in its ad hoc form) produces solutions that are neither precedent-setting nor definitive. Strategies and concepts used to resolve similar disputes are often different. At the very least, the elements of each settlement must be reconsidered, in each case.

EDR can also appear expensive in terms of the front-end investment of time required. A thorough pre-mediation assessment of the conflict from each side's perspective is vital if the mediator is to prove effective. However, conflict assessments take time and consume resources. It may also be necessary to train the stakeholders in dispute resolution or consensus building techniques before actually beginning an EDR process. These costs may ultimately be viewed as minor, in comparison to court costs, litigation fees, opportunity costs, environmental losses (irretrievably lost habitat, continued poor air quality, etc.) or irretrievably ruptured relationships.

EDR is still poorly understood by the public (although this is beginning to change). Thus, stakeholders' suspicion of the process can make them reluctant to participate. EDR also requires the involvement of neutrals.[67] Some parties perceive such helpers as threats to their control of the policy debate and its settlement. In addition, some agencies still perceive the participation of a neutral as sapping their power. However, government officials are rapidly learning that this is not the case. Continuing education in, and experience with, the EDR process should ameliorate this problem in time. Agencies often find settlements arrived at through EDR hard to disapprove, precisely because they represent substantively better outcomes than might have been produced by litigation; but they must meet all regulatory requirements and agencies cannot accept them merely because they have been reached by consensus.[68] As noted earlier, ad hoc EDR processes produce discrete agreements that are not themselves enforceable if violated. In fact, parties may not be able to resolve their disputes with finality through EDR. Environmental disputes generally come under the jurisdiction of state or federal agencies, or both. Thus, a solution built through consensus may break down if a government entity refuses to ratify it.[69] However, such an outcome can be avoided if the parties involve the agency as a stakeholder from the outset. Moreover, even if the agency does not participate and does not ratify the final settlement, agreement among the stakeholders will often resolve many of the key issues dividing them.

Mediators are, as a rule, not legally accountable to courts or the parties involved; there is no enforceable or even nationally recognized code of ethics or measure of competence that constrains the selection of environmental mediators. Codes for mediators are constantly being debated. However, the question of enforcement and what constitutes good practice and accountability are still unresolved.

Bad agreements arrived at through the involvement of incompetent mediators must be expected or ultimately litigated; this, after investing considerable effort and resources. However, bad agreements are no more likely to occur through the use of EDR than in court or via traditional political give-and-take negotiation. In fact, given the collaborative nature EDR, the odds of coming to a bad agreement are significantly lower.

EDR may be unsuitable in situations involving dramatic asymmetries of power; only rights-based forums (i.e., courts) can adequately protect the interests of the powerless. Indeed, it is possible that the absence of counselors/lawyers may disadvantage less sophisticated stakeholder groups in negotiations with other, more sophisticated, parties.[70] On the other hand, parties are entitled to be represented by counsel in mediation if they so choose, as long as the principal is present as well. Further, "...the notion of power - undifferentiated and in the abstract - is not particularly helpful in understanding its role in mediation, or its relative distribution between environmental disputants."[71]

"Firstly, it must be emphasised that most environmental mediation takes place "in the shadow of the law".[72] Unlike the mediation of say industrial collective bargaining disputes, the fact that in the absence of a settlement there will be a...determination in accordance with law is known, even if the outcome is uncertain. Not only can the parties look over their shoulders at what they can reasonably anticipate the court or other authority would impose in the absence of an agreement, they can test out each and every proposal during the course of the negotiations with a representative of the regulatory agency present at the table. Power is therefore not exercised at large in environmental mediation but within a realm tightly prescribed, not only by law, but also by official policy."[73]

Some observers claim that the absence of procedural safeguards offered by courts disadvantage weaker groups. Mediators are attempting to address this by including in their contracts an explicit responsibility for training the parties (who want or need help) and by developing codes of conduct requiring a mediator's withdrawal when power imbalances are too severe to allow meaningful dispute resolution to occur.[74]

Unless there is a need to set precedent or establish specific rights, courts are not well suited to resolving environmental issues. Courts put little or no emphasis on determining or enhancing the parties interests or preserving vital relationships. Less powerful groups will be significantly disadvantaged in court by a lack of funds or expertise. Mediation, on the other hand, does not eliminate anyones legal rights. A party is always free to withdraw from an ad hoc process and head to court at no disadvantage.

Environmental disputes often feature stakeholder groups that lack cohesion. When a solution is reached that a subset of a particular group disagrees with, those participants can form a new splinter group and undermine consensus. Indeed, dissatisfied parties appeal court decisions as well. Powerful losing parties in a lawsuit can frustrate apparent court victories via political means - witness the activities of Greenpeace, Earth First and so on. They can do the same in EDR, although EDR strives to identify and respond to all parties and their interests. This minimises the likelihood of splinter groups forming after-the-fact.

9. The Transferability of EDR Theory as Practised in the United States: What Can be Learned From the American Experience?

The concept of EDR is attracting worldwide attention. Throughout Europe, experiments with EDR (along the lines of those in the U.S.) are well underway. In Great Britain, Spain, Germany and the Netherlands there is already documentation of successful EDR efforts.[75] In Central and Eastern Europe, training is underway in the hope that the availability of mediators will engender experimentation with EDR over the next few years.

These preliminary efforts suggest that environmental mediation will be much more agency-controlled in Europe than in the United States. This fact alone is likely to lead to significant differences in practice. For example, neutrals in Europe are more likely to be selected or designated by the relevant agency. All stakeholders are not as likely to be invited to participate. The process is more likely to take place behind closed doors than in the United States[76], and a greater share of the costs will probably be covered by governments.

The presumption throughout Europe is not likely to be that mediation is desirable because it avoids litigation. The fact is, the rules of court standing and the operation of administrative law are such that few of the parties that can litigate in the United States will have that right in Europe. On the other hand, as in Canada, where the practice of environmental mediation has grown quite rapidly, the strongest argument for mediation is that EDR produces agreements that better satisfy the interests of the parties than traditional administrative procedures (and thereby head off endless political or parliamentary wrangling). While mediation is often understood as an alternative to litigation in the United States, it is probably more realistic to see it as an alternative to extended political and parliamentary confrontation throughout Eastern, Central and Western Europe.

Environmental mediation has also been tried in Asia, Africa and parts of Central and South America. What is most interesting in these settings is that mediation has deep cultural antecedents that have nothing to do with the way it is practised in the United States. In Japan, China, Indonesia and parts of Africa, what Westerners call mediation has been practised for centuries under other names. Consensual approaches to resolving differences - often involving the use of natural resources - are part of the way tribes, families and communities have traditionally worked out their differences. The reliance on elders or community leaders to assist in the reconciliation of differences is quite common. Westerners may think they have invented mediation, and believe that it is a social technology that ought to be shared with the rest of the world. We would do well, however, to study indigenous dispute handling procedures in the contexts in which they evolved to see what the West can learn from these experiences, rather than teach.

The developing world is under increasing pressure to harmonise its environmental regulatory standards with those of the developed nations in line with a growing range of multilateral environmental agreements. At the same time, agencies like UNDP (United Nations Development Programme) and the World Bank are feeling increasing pressure to take account of environmental concerns in the granting of development assistance. These trends make it likely that environmental mediation, as it has come to be known in the West, will be exported to the developing world. It would be strange, though, if these concepts were imposed from outside without attention to the counterpart notions that have a long history outside North America and Europe.

10. Obstacles to the Development of Indigenous Theory

The developing world is now considering whether and how it wants to use environmental mediation as it has come to be understood in the United States. In doing so, it must confront the reasons why direct application of these American concepts may be inappropriate. Five points illustrate why this is true.

10.1 Neutrality

The sources of credibility and legitimacy for neutrals in the United States are professional expertise, a reputation for evenhandedness and experience. In other parts of the world, the primary source of acceptability is often social standing. Such status may be the result of age or accomplishment in other arenas. The notion of neutrality, itself, may have little or no meaning in some cultures. Success as a mediator may have more to do with the resources or leverage one can bring to the negotiating table than with the concept of neutrality.

10.2 Transparency

In the United States, there is a premium on openness and accountability. Indeed, the credibility of decision-making in the public sector often depends more on the attributes of the process than on the outcome! In settings in which the history and style of governmental decision-making are different, an emphasis on transparency is inappropriate, even unacceptable.

10.3 Commitment

Mediators in the United States typically rely on contractual arrangements and litigation to ensure that agreements are honored. In other countries, reliance on lawyers, contracts and courts might not have the desired effect of forcing negotiators to live up to their negotiated commitments. On the contrary, such arrangements might undermine the informal bonds of trust that are essential to the success of the EDR process.

10.4 The Role Of (And Belief In) Science

The majority of American citizens are willing to entertain arguments on the merits when it comes to protecting natural resources, or determining acceptable levels of risk or environmental impact. They expect experts to offer such assessments; indeed, the public gives expert advice great credence. In the United States, the scientific method is accepted (perhaps too uncritically) by the average citizen; the role of non-objective judgments, personal bias and cultural values in science-intensive policymaking are all-too-often overlooked.

In other parts of the world, non-scientific forecasts and assessments of the desirability of proposed actions are given more credence. This is not to say that all non-Western cultures have an anti-science bias; rather, there is often a willingness to give additional weight to non-scientific beliefs and interpretation in non-Western settings. Unless environmental mediators takes account of this difference, an over-reliance on scientific expertise is not likely to produce acceptable results in some non-Western forums.

10.5 The Role and Responsibility of Government

In Western settings, there is an accepted role for government in enforcing environmental protection; this remains true despite current trends towards deregulation and privatisation. In some non-Western countries, where poverty and economic distress top the list of local concerns, efforts to generate agreements aimed at balancing environmental concerns with demands for economic growth will not be accepted. Environmental mediators working in such settings must recalibrate their sense of what is most important.

From an international perspective, mediators must be sensitive to the alternative developmental paths that some countries have chosen. The success of the environmental mediation movement in the United States is not, in and of itself, a justification for the export of the American model to other parts of the world. Mediators working in other cultures must build indigenous theories that take account of these important differences.

Bibliography

Administrative Conference of the United States (ACUS), chaired by Thomasina V. Rogers, *Toward Improved Agency Dispute Resolution: Implementing the ADR Act* Washington, DC: US Government Printing Office, 1995.

Alexander, AA Promising Try at Environmental Detente for Coal, *Fortune Magazine*, Feb. 13, 1978.
American Management Systems Inc., *Conversion to Coal At Brayton Point: Final Report to the New England Energy Task Force*, October, 1978.

Amy, Douglas J. *The Politics of Environmental Mediation*, New York: Columbia University Press, 1987.

Arrow, Kenneth et al. *Barriers to Conflict Resolution*. New York: W.W. Norton & Co., 1995.

Bacow, Lawrence and Michael Wheeler, *Environmental Dispute Resolution*. New York and London: Plenum Press, 1984

Bingham, Gail and Leah Haywood. "Environmental Dispute Resolution. The First Ten Years" *The Arbitration Journal* December, 1986.

Bingham, Gail. *Resolving Environmental Disputes: A Decade of Experience*. Washington, DC: Conservation Law Foundation, 1986.

Carpenter, Susan and W.J.D. Kennedy. *Managing Public Disputes*. San Francisco: Jossey-Bass, 1988.

Collins, Richard and Bruce Dotson *Negotiating Public Policy Issues*, Washington, D.C: National Institute of Dispute Resolution (NIDR), 1986.

Bush, Baruch and J. Folger. T*he Promise of Mediation: Responding to Conflict through Empowerment and Recognition.* San Francisco: Jossey-Bass Publishers, 1994.

Collins, Richard and Bruce Dotson. "Sharing the Pain in Virginia. New laws to Protect Instream Flow, Consensus July, 1990.

Cormick, Gerald. AMediating Environmental Controversies: Perspectives and First Experience, 3 *Earth Law Journal* 215 1976.

Davy, Benjamin. *Essential Injustice: When Legal Institutions Cannot Resolve Environmental And Land Use Disputes.* Vienna and New York: Springer-Verlag, 1997.

Detailed Reports Of The Task Forces: Two Volumes And A Summary (F.Murray ed.) published by the National Coal Policy Project, CSIS, Georgetown University, 1800 K Street NW, Washington, DC 2006, April 1978.

Dinell, Tom and John Goody. *A Source Book on Dispute Resolution in Planning School Curricula*, Washington, DC: NIDR 1987.

Dukes, Franklin E. *Resolving Public Conflict: Transforming Community and Governance*. (Manchester and New York: Manchester University Press, 1996).

Duve, Christian. *Study of Special Masters in Complex Environmental Disputes*, draft paper prepared for the Public Disputes Program, Program on Negotiation at Harvard Law School: June, 1997.

Fisher, Roger. ANegotiating Power: Getting and Using Influence, *American Behavioral Scientist* Nov. 27, 1983 no.2; pps. 149-66.

Forrester, J. and D. Stitzel. ABeyond neutrality: the possibilities of activist mediation in public sector conflicts, *Negotiation*, 5(3) (1989).

Glasbergen, Pieter. *Managing Environmental Disputes: Network Management As An Alternative*. Dordrecht and Boston: Kluwer Academic Publishers, 1995.

Goldberg, Stephen B, Frank E.A. Sander and Nancy H. Rogers. *Dispute Resolution: Negotiation. Mediation and Other Processes*, Boston: Little, Brown and Company, 1992.

Harrison, John AEnvironmental Mediation: The Ethical and Constitutional Dimension, 9 *Journal of Environmental Law* 80.

Huelsberg, Nancy A. and William F. Lincoln (eds) *Successful Negotiating in Local Government*, ; Washington, D.C.: ICMA / Practical Management Series, 1985.

Kolb and Associates, *When Talk Works*, San Francisco: Jossey-Bass, 1994.

Lax, David A and James K. Sebenius. *The Manager As Negotiator*. New York: The Free Press, 1986.

Macfarlane, Dr. Julie. *1995 Evaluation of Canadas Ontario Court (General Division)s ADR Centre*; Faculty of Law at the University of Windsor, Ontario; on-line at the Access to Justice Net site: Awww.acjnet.org/docs/minagont.html.

Mernitz, S. *Mediation of Environmental Disputes: A Sourcebook*. New York: Praeger, 1980.

Mnookin and Kornhauser. ABargaining in the Shadow of the Law,88 *Yale Law Journal* 950, 1979.

National Institute of Dispute Resolution (NIDR), *A Decade of Progress*, Washington, DC: NIDR, 1993.

OConnor. "Environmental Mediation: The State-of-the-Art" *E.I.A. Review* No.2, Oct. 1978 note 11, at 2. (published by the Laboratory of Architecture and Planning, Massachusetts Institute of Technology).

Primm, Edith. AThe Neighborhood Justice Center Movement, *Kentucky Law Journal* 81, 1992-1993.

Raiffa, Harold. *The Art & Science Of Negotiation*, Cambridge: Harvard University Press, 1982.

Regional Part 22 ADR Policy, June 23, 1997; US Environmental Protection Agency, Region I. (On file with the authors and available through the US Environmental Protection Agency).

Rubin, Jeffrey Z. and Frank E.A. Sander. AWhen Should We Use Agents? Direction versus Representative Negotiation," *Negotiation Law Journal*, October, 1988.

Ruckleshaus, William. AEnvironmental Protection: A Brief History of the Environmental Movement in America and Its Implications Abroad, 15 *Environmental Law Journal* 455, 1985.

Schoenbrod, David. ALimits and Dangers of Environmental Mediation, 58 *New York University Law Review* 1453, 1983.

Society of Professionals In Dispute Resolution (SPIDR), *Ethical Standards of Professional Responsibility*, adopted June, 1986.

Stulberg, Joseph B.. AThe Theory and Practice of Mediation: A Reply to Professor Susskind, 6 *Vermont Law Review* 1978.

Susskind, Lawrence. AEnvironmental Mediation and the Accountability Problem, 6 *Vermont Law Review* 1978.

Susskind, Lawrence and Alan Weinstein. AToward a Theory of Environmental Dispute Resolution, *Boston College of Environmental Law Review* 9/2 1980.

Susskind, Lawrence and Gerald McMahon. AThe Theory and Practice of Negotiated Rulemaking, 3 *Yale Journal of Regulation* 133 (1985)

Susskind, Lawrence and Laura van Dam. "Squaring Off at the Table, Not in the Courts, *Technology Review* July, 1986.
Susskind, Lawrence. "NDIR's State Office of Mediation Experiment, *Negotiation Law Journal* 2(4) October, 1986.

Susskind, Lawrence and Jeffrey Cruikshank. *Breaking the Impasse: Consensual Approaches to Resolving Public Disputes*. Cambridge: Basic Books, 1987.

Susskind, Lawrence and Susan Podziba. *Affordable Housing Mediation: Building Consensus for Regional Agreements in the Hartford Greater Bridgeport Areas* Cambridge: Lincoln Institute of Land Policy, July, 1990.

Susskind, L.E., E.F. Babbit and P.N. Segal. AWhen ADR becomes the Law: a Review of Federal Practice". *Negotiation Journal*, 9(1) 1993.

Susskind, Lawrence and Patrick Field. *Dealing With an Angry Public: The Mutual Gains Approach to Resolving Disputes*. New York: The Free Press, 1996.

Susskind, Lawrence E. and S. McKearnan. AThe Past, Present, and Future of Public Dispute Resolution in the United States " *University of Texas Journal of Architecture and Planning* (JAPR), forthcoming in 1998.

Wheeler, Michael. ANegotiating NIMBYs: Learning from the Failure of the Massachusetts Siting Law, *Yale Journal on Regulation II* Summer, 1994.

Endnotes

[1] In recounting the early history of environmental mediation, we wish to acknowledge our reliance on the work of Gail Bingham and Franklin Dukes. See Bingham and Haywood, December, 1986; Dukes, 1996.

[2] In general, these public dispute resolution pioneers worked in four distinct areas: environmental dispute resolution, negotiated investment strategies, negotiated rule-making, and community dispute resolution. See Susskind and McKearnan,1998. (This paper is also available through the Program on Negotiation at Harvard Law School.)

[3] The first suggestion for environmental dispute resolution is found in Foster's 1969 article, "A case for environmental conciliation". See Mernitz, 1980.

[4] See Susskind and Weinstein,1980: pp143-196.

[5] The Snoqualmie River mediation was sponsored primarily by the Ford Foundation to expand the range of applications of dispute resolution procedures from the labour-management arena to neighborhoods and communities. "In fact, many of the first environmental dispute resolution exercises were 'showcase' examples, intended to demonstrate to a variety of interested parties in fields not familiar with its philosophy or practices the feasibility of conflict resolution. These were efforts to introduce the concepts of consensus, participation, integration, and interest-based negotiation to individuals and institutions more accustomed to adversarial modes of thinking and practice." See Dukes, 1996: pp. 31-32.

[6] See Cormick, 1976; O'Connor, 1978.

[7] The mediation resulted in a number of agreements, some of which were never implemented. See Bingham and Haywood,1986 p.6. Also see Bacow and Wheeler, 1984 pp.113-116.

[8] See Bingham and Haywood, 1986. Also see Detailed Reports of the Task Forces, 1978, and Alexander, 1978.

[9] Other important early policy dialogue experiments included the Center for Negotiation and Public Policy's facilitation of discussions between New England power company officials and regulators to discuss the conversion of power plants from oil to coal. This discussion developed into the successful mediation of the dispute over the conversion of the Brayton Point power plant. See Bingham, 1986 at p.20. For a full account of the Brayton Point mediation, see Bacow and Wheeler, 1984 pp.58-184.

[10] Bingham, 1986.

[11] The significance of the Storm King mediation was soon affirmed in Colorado, during one of that state's plethora of water policy and planning controversies, known as the Two Forks Dam dispute. The metropolitan Denver area's projections of future water needs constantly outstrip the current or (planned) supply. As a result, major new water storage and diversion projects were proposed throughout the 1970s and 1980s; projects that were condemned by environmentalists for their potential negative impact. Facing this problem, 31 elected and private sector policy-makers began meeting in October, 1981 in an

innovative attempt to build consensus on how metropolitan Denver might meet its future needs. "From the beginning, the difficulties that the roundtable faced were similar to those in many other natural resource controversies across the nation. Many individuals and groups had competing interests in the allocation of the state's water resources. No mechanism or planning procedures for bringing these groups together existed previously, and the issues themselves were quite complex." - Bingham, 1986 at p.38. For an excellent account of how these difficulties were partially surmounted, see Bingham at pp.37-41.

[12] See Amy, 1987.

[13] See Bingham, 1986 p.129.

[14] See Dukes, 1996.

[15] The Ford Foundation funded the American Arbitration Association (AAA), the National Center for Dispute Settlement, New York's Institute for Mediation and Conflict Resolution, the Community Crisis Intervention Center at Washington University in St. Louis, Missouri and the Center for Community Justice, all of which were involved in community disputes.

[16] See Bingham, 1986 pp.24-25; Dukes, 1996 pp.33-34.

[17] "In the environmental field, the Ford Foundation tended to fund pioneers in more formal dispute resolution efforts. The Hewlett Foundation, on the other hand, tended to fund less formal processes designed to build relationships which could sustain the tensions of subsequent decision-making processes." Dukes, 1996 p.34.

[18] The William A. and Flora Hewlett Foundation's Ann Firth Murray, quoted in Bingham, 1986 p.25.

[19] See Dukes, 1996 p.34.

[20] See Susskind, October, 1986 pp.323-327; also see Dukes,1996 p.34.

[21] See Dinell and Goody, 1987. See also Collins and Dotson, 1986.

[22] Prominent examples include Bingham, 1986; Bacow and Wheeler, 1984; Susskind and Cruikshank, 1987; and Carpenter and Kennedy, 1988.

[23] By specifying the procedural requirements that must accompany various types of agency action (particularly rulemaking) Congress attempted to restrict agen-

cies' exercise of discretion. However, the procedural burdens imposed by the APA has made rulemaking "excessively costly, rigid and cumbersome...it imposes perverse incentives that conspire to undermine sound public policy." See Jody Freeman, "Collabourative Governance in the Administrative State," 45 U.C.L.A. L.Rev 1, 5 at footnote 18. To illustrate, in the late 1980s, up to 80 % of the rules promulgated by EPA were challenged in federal court. See Ruckleshaus, 1985.

[24] ACUS served as the federal government's "watchdog" agency until 1995, when it went out of existence as the result of budget cuts. This agency, whose staff was appointed directly by the President, was charged with eliminating waste and encouraging efficient management of all federal agency operations.

[25] See Susskind and McMahon, 1985; Susskind and van Dam, July 1986 pp.39-40.

[26] See '303, the Negotiated Rulemaking Act of 1990, Public Law 101-648; also see Susskind, Babbit, and Segal, 1993 pp.59-65.

[27] See ACUS, 1995.

[28] See Wheeler, Summer 1994 pp.241-290.

[29] See Susskind and Podziba, July 1990; see also Susskind, October 1986 pp.323-327.

[30] Civic experiments with ADR originated with the Kettering Foundation's support of the Negotiated Investment Strategy (NIS) in 1978. NIS uses conflict resolution to craft consensus agreements about policy on future investment by cities and states. See "Negotiated Investment Strategy". Kettering Foundation, Dayton, Ohio, 1982. For a general overview, see Huelsberg and Lincoln, 1985; also see NIDR, 1993 p 4.

[31] See Primm, 1992-1993 p.1068.

[32] Collins and Dotson, July 1990 p.5.

[33] Resolve, a Washington-based group that began as part of the Conservation Foundation in 1977, is an example of an organization that has elected to broaden its focus from environmental to public dispute resolution. See Dukes, 1996 pp.38, 78.

[34] For detailed profiles of the careers and accomplishments of the first practitioners, see Kolb and Associates, 1994.

[35] For a full account of the activities of various state offices of mediation, see Dukes, 1996 pp.80-82.

[36] See the Resources Directory of *Consensus.*

[37] NIDR, 1993 p.4.

[38] The SPIDR Sector on Environmental and Public Dispute Resolution is the only association specifically devoted to public conflict resolution. See Dukes,1996 pp.38, 44.

[39] See American Management Systems Inc., October 1978; also see Susskind, 1978 pp. 24-37.

[40] See the discussion on the Snoqualmie dam dispute, supra.

[41] For interesting discussions of the principal-agency problem, see Lax and Sebenius, 1986 pp.306-314; Rubin and Sander, 1988 pp.395-401; Arrow et al, 1995 pp.95-202.

[42] See Susskind and Cruikshank, 1987 p.192.

[43] Practitioners and scholars still disagree on the ideal number of participants, the best way to choose participants (i.e., self-nomination vs. invitation), the best way to select and pay the mediator, and the need for the mediator to perform all the pre-negotiation tasks. However, the authors believe that it is always better to include too many people or groups than too few - especially at the outset. Although there is a logistical advantage in limiting the number of voices directly involved, that advantage is outweighed by the problems that arise if someone decides that they have been unfairly excluded. The authors also recommend that each coalition nominate its own representatives. Ad hoc selection processes must sometimes embrace elabourate selection procedures if they are to overcome the charge that they are less representative than conventional processes. See Susskind and Cruikshank, 1987 pp.101-108.

[44] See Susskind and Field, 1996 pp.38-39.

[45] See Susskind and Cruikshank, 1987 p.221.

[46] See Susskind, 1978.

[47] The FMCS is an independent executive agency of the federal government created in 1947 to facilitate the resolution of labour-management conflicts. Its primary duty is to promote labour-management peace. This responsibility is fulfilled by providing mediation assistance in preventing and resolving collective bargaining disputes. For this purpose, FMCS stations federal mediators strategically throughout the country. Service mediators are carefully selected and trained. Most mediators have backgrounds in management or labour, and many have some experience in both. Mediators are selected for the job because of their demonstrated skills in collective bargaining. The AAA is a public-service, nonprofit organization founded in 1926, with headquarters in New York City. Its main goal is the resolution of disputes of all kinds through the use of arbitration, mediation, democratic action, and other methods. Although AAA has moved gradually into the mediation of environmental disputes, most of the disputes it mediates involve a limited number of parties and easily identifiable issues. (i.e. wages, working conditions and benefits).

[48] See Susskind, 1978.

[49] However, a number of states and court rules make mediators generally accountable for the course of mediation, and, occasionally, laws specify consequences for mediators who breach specified duties. However, certain states provide mediators legal immunity. See Goldberg, Sander and Rogers, 1992 pp.176-77.

[50] For a full explanation of the theory of "pareto optimality" as it applies to negotiation, see Raiffa, 1982.

[51] See SPIDR, 1989, reproduced in Goldberg, Sander and Rogers, 1992 pp.164-171.

[52] See the discussion of the mediation of the Foothills Water treatment project Congressman Timothy Wirth, in Bacow and Wheeler, 1984 pp. 195-240; Susskind, 1978 pp. 30-37.

[53] See Dukes at p. 181.

[54] On this subject, the New York State Unified Court System's (UCS) certification program may provide a model for future attempts at certification. For more information, see: NYS Unified Court System/ Community Dispute Resolution Centers Program, PO Box 7039 - AESOB, Albany, NY 12225. Phone: 518-473-4160/FAX: 518-473-6861.

[55] Such agency involvement would also solve the financial problems that continue to plague ad hoc attempts at mediation. This problem is endemic to the entire field of public conflict mediation, as well as the environmental field. Mediators cannot insist that all parties to environmental disputes pay for their services, since many of the parties do not have resources. Mediators are understandably uncomfortable with the thought of collecting fees from only those parties that can afford to pay, thus jeopardising their apparent neutrality. Even government grants are problematic since regulatory agencies are often among the parties-at-issue. For a complete analysis of the experience in using court appointed "special masters" to mediate environmental disputes, see Duve, 1997.

[56] See Susskind, 1978.

[57] Such actions are filed pursuant to procedures set in the US Code of Federal Regulations (CFR). See 40 CFR Part 22, which sets out the administrative "civil procedure" governing administrative litigation brought by the EPA.

[58] For Part 22 cases, there is a presumption that the case team will offer mediation to the Respondent if the case has not settled (and settlement does not appear imminent) within 90 days after the answer is filed. The presumption that the offer to mediate will be issued may be overcome under certain circumstances (e.g. where there are ongoing, productive settlement discussions or where the Region believes that it is important to obtain an administrative ruling on a particular issue).

[59] See "Regional Part 22 ADR Policy," (June 23, 1997), which "...sets forth the Regional policy regarding the use of Alternative Dispute Resolution (ADR) in Part 22 penalty cases and other administrative enforcement matters."

[60] See Macfarlane.

[61] See the Federal Court of Australia Act 1976, Section 53A.

[62] The new sub section (53(1A)) reads as follows:

Mediation and arbitration 53A. (1) Subject to the Rules of Court, the Court may, by order, refer the proceedings in the court, or any part of them or any matter arising out of them, to a mediator or an arbitrator for mediation or arbitration, as the case may be, in accordance with the Rules of Court. (1A) Referrals under subsection (1) to a mediator may be made with or without the consent of the parties to the proceedings. However, referrals to an arbitrator may be made only with the consent of the parties. (2) The Rules of Court may make provision for the registration of awards made in an arbitration carried out under an order made under subsection (1).

For more information, contact the Executive Officer, International Institute for Negotiation and Conflict Management, on the world wide web: "iincm.glblaw.uts.edu.au".

[63] There is precedent. For instance, EPA provides access to funding through CERCLA technical assistance grants (TAGs) of up to $50,000 to communities engaged in hazardous waste remediation. See 42 U.S.C. 9617(e).

[64] However, closed meetings are more acceptable if the agreements negotiated are subject to public scrutiny during parallel regulatory hearings. There is substantial disagreement among public sector mediators regarding the advantages of open versus closed meetings. The majority view is that all contact with the media should be avoided until after a settlement is reached. This traditional view assumes that all the appropriate interests are adequately represented behind closed doors.

[65] This position has created a significant amount of controversy. For an interesting debate on mediator accountability, see Goldberg, Sander and Rogers, 1992 pp. 171-178; also see Stulberg, 1978; and Amy, 1987.

[66] See Bush and Folger, 1994. For a thorough discussion of the transformative aspects of public conflict resolution and the writings of its adherents, see Dukes, 1996 pp.119-184.

[67] See Forrester and Stitzel, 1989 pp. 261-64.

[68] "Bingham's research...demonstrate[es] that when regulatory agencies are not involved in mediation they do not simply rubber stamp the outcome and do indeed feel free to reject negotiated outcomes. Agreements were actually implemented in 85% of cases where officials participated, but in only 87% of cases where they did not participate. Partly as a result of this finding, formal mediations now rarely exclude regulatory officials. Indeed, with the growing institutionalisation of consensus seeking approaches environmental mediation is now most commonly initiated by officials." See Harrison at p. 91.

[69] Some commentators claim that the primary danger of EDR is that the settlement process may bypass the regulatory process in which the public interest, not necessarily represented by the parties to a negotiated settlement, can be aired. However, in the US at least, there is no reason why the outcome of a negotiated process should not include the relevant regulatory bodies; nor does EDR

between all parties except the relevant agency abrogate that agency's power to affect the terms of the final settlement. See Schoenbrod, 1983.

[70] However, Roger Fisher presents an alternate view of what constitutes true negotiating power. See Fisher, 1983.

[71] See Harrison p.96.

[72] See Mnookin and Kornhauser, 1979.

[73] See Harrison p. 96. Also, most practitioners agree that parties only agree to negotiate if they perceive a relative balance of power; that they are in an inter-dependent relationship with one another such that everyone has some power to prevent or constrain at least some of the others from acting wholly unilaterally. On this point, see Susskind and McMahon, 1985 pp.153-5. Also see Fisher, 1983.

[74] "...If the neutral is concerned about the possible consequences of a proposed agreement, and the needs of the parties dictate, the neutral must inform the parties of that concern. In adhering to this standard, the neutral may find it advisable to educate the parties, to refer one or more parties for specialised advice, or to withdraw from the case." See SPIDR, 1986 para.6.

[75] See, for instance, Glasbergen, 1995; Davy, 1997.

[76] "Critics of environmental mediation charge that the mediation process is hidden from view, and that the public is therefore denied opportunity to hold regulatory agencies to account...It is true that the conventional model of mediation in say the context of commercial, family or labor relations disputes, suggest a purely private negotiation behind closed doors. Indeed this is frequently cited as a major advantage over court proceedings. And in the UK, one of our few institutionalised mechanisms for the consensual resolution of planning disputes...has had a chequered history characterised by suspicion of backroom deals. In contrast, environmental mediation in the US could not practically aspire to confidentiality or privacy, even if that were thought to be desirable." See Harrison at pp.88-9.

CHAPTER II
ENVIRONMENTAL CONFLICTRESOLUTION IN GERMANY

ENVIRONMENTAL CONFLICT RESOLUTION IN GERMANY

Helmut Weidner

1. Introduction

The foundations for a modern, independent German environmental policy were laid in the early 1970s with the launch of a variety of government programmes, the establishment of several institutions and the promulgation of a comprehensive body of law. Nonetheless, the 1970s also mark the starting point for a long string of environmental conflicts in Germany, accompanied by an increase in the size and strength of the environmental movement. The establishment of a "green" national political party, which entered the national parliament in 1983, successful protests against some of the environmentally harmful activities of private and public bodies, and an increasing use of the courts, forced the government to give more emphasis to environmental protection and encouraged experimentation with new approaches to environmental conflict. The first major negotiation-based, consensus-oriented procedures organised by a neutral third party were initiated in 1990. Both dealt with waste management conflicts. They were structured as mediation procedures. The basic impetus for this development came from the use of Environmental Dispute Resolution (EDR) techniques in the US, which were, and still are, the main model for the design of environmental conflict resolution (EDR) procedures in Germany.

Since then, a number of similar procedures have been conducted, covering a broad range of problem areas (e.g. transport, land use, contaminated landfills, airport siting, risk assessment for genetic engineering). However, although there is an increasing number of all types of negotiation-based, informal procedures aimed at increasing substantive participation, the absolute figures are small and do not bear out the expectations of proponents of alternative procedures. Despite the fact that the capability and willingness of the relevant parties in environmental conflicts (public administration, non-governmental environmental organisations, business) have been growing for several years now, the influence of certain restrictions remains strong. This is due mainly to specific features of the politico-administrative and legal culture in Germany, and the generally unfavourable conditions for progressive environmental policy resulting from the deepest economic crisis since World War II. The mixed experience with actual cases, particularly that of disappointments due to unrealistic expectations, is also responsible for this very slow, albeit steady, increase. However, when assessing the results achieved so far, the overall balance is promising. It is obvious that better results could be reached, if the techniques for settling disputes were more refined, participants (and mediators) better trained and some legal and institutional framework conditions modified. Activities in this direction have been already initiated with growing support from government bodies, academic organisations and influential legal experts.

This leads one to expect that, as environmental policy is reorganised and made more flexible - a process begun recently - EDR will also become an officially recognised instrument, i.e. embedded in the existing legal and institutional framework. Such a conclusion is also supported by the fact that reports commissioned to examine this question have responded positively, and that the professionalisation of mediators, who all started out as amateurs in this area, has accelerated rapidly. However, it is still impossible to say whether the seriously deteriorating economic situation will be exploited by businesses and some areas of government to reduce the level of environmental protection. In this case, the (fragile) trust of environmental organisations and the concerned general public in co-operative EDR procedures which has been built up in the past would probably suffer greatly.

2. The Politico-administrative and Legal Context
2.1 Development of Environmental Policy in Germany: A Brief Overview

About 25 years ago, the foundations for a modern environmental policy in Germany were laid with a variety of government programmes, such as the "Quick-start programme of 1970 and the "Environment programme" (1971), and with a comprehensive body of law. This was achieved within a relatively short period in a show of legal and institutional strength from the left-liberal (SPD/FDP) coalition (1969-1982). The political administration was also very much going it alone in this, as there was no massive popular pressure in this direction at the time. The stimulus in Germany had been developments in environmental politics abroad, particularly in the US, which were taken up by a coalition government almost overjoyed at the prospect of bringing in new reforms. In close co-operation with large business organisations and scientific experts, an environmental policy concept and body of regulations were produced which were, for their time, very demanding[1].

The dominance of legal experts among the state agencies, and the then especially pronounced "statist ideology", which viewed the government as a control centre for society, both responsible for and competent at drawing up and supervising detailed matters in complex political areas, had a profound influence on the character of the programmes and laws. The result was thus an ambitious but hierarchical regulative approach to environmental policy, whose regulatory instruments were mainly of the "command and control" variety, with their roots in the prevailing legal dogma (especially policing law) in the area of nature protection and public health & sanitation policy.

The economic turbulence in the wake of the 1973 oil crisis quickly showed up the weaknesses of a plan which made the realisation of environmental protection targets essentially dependent upon complex state and regulatory measures, but gave little legal or institutional opportunity for social agencies representing environmental protection interests to exert their influence. And so, as early as the mid-1970s, with a number of agreements between trade union and business leaders and the high-ranking members of the political and administrative system, came stagnation in the development of environmental policy and considerable failures in its implementation.

The task of making political issues out of what were now widely-felt environmental fears and demands in German society was taken up more and more by the so-called new social movements, from which green alternative parties finally grew, with growing electoral success. The constitution of a "green" national political party,[2] as well as increasingly successful protests and demonstrations against environmentally harmful activities by business and public bodies, forced the established parties and government to give environmental protection more weight. The speed and extent of these course corrections can only be explained by the massive visible and tangible effects of pollution (for instance smog, dying forests), and by extensive critical reporting in the media on environmental problems.

The conservative-liberal (CDU/CSU/FDP) government coalition followed, at the end of 1982. It reacted to the challenges in the political arena represented by the environmental movement, green parties, an ever greener social democratic party (which was by then marching under the banner of "environmental modernisation") and also by the Chernobyl disaster, and put pioneering new legislation through parliament in a relatively short space of time, achieving massive reductions in the pollution in specific problem areas. In doing so, it also stimulated environmental politics in the EU and farther afield. And German environmental policy was awarded high marks in an OECD status report in 1993.

Comparing the strategic approaches and environmental policy instruments of the conservative-liberal government and its social-liberal predecessor, one is led to conclude that things have remained broadly, for a long time at any rate, very much the same. The dominant policy style is still a regulatory one, with the emphasis on command and control. The opportunity for a radical shake-up of the ossified elements in the environmental regulatory system, which the process of German reunification after 1989 brought with it, was more or less completely missed.

However, tendencies towards a transition from overwhelmingly reactive, curative measures and bureaucratic regulatory instruments to flexible, root-cause oriented approaches of conserving resources and the environment have been evident for a number of years. The redrafting of environmental liability law in 1990, the easing of the rules of evidence in proving causation and the extension of liability to cover even proper operation of a plant, all point in this direction. And the strongly promoted Eco-Audit System, as well as some further instruments along these lines, increases flexibility in the business sector and the transparency of entrepreneurial environmental activities and their effects.

These are all certainly promising beginnings. However, further opportunities initiated by the European Union (EU) to change the existing patterns in the environmental policy system in favour of environmental needs, such as for example the Directive on public access to environmental data, have been little exploited. Regulations to promote public participation or improve the legal status of groups representing environmental interests, for example through the introduction of a right of action for environmental associations ("class action"), found no majority support in the government. The conservative-liberal government reacted to the rising pressure for political action on the environment chiefly by extending the range of conventional (regulatory) legal instruments. In the course of its term of office it even increased the level of legislative density and detail in environmental policy instruments, in what the independent Council of Environmental Advisors (*Rat von Sachverständigen für Umweltfragen*) described in 1994 as "almost hectic legislative activity over recent years".

2.2 Policy Style and Legal Climate

This continued heavy reliance on a conventional regulatory approach contradicts not only the recommendations of experts, but also the results of more recent findings in environmental and other policy research. Within all the variety of current political theory there is virtually total agreement that the need for government leadership on the environment has risen dramatically, but that the forms of control which have dominated up to now have increasingly shown themselves to be inadequate, and therefore that non-hierarchical, framework-building means of ("soft") control (such as through information, decentralisation, and procedural initiatives which, for example, set up dialogue or discourse-based procedures) as well as economic instruments should be used more intensively.

The German government instituted a systematic examination of the instrumental and procedural elements of its current environmental policy approach, and a test of the utility of alternative instruments and procedures. Its conclusions to date are not entirely promising: on the one hand, sharp criticism of over-complicated environmental protection procedures from the business sector appears to have opened up the way to new changes, e.g. in planning permission law through streamlining, so-called speeding-up laws (*Beschleunigungsgesetze*), including a reduction in public participation rights in planning and implementation areas; on the other hand, other recommended alternatives are the subject of rather muted discussion. Approaches involving economic instruments based on the "polluter pays" principle, and on the use of targeted information campaigns to sway opinion, are being used increasingly, but still play a less important role than in other progressive countries (e.g. the Netherlands, Denmark and Sweden). The existing procedures for public participation in decision-making and implementation are rather limited and criticised as being merely symbolic. However, with respect to the participation of environmental organisations and critical academic institutions in policy formulation, the situation improved considerably during the 1980s.

This hesitant and ambivalent attitude towards structural innovation in environmental law and policy is not only the result of a strong interest in maintaining existing structures of power and influence, but is also a consequence of the politico-administrative culture, one dominant factor of which is the legalistic and hierarchical thinking in the upper echelons of the bureaucracy.[3] Correspondingly, conventional environmental regulations still make up the majority of the government's range of standards.

A systematic change towards more flexible approaches is also hampered by the legal and institutional complexity of the environmental policy system, and the manifold formal and informal practices and relationships which have evolved within this system over time, involving administrators at all government levels, business federations, trade unions and "established" scientific institutions.

The complexities of a three-tier federal system with separated and overlapping powers of jurisdiction, as well as of implementation and enforcement, require a high level of vertical and horizontal co-ordination and co-operation. The attempt to achieve a high degree of uniformity in implementation is encouraged by common bureaucratic traditions within state governments and the predominant legal background of senior officials. Furthermore, the employment of senior officials on a permanent basis allows for the accumulation of basic expert knowledge and favour the establishment and maintenance of informal communication networks.

Overall co-operation in the field of environmental policy bears the hallmark of Germanys particular brand of federalism[4]. Features of this are the strong interdependence between executive institutions at all levels, and the co-ordination mechanisms which have developed in particular between the central government and the states. Complex procedures of representation and consultation are fundamental to this system. Many legislative and other important decisions result from bargaining behind the scenes, and, within the various institutional bodies, between politicians (of the government and the opposition) and administrators.

The system is in fact even more complex, as it is also closely interwoven with neocorporatist[5] elements in industry and society: Germany has a powerful system of interest group organisations, recognised in law and with close links to the political parties. It includes statutory chambers of trade and industry, and trade union and voluntary bodies associated with the churches. They work through a complex network of consultative procedures which underlie and interlink policy-making at all levels. The interweaving of interests and influence between sectors and levels of government and society is a key aspect of German political life.[6]

Other forms of judicial control of governmental actions and conflict settlement are laid down in the public (administrative), civil and criminal law, for each of which different sets of courts are responsible, both at federal and state level. Up to now, criminal law and the civil courts have played only a minor role. The administrative courts exercise comprehensive judicial control over administrative actions whereby the rights of individuals have been violated (Art. 19GG; Federal Administrative Court Procedure Act). They hear cases brought by individuals to prevent, control or reverse the act of a public agency or a private organisation with public functions. Not only those affected by pollution but also "the polluters" (the regulatees) may initiate court action and frequently do so. Taking legal action is only possible if the injured party's individual statutory rights have been unlawfully harmed by the act or omission of the administration. This concept of the judicial review of administrative action is reflected in the restrictive criteria for access to administrative courts which, for example, do not allow class action or "altruistic" action by an individual.

As a rule, and this is provided for in several specific regulations and laws, planning or licensing procedures for activities on a certain scale must be open to public participation. During a set period anyone can lodge objections against the development project with the responsible authority. After that the licensing authority must discuss the objections with the applicant, and with those who have lodged objections, at a public hearing. The decision is then taken through an internal administrative process. The decision must be made public. Only the applicant and those with a direct, individual interest with a basis in law are allowed to initiate court procedures. In stark contrast to the situation in the US, further obstacles to substantive participation or influence are presented by limited public access to administrative and private information relevant to the case (this applies to environmental organisations too), although implementation of the EU Directive on access to environmental information has brought about an improvement. In general, as characterised by an expert from the US, and especially compared with the situation there, "an important weakness of the German administrative law system is its failure to require an open and transparent process of rule-making. The Environmental Ministry may consult with outside groups and individuals if it wishes before promulgating regulations, but even where such consultations are statutorily required, they are not judicially enforceable ... The role of the administrative courts should be rethought to provide them a limited role in overseeing the procedural integrity of the regulatory process".[7] In addition, as already mentioned, even this weak protection of environmental interests appears to be being eroded with the enactment of "speeding-up" laws designed to streamline the permission procedures for certain large-scale projects.

Overall, the legal powers underpinning environmental interests are clearly considerably weaker in Germany than in the US. This may also explain the later development in Germany of EDR procedures.

Nevertheless, administrative courts play an important role in environmental policy and conflicts. They are often mobilised by third parties before, during and after licensing or planning procedures, with the aim of achieving tighter environmental standards or stopping projects or operating plants. The lower courts in particular have often ruled in favour of environmental concerns. They also started quite early with a thorough review of the interpretation and application of broad statutory terms by the administration as well as the adequacy of standards set in administrative directives. Quite often they have challenged the administration's decisions and proceeded to develop standards on their own initiative. This has resulted in a heated debate on the administrative courts' increasing intervention in the governments areas of competence. Finally, decisions by the higher courts and the Federal Administrative Court have emphasized and strengthened governmental powers for making standards more specific, while a Federal Supreme Court decision in 1984[8] and the Environmental Liability Act of 1990 relaxed certain restrictions concerning negligence and burden of proof.

Overall, the higher courts have not played a major role in *actively* shaping environmental policy. Nevertheless, some decisions have had considerable impact on governmental policy-making, e.g. the *Voerde* decision by the Federal Administrative Court (concerning a fossil-fuelled power plant) which led to stricter emission standards within the statutory framework.[9] In several instances, the federal courts have also stressed the government's duty to strive for a precautionary environmental policy, which has brought about the re-interpretation of this principle in an environmentally positive direction. However, there is a clear tendency not to encroach too far on the governments powers of active policy design and to limit such encroachment by the lower, especially administrative, courts by case law.[10]

2.3 Changing Conditions for the Context for Environmental Co-operation

Current government environmental policy is characterised by an inherent contradiction. It resorts simultaneously to obsolete and to modern, innovative environmental policy plans. It alternates between stimulating and dampening down the now considerable potential for environmental modernisation in business and society, and it does not make adequate (at least, as compared internationally) use of the large environmental policy capacities which have been built up in recent years by the central agencies ("environmental proponents").

This could largely be explained by the peculiarities of the German political system, which make it difficult to bring about swift, radical change in environmental policy. This is so even though while favourable conditions for a modernisation of environmental policy already exist within society and its institutions, as well as in the political and administrative system and in important economic sectors. These favourable conditions include a broad distribution of environmental expertise, many varied forms of co-operation between environmental policy innovators from all areas of society, a large amount of technical and informational resources, well-organised networks of environmental interests and, not least, a relatively broad and stable consensus as to the necessity of an environmental modernisation of industrial society. The old neocorporatist mode of co-operation of the post-war period, between state, business associations and unions (the "iron triangle"), is gradually developing into a network (the "green triangle") in which organisations representing specifically environmental concerns are now also able to participate in political decisions.

The slow pace of change in environmental politics fits with the general hypothesis that the institutional conditions in German politics make a fundamental change of strategy a long-drawn-out process. Major changes require as a rule a very broad political and social consensus, which is typically gained through a complicated and time-consuming process. The roots of this are in the neocorporatist pattern for solving problems and in the associated institutional fabric, for example in the specific form of German federalism, in the requirement for the rule of law and the constitutional opportunities to scrutinise fundamental political decisions which this entails, as well as in the proportional voting system, which seldom leads to clear-cut political majorities.

Thus the political scientist Manfred G. Schmidt describes the broad characteristics of action by the German state as a "politics of the middle way"; it is characterised by two starkly contrasting elements: on the one hand, it is almost incapable of rapid changes of course, while on the other hand, it has a notable capacity for long-term, gradual, "silent change", and on this basis possesses a considerable ability to take into account new challenges, issues and solutions.

Against this background, it seems plausible to regard the increase in EDR procedures over recent years (the majority of the cases were initiated by public authorities) as the expression of just such a "silent change" in environmental politics.

This assessment is supported by, among other things, the following developments:

(1)   There is now in Germany a broad base of sometimes highly organised proponents of progressive environmental policy, and this base covers all areas of society. The main winner as regards environmental protection, the eco-industry, still has a keen interest in stringent environmental policy creating new markets and expanding those already established.[11] Recently, there has also been a sharp rise in the growth of a new "environmental market", which has established itself alongside the traditional market for technology. It too is expected to grow in the coming years, partly as a result of the introduction of new policy instruments, and partly because of the need for new approaches in solving environmental problems. This growing sector could be called an "environmentally proactive business sector", since most of the organisations and groups of which it is made up have strong links to the environmentalist movement and equally strong opinions concerning ecology. This "environmentally proactive business sector" is not simply selling environmental products and services, but is doing so with a committed environmentalist approach. The "greening" of (normal) enterprises is contributing to the growth of this sector. Furthermore, an expanding, independent, highly specialised "eco-bureaucracy" has arisen, and is developing its own esprit de corps. It has opened the doors to a new kind of employee: an expert with a specialised environmental education gained both before and during employment, younger and often highly motivated, and brought up in a social atmosphere of increasing "greenness". Membership of environmental organisations is no longer a rarity. Co-operation with such organisations is no longer a problem for these administrators.

(2)   In the course of environmental policy development over the last decade an essential change has taken place in the constellation of agencies and in the dominant environmental policy paradigm. This is above all the result of a greatly increased need for co-operation in the field of environmental policy, and a

correspondingly greater ability of central groups of agencies to co-operate with one another. The reason for the increased need for co-operation is partly a change in the nature of environmental problems, and partly the increased influence of well-organised environmental proponents and the emergence of a new environmental policy approach, "environmental modernisation" or "sustainable development". In many environmental policy fields, public authorities and industry are having to rely to an increasing extent on information and co-operation from many individuals, social groups and environmental organisations. None of this can be achieved through "giving orders" alone. Parallel to the rising *need* for cooperation, the *ability* of central groups of agencies to co-operate has also grown in recent years. This applies to business, public authorities and political parties as much as to environmental organisations. Furthermore, there is perceptible movement among all groups towards an increasing preference for flexible and co-operative problem management instruments and for breaking down the powerful barriers to communication and mutual aversion which once existed. To nearly all agencies, cautious co-operation now appears more attractive than traditional conflict management, with its final port of call usually the courtroom. Most of the significant agency groups support the idea of sustainable development. Resulting from such an agreement in principle are many varied possibilities for co-operation between otherwise conflicting agencies, since the anti-communicative caricatures of the other side and its ideology can now be construed and credibly expressed only with the greatest difficulty. There have already been numerous cases of co-operation between the main agencies as a result of these developments[12], especially with respect to Local Agenda 21 procedures.

Whether this development will continue under the present unfavourable conditions - an increase in social and economic policy restrictions, which are likely to remain in place for some time to come - will depend greatly on the opportunities for environmental organisations to achieve results with these new forms of co-operation (including EDR procedures) which are acceptable to their membership and the public, and on the responsible authorities as well as the business sector supporting this by guaranteeing fair negotiations (and an adequate implementation of agreements).

3. The Development of Environmental Dispute Resolution (EDR)
3.1 A Difficult Starting Point

Negotiation-based dispute resolution has always been a cornerstone of environmental policy. Until recently, however, with rare exceptions, only regulators and regulatees (and their interest organisations) participated in the informal negotiations which took place before and in parallel with planning, licensing, abatement (clean-up), etc. procedures as well as during rule-making processes. Some regulations were enacted to formalise this informal, but close and opaque interaction, in which essential elements of the formal process were often pre-determined. But very soon it became apparent that these regulations were no powerful remedy.

Until recently, citizens and environmental organisations concerned about pollution had only very limited legally instituted means for influencing government policy, the environment-related activities of public authorities and the behaviour of emitters. And there were considerable legal barriers to seeking a remedy for damage (or its prevention) through court action. This situation improved with some legal measures which generally strengthened the position of so-called third parties (e.g. access to information, lighter burden of proof, stricter liability clauses, environmental impact assessment regulations), and the development over time of better relationships between environmental organisations, responsible authorities and business. However, their actual influence has remained weak, because the long-standing relationships between authorities and industry still dominate. The environmental movement has used its increased organisational and legal power to challenge projects and decisions by means of blockades, demonstrations (sometimes quite militant) and court action.

In the past, some areas of environmental conflict have proved to be particularly resistant, even allergic, to any attempts by environmental policy-makers to exert control over them. These include large industrial and public projects where people are afraid of negative consequences for public health and the environment. Because they are as a rule facilities and infrastructural projects which are crucial to the functioning of an industrialised society (projects such as landfills, waste incineration plants, airports, motorways, dams, power stations), disturbances which may be ecological in origin also cause major political and societal conflicts in which powerful economic interests and state institutions are actively involved. The projects are opposed not only by citizens who could be adversely affected and by environmental organisations, but also increasingly by local public authorities and politicians, which makes delicate procedures and hard enforcement of decisions using conventional instruments considerably more difficult than if it were a case of merely dealing with societal representatives and their organisations. Opposition from parties which understand all the intricacies of the political and legal system must therefore also be taken into account.

If, as is increasingly the case, the project is not dropped due to these conflicts, its realisation often becomes a very time-consuming and expensive business, the original objectives are watered down, the conflicts are shifted to the implementation phase, which in turn causes enforcement deficits, and the groups involved become embittered. And this ignores the destructive effect on social relations within the town or region affected. In short, the traditional instruments at the disposal of governments for implementing their public policy objectives and responsibilities are proving to be increasingly unsuitable in major environmental disputes for achieving solutions which are not only economically viable, but also compatible with the needs of the environment and the wishes of society.

As a rule, none of the groups involved in the conflicts is happy with the situation. This is evident from the reciprocal accusations made. Industry is accused of market failure and ignoring the environment out of economic principle; the environmental groups are accused of hysteria and inability to enter into dialogue with others; politicians and public administrators are criticised from all quarters as lacking impartiality and being incapable of taking decisions; critical scientists are even talking in terms of the failure of the state to protect the environment.

Virtually all major environmental disputes until recently ended up in court. It is seldom, however, that a court ruling will satisfy all parties to the conflict, and even the winning party is rarely completely satisfied. Court rulings often lead to long-lasting resentment on the part of the weaker party, and they do not exclude the possibility of subsequent implementation deficits. Using the instruments of legal and political power to implement less than optimal decisions in cases of dispute clearly undermines trust in the capacity of state institutions to solve problems and in their impartiality. One side complains about the weak state (and calls for privatisation and de-regulation), while the other side sees the state as an advocate of the economically strong that jeopardises the ecological future of everyone for the sake of short-sighted profit interests or even self-interest.

Under these conditions, conventional procedures for decision-making face increasing criticism of their fundamental principles. Some critics see these procedures as inefficient relics of an overly bureaucratic view of the state; others see them as ecologically blind instruments which systematically favour economic interests. Conventional procedures have such a poor reputation that it hardly seems possible that this could be repaired adequately in the short to medium term.

Almost everyone complains of the lack of appropriate instruments for mastering the challenge to implement effective environmental policies. This creates an openness towards unconventional instruments and encourages (by virtue of necessity) a willingness to take new approaches to dealing with environmental disputes. Since 1990, an ever-growing interest in alternative forms of conflict management can be identified.

Progress has been rather slow, especially when compared to that in the US and Canada. This is partly due to legal restrictions but is also bound up with the still prevalent specifically German statist ideology (according to which public authorities must be impartial towards all groups and individuals) and with past experiences with negotiations under the officially formalised co-operation principle.[13]

Although negotiated solutions as such are hardly a matter of dispute any more as regards the implementation of public policy, including in the field of environmental protection, they nevertheless have quite a poor reputation in Germany. Environmental activists and organisations often view negotiating processes as something of a fiddle, a secret pact between those parties to whom economic considerations are more important than what is ecologically required and possible. This criticism is not, as the counter-criticism runs, a nebulous suspicion without a real specific basis. There are good reasons for their criticism of an interpretation and implementation of the co-operation principle which favours polluter interests. A good number of negotiated solutions which, for example, were worked out in the form of what are known as sectoral agreements (i.e. concerning a particular industry) did little more than set out on paper what is already common practice, were simply not adhered to, or granted the companies causing environmental pollution generous grace periods for changing their policy (resulting in contaminated sites which had been given advance approval). The agreements with the automobile industry on reducing exhaust fumes and with the packaging and asbestos industries are prime examples of this.[14]

Formal participation procedures, particularly those involving the general public in cases likely to cause a good deal of conflict (such as nuclear or conventional power stations, waste incineration plants, airports), are perceived as being mere tokenism, bringing nothing but a veneer of public participation and a preprogrammed outcome.

At central government level, where laws, regulations and the most important environmental standards are decided upon, it is primarily the environmental organisations who had bad experiences with participation procedures, and also realised that the representatives of the state in the numerous standards and other committees could often not compete with the expertise available to the companies affected by environmental legislation.

In addition to this, many high-ranking bureaucrats, and in particular legal experts, were against real negotiation and alternative, not legally structured, dispute resolution procedures. Finally, influential representatives of the industrial sector also suspected that the inclusion of environmental interest groups in negotiations would only lead to emotional and irrational discussions.

Against the background of these institutional and practical starting conditions, and of conflict and unfortunate experience, the increase in consensus-oriented and dialogue-style procedure since 1990 can be considered fairly remarkable.

3.2 Overview

Although some EDR procedures had taken place in the years before an intensive debate began in academic circles and in the relevant institutions[15], there were two major cases of mediation which stimulated the establishment of similar procedures in other environmental areas. Both these were concerned with waste problems. The mediation procedure in the village of Münchehagen started in 1990, the other in the district of Neuss in 1991. The Neuss mediation is described in detail in Section 4 of this chapter, and therefore this overview will focus mainly on Münchehagen.

The reason for setting up this mediation procedure was a controversy which had raged for years over the hazardous waste landfill in the tiny village of Münchehagen in Lower Saxony, concerning suspicions of illegal dumping, contamination of soil and water and danger to public health. There was much dispute between the public authorities at different levels, there were internal administrative conflicts, and disputes among citizens' groups, environmental organisations and the responsible authorities and villages concerned. The media showed a keen interest in the case. The heart of the conflict was the question of how quickly and thoroughly the landfill should be cleaned up. The responsible bodies here were the district and state authorities, who behaved at first in a highly restrictive fashion, not least because it was likely that a comprehensive rehabilitation of the site would become extremely expensive.

On the initiative of a member of staff at the Evangelische Akademie in nearby Loccum, a mediation procedure was begun at the end of 1990, and its instigator (Meinfried Striegnitz) became the first environmental mediator in Germany. He was in no sense a professional mediator. However, he prepared both the procedure and his own role very thoroughly. For example, he took part in conflict resolution seminars in the US and Canada, and organised several conferences in Germany on consensual dispute resolution procedures, at which experienced mediation experts from abroad also took part.

The participants in the Münchehagen mediation included representatives of various departments of the local authorities, pressure groups, environmental organisations, the district council and state government, as well as politicians from different parties and concerned members of the public. On the mediation committee, about 15 people represented the principal parties in the conflict; in the plenary sessions, a broader circle of interested parties (around 25) was gathered together. The procedure was financed by the state of Lower Saxony, the environment ministry of which advocates and funds dialogue-oriented procedures which offer opportunities for broader participation. On the basis of a draft by the mediator, a detailed agenda, setting out in particular the goals of the procedure and how to handle publicity issues, was accepted by all participants. Particular importance was attached to the confidentiality of the discussions within the mediation committee, and this was maintained throughout the procedure. The committee was nevertheless also obliged to keep the public regularly informed about the procedure. The participating responsible authorities had not made any prior commitments to accept the recommendations of the committee, but they had expressed their willingness to look closely at them and implement them as far as the law permitted. Both committees met and are still meeting very often, on average once a month (mediation committee) or every two months (plenary committee). Numerous agreements have been reached, in particular on questions of the technology and extent of the clean-up. The first steps in implementing these agreements have been taken, but there are still further unresolved questions under negotiation.

Even though the procedure has not yet been concluded, the participants, whose positions were originally more or less entrenched, view it for the main part as a positive experience. Particular emphasis is given to the fairness of the procedure, the communicative competence of the mediator, and the fact that an extremely confrontational situation at the outset has been successfully transformed into a highly cooperative, consensus-oriented one.[16]

Nevertheless in Germany, mediation procedures in the strict sense of the word (i.e. organised and directed by a mediator accepted by all parties) are still relatively uncommon in the field of environmental protection, although numerous similar procedures do exist, and, in total, there have been more cases than in other European countries. Overall, the trend towards all types of procedure which are negotiation-based, informal and aimed at increasing participation has gained noticeably in popularity.

Apart from these two major mediation procedures, there are a number of small to medium-sized procedures which are extending the idea of co-operation, and are trying out or have tried out new forms of dispute resolution either before or in parallel with formal procedures. Some examples are: the search for a landfill site for household and similar waste in the area of Hildesheim, for a hazardous waste landfill in the district of Arnsberg and for a landfill in the district of Schleswig-Flensburg; risk estimation, making safe and cleaning up populated contaminated areas in Wuppertal, Essen and Hamburg; making safe and cleaning up the Vorketzin landfill in Brandenburg; cleaning up a sludge landfill in Bielefeld; modifications to a waste incineration plant in Bielefeld-

Herford; the search for a landfill site for dredged sludge from the Hamburg harbour in Lower Saxony; modernisation and extension of the waste-fired heating and power station in Iserlohn; cleaning up and re-planning a landfill within a citizens' forum in Dortmund; a "round table search for a site" accompanying a formal siting procedure for a household waste disposal centre in the rural district of Märkisch-Oderland; setting up a transport forum to draw up a long-term traffic plan for Heidelberg; dispute resolution in the wake of open-cast lignite mining in the Niederlausitz area; the development of a hazardous waste plan for Lower Saxony; cleaning up kindergartens in Hamburg contaminated by dioxins; clean-up measures near the North German refinery in Hamburg, and a dialogue-oriented task force on waste management in the rural district of Osnabrück.

New (informal and negotiation-based) conflict resolution procedures are being implemented in virtually all areas of the environment, but primarily in the area of waste management. The examples are connected with regional planning and environmental impact assessments, with the necessity for plans, licensing, siting, clean-up and general planning procedures. They take place either before or in parallel with these procedures. Political discussions on delicate subjects have also taken place. A project group from the Berlin Social Science Research Centre co-ordinated, for example, a moderated dialogue (round table) on the risks involved in cultivating plants with genetically engineered herbicidal resistance, in which representatives from science, industry and environmental organisations took part.[17]

In the area of waste management, two procedures which were very similar to mediation were organised by private companies to consider sites for landfills in the states of Saxony and Bremen, and led with relatively little friction to a consensus amongst participants; both companies are now specialising in environmental mediation procedures. Neither the degree of complexity, the social and political delicacy of the object of conflict, the size of the planned investment (and as a consequence the extent of the economic interest) nor the length of time which will probably be required seem to form a barrier to using EDR procedures. The public dialogue procedure initiated to find a site for a major airport for the region of Berlin and Brandenburg, which has been supervised by a private mediation company since autumn 1993, is by far one of the most complex and therefore daring forms of EDR seen in Germany. Recently (May 1998), the state government of Hessia decided to organise a mediation procedure for the planned expansion of Rhein-Main airport in Frankfurt. They otherwise feared major, maybe even violent, conflicts with citizens' action groups and environmental NGOs: similar conflicts had arisen years previously in connection with the construciton of an additional runway. The Hessian government now proposed to set up a three-member mediation team and to limit the duration of the process to eighteen months. It also promised that during that period there would be no decision taken by any authority which might narrow the scope of possible decisions for those participating in the mediation.

Since 1990, about 50 EDR procedures (supported by moderators, facilitators or mediators) have taken place or are still underway in Germany[18]. According to a (partial) survey, the environmental fields of application for EDR are as follows[19]:

Contaminated sites

Experience with mediation procedures came primarily in the clean-up of populated contaminated sites. In this area, conflict mediation starts out with relatively good framework conditions, because the legal regulations for this environmental problem are not as tight as others. In more than ten cases the participants mostly sought agreements on clean-up measures, risk estimation, and compensation.

Waste

Waste management problems have emerged as the largest field of application for EDR, especially mediation, to date. Here the disputes between project managers, local and state authorities, environmental groups and affected parties are often so intense, and lack of trust in the impartiality of authorities so strong that a neutral mediator represents the last resort. Prominent issues for negotiation include the siting and enlargement of waste incineration plants and landfills, risk estimation, policies for waste reduction and prevention, forecasts on the future development of waste volumes, monitoring, pollution abatement technology, possibilities of new (e.g. bio-) technologies and climate change. Conflicts about waste management are usually highly politicised because NGOs consider waste policy an appropriate way of forcing policy-makers and industry to move towards ecological modernisation. About twenty medium to large-scale EDR cases have been reported. These include not only concrete projects but also policy dialogues on future waste management strategies

Transport

To date, EDR on transport issues has taken place primarily at the level of mediated or moderated policy dialogues and of so-called planning cells (*Planungszellen*) where randomly selected citizens draft a policy with the help of facilitators (about ten cases). There also have been local uses in siting and discussion of compensation measures, which includes the most complex mediation procedure in Germany so far (the planning of a major airport in Berlin/Brandenburg).

Pollution of indoor atmosphere

One case, concerning the risks arising from wood preservatives in nursery schools, has been reported, but there are probably several more (e.g. on asbestos) which are not known outside the region concerned.

Energy

The only example from the field of energy policy reported is the consensus talks on future national energy policy, which have been underway for some time, and which are periodically and acrimoniously broken off.

Chemicals

EDR procedures in this field (about five) cover mediated or moderated negotiations on industrial projects, production of specific chemical substances (e.g. herbicides) as well as moderated dialogues on genetically manipulated substances (e.g. crop plants, enzymes for washing powders).

Nature conservation

Five large cases have been reported (although there may be some more medium-sized cases). Among the issues dealt with are establishment of a national park and of a major protected area.

In almost all cases the EDR procedures take place before, after or in parallel with formal procedures and only very rarely, in negotiations with private parties, in place of them. Regulatory negotiation (RegNeg) in the strict sense i.e. procedures for establishing legally binding standards, guidelines, etc., has not until now taken the form of EDR procedures in Germany. This is due partly to the associated serious legal problems, but also to the fact that, in this area, there have long been informal consultation and negotiations between the responsible administrators and economic or professional interest groups.

3.3 Regulatory Action and Standard-setting

Currently, EDR techniques are applied only relatively seldom in the field of regulatory activity. This is by no means because conventional procedures are functioning well or organisations representing environmental interests are satisfied with the results. On the contrary, there is frequently conflict between the authorities and those affected by enforcement actions, and in almost every major case, environmental organisations are critical of both the tardiness of authorities responses and the inadequacy of the measures then taken. Furthermore, representatives of the scientific community, and independent groups of experts (in particular the government committee of environmental experts) have also long been critical of the various standard-setting and decision-making procedures where standards, often of a technological or scientific nature, are set. These standards are important (in terms of legal implementation) for environmental policy planning, but especially for permissions and enforcement activities. The criticisms are directed above all at the fact that these procedures are to a great extent non-transparent, that participation by environmental organisations is extremely limited, and that the environment and public health are given insufficient consideration in favour of the interests of economic agency groups.

The above problems would in themselves offer enough potential for conflict to stimulate a search for alternatives to conventional procedures. However, this is only the case to a limited extent, if at all, and there are two important reasons for this. On the one hand, "alternative procedures" have long been widely practised with respect to enforcement actions (known in Germany as "informal administrative activity"), reducing the problems found in conventional procedures - but, as will be shown, generating new problems - and on the other hand, standard-setting procedures are conducted predominantly with consensus between participating parties, offering scarce opportunity for external critics to disrupt them seriously through political or legal intervention. Unlike in the US, groups who are unhappy with the resulting norms cannot file lawsuits to challenge them.

3.3.1 Enforcement and Informal Administrative Activity

Because of the variety of difficulties experienced by the implementing authorities in efficiently pushing through complex, sometimes highly detailed, sometimes vague, sometimes contradictory environmental regulations, and their corresponding interest in avoiding challenges in the courts, informal procedures have developed since the very start of modern environmental policy whereby the authorities discuss problems with those affected from outside the formal procedures, and negotiate possible solutions in order to arrive at written and oral agreements which, however, are not legally binding.[20] These negotiations take place before (and during) permissions procedures, in enforcement actions (e.g. putting a halt to impermissible environmental pollution, clean-up measures) and in the implementation of environmental protection measures which have insufficient or no basis in law. This type of "informal activity" is very widespread, taking place in practically every medium to large case.

While these informal compliance agreements are mostly concluded between enforcement authorities and individual companies, another form, the "informal regulatory agreements", takes place between the federal or state environmental ministries and business organisations or large companies, such as energy providers. These cases involve additional monitoring programmes, using substitutes for toxic substances, raising recycling rates or installing anti-pollution technology. As a rule, the authorities then - temporarily - renounce their corresponding legislative activities. These voluntary commitments have been on the increase for a number of years; the present government sees them as offering a promising approach to deregulating environmental policy and making it more flexible. Furthermore, administrators estimate - statistics are not collected - that so-called administrative contracts (a special form of public contract) are also relatively frequent. They are concluded between the administration and private agencies and exist alongside, in combination with, and in place of formal administrative action.[21] In larger-scale cases, experts in administrative law are often brought into the procedure by the negotiators, in order to avoid legal problems, but not to act as mediators.

Even in the other areas of informal administrative activity mentioned above, neutral third parties have up to now been used only seldom as mediators or moderators. This is generally thought to be due to the fact that the agency groups are only small and very homogenous: representatives of the public administration and of private companies. There is no provision for the inclusion of further agencies, which is often - especially in relation to environmental organisations - also undesirable. Only where this is unavoidable, or where a conflict situation or lack of trust exists between representatives of the authorities and the businesses themselves, is a mediator occasionally called in.

A typical example of this can be found in the clean-up of a large old copper smelter (Norddeutsche Affinerie) in Hamburg. Environmental quality measurements revealed extremely high soil and air pollution from heavy metals in the vicinity of the plant, and the ground water was polluted with arsenic. This led to a heated debate within parliament and in the public arena. More and more groups demanded the decommissioning of the plant and criticised the environmental authority for hesitancy and taking inadequate action; the media carried reports of a "cosy relationship with polluters". Opposition parties in government demanded closure of the factory, which would have meant the loss of 3,000 jobs. The factory's management played for time. It expected that public outrage would soon subside, and feared that taking rapid corrective action without being legally obliged to do so might be interpreted as an admission of legal guilt. In addition, the costs of clean-up measures were expected to be extremely high, and there was mistrust of the environmental authority, which was believed to have been developing its strategy in order to close the factory. The authorities, in turn, were under enormous political and public pressure to introduce convincing measures as soon as possible. They wanted to avoid closing the plant at all costs, to protect the jobs there. The measures necessary to achieve clean up of the site would have required a large of detailed clean up orders, but in view of the complex issues involved the experts considered it unrealistic to frame these in a legally watertight way. It was clear that such a case would end in a long drawn-out court procedure. Faced with this situation, the environmental authority called in the Institute for Communications and Environmental Consultation (*Büro für Kommunikations- und Umweltberatung*). Its mediator was able to initiate discussions in an atmosphere of trust. The director of the responsible department in the environmental authority put it thus: "The gradual easing in the atmosphere took hold of employees and managers, negotiations grew into discussions, discussions into collaboration, and out of this emerged a common clean-up plan."[22]

The plan provided for complex modernisation, including the use of completely new processes, at a cost of well over DM 100 million. The agreement was laid down in detail and in writing, but not as a legally binding contract. The public was informed about the clean-up plan in a 30-page leaflet, and the municipal government presented a comprehensive annual report on its implementation to the public and parliament. Implementation was relatively free of friction and led to the plants being upgraded to the most modern level of environmental technology, during which the legally required permits were issued step by step. The responsible director from the Hamburg environmental authority rated the procedure as highly successful and, based on his experience, recommended that "EDR, sometimes even with the use of neutral third parties, should always be tried when a planning or permissions procedure reaches an impasse, be it during preparatory stages or the procedure itself. EDR should be understood as a complement to traditional administrative activities and conducted as such. The administration should be organised in such a way as to favour mediation as a form of activity." [23]

Despite the overwhelmingly positive assessments of EDR procedures given by participants in permissions and enforcement procedures, criticism is often made, politically and legally speaking, "from outside", although this is mostly phrased in general terms. It applies on the one hand to the fact that the relationships are bilateral - between authority and immediately affected party - and that social groups such as environmental organisations in particular are not included, and that - even where the outcome of negotiations is made public - the procedure is transparent to a very limited extent for outsiders. The neutral third parties (mediators, etc.) are not considered a guarantee that the procedure is oriented towards the public interest, as they have the trust only of the two participating actor groups, are paid by them, and are not obliged to account for their actions to the public. The key point of legal criticism is that, under the German legal system, public authorities are granted a position of strength and a large degree of independence with respect to both those affected by the regulations themselves and those affected in general, as their decisions - even in permissions and clean-up measures - must always be taken in the public interest. It is claimed that "opening up" negotiation procedures - whether through EDR or in informal administrative activities - thus leads unavoidably to the administrations delegating this key function to third parties, or relegating itself to the status of the other negotiating parties. It should however be pointed out that this strict interpretation of the legal position, based as it is on the fiction of an entirely independent, omnipotent authority, capable of discerning a single "genuine" public interest, has few adherents now, precisely because of the many contrary experiences in the complex area of environmental policy. The trend is now towards enabling administrations to act co-operatively and flexibly and to seek the public good in consensus with all relevant groups.

3.3.2 Norm and Standard-setting Processes (Reg Neg)

There are various processes in Germany for developing and determining standards (*norm* in German), applying to a number of different parties or thematic areas, i.e. not just to a single case. In comparison to those in the US, the processes are considerably less formalised or determined by legal requirements, and there is only a small possibility of legal intervention. This is the case in both of the significant procedure types into which the processes can be broadly divided: executive or parliamentary decrees of directives and standards and the setting of more or less technical standards by specific private and public institutions.

(1) Standard-setting

This chapter will not deal with the general legislative process, but with standards that fix goals and general clauses in environmental law, so that legal implementation becomes possible for the responsible authorities. Before an ordinance or administrative directive is decreed, interested parties are generally given a say. The Federal Air Pollution Control Act (*BundesImmissionsSchutzGesetz* - BImSchG), for example, lays this down in Article 51 which refers to representatives of the scientific community, affected parties, business, transport and the responsible higher state authorities. The Act does not include concrete direction on this, nor are there regulations as to the form of the hearing. Even if the requirement to listen to representatives of these interest groups is not met, this does not necessarily vitiate the standard in a legal sense.

Administrative directives (*Verwaltungsvorschriften*) play an extremely important role in the enforcement of environmental policy. In principle they are only binding on authorities (because they are directed at the administration), but in practice they have a sizeable external effect, as the authorities must comply with them in their activities (planning, permissions, clean-up orders, etc.). For this reason, affected parties take them into account immediately. In significant areas they define Best Available Technology, frequently in some detail.

The procedure for issuing administrative directives is controlled by law. In certain cases, the kinds of interest groups and institutions which should be allowed to participate is laid down. In particular environmental areas, formal standing committees (*Technische Ausschüsse*) are set up to conduct standard-setting. In addition, a hearing for the interest groups to be involved ("participating circles") takes place before an administrative directive is issued, and since the 1980s this has included environmental and consumer groups. The administrative directive sometimes refers to or includes technical standards developed by private institutions.

Although environmental groups are involved in "big decisions" (e.g. on a wide-ranging directive on waste management), the standard-setting process is nonetheless concentrated on technical, scientific and economic aspects. Legal intervention on the grounds of procedural error is virtually impossible. For this reason, the standard-setting process is very much characterised by co-operation and negotiation. This presumably explains why EDR procedures, such as regulatory negotiation, which is used especially by the US Environmental Protection Agency, are not present, and why the administrative, scientific and economic interest groups have little interest in the process.

(2) Technical Standard-setting

The development and laying down of sector-wide (*überbetrieblich*) standards, which apply to a group of companies, a class of plant, etc., are conducted to a great extent by private organisations, such as *Deutsche Industrie-Norm Ausschuß* (DIN), *Verein Deutscher Ingenieure* (VDI) or *Abwassertechnische Vereinigung*. They are thus internal technologically based standards. They are not in themselves legally binding but are of great importance in practice, as they are held to be a generally agreed product of the best available technical and scientific knowledge. Moreover, they often have an indirect legal significance, where they are, for example, included lock, stock and barrel in laws and ordinances, or where ordinances and administrative directives refer to them for orientation. Conflicts between those participating in standard-setting which cannot be resolved internally (including internal mediation and arbitration) are extremely infrequent. Internal use of the courts to push through a particular interest is impossible, and there is - with a few minor exceptions - no legal regulation of the procedure. The procedures are generally determined by the organisations themselves, standard-setting is heavily characterised by technical (and economic) considerations and industrial interests are mostly over-represented. With few exceptions (e.g. DIN), environmental organisations are not represented. The participants show no interest in alternative procedures using neutral third parties: the standards are considered to be the broadest possible consensus between relevant experts. Outsiders have virtually no means of intervening to exert pressure for procedural change.

All in all, it can be said of standard-setting that co-operative negotiation procedures take place to a great extent, and that technical and economic aspects or interests clearly predominate. Internal mechanisms result in the participants generally coming to a consensus. The rights of excluded or insufficiently included interests to information, participation or appeal are so minimal that significant external pressure cannot be exerted. The lack of legal regulation of standard-setting in Germany has historical reasons. German administrative law has always concentrated on a single procedure: the "decision to enforce a standard." Thus procedural and participatory problems in standard-setting generally emerge only when administrative decisions on permissions or enforcement are challenged, and the courts examine the standard-setting procedure as well. However, this occurs extremely seldom, compared with the US, and with less rigour. In general, far stronger procedural control is exerted by the US courts than by German ones, where the content or material aspects of a decision is more closely considered instead. A tendency towards taking more account of procedural aspects has been observable in German courts for some time, but there is a long way to go before this attains a level comparable to that in the US. In this respect, this trend cannot be expected to offer a significant stimulus to the use of EDR in standard-setting.

3.4 Alternative Dispute Resolution (ADR) in Other Areas

In other political and legal areas, unlike the case of the environment, there has been an upswing in ADR, i.e. in particular the resolution of conflicts without a legal judgement, whether within or outside the courts. Here too, this was preceded by powerful stimuli from the US. In Germany, this form of dispute resolution has a longer tradition in the areas of civil, criminal and public law, concerning divorce, family disputes, compensation of victims, disputes at work, ombudsman systems for dealing with customer complaints (especially in the banking sector), tribunals and arbitration in various sectors (in particular dealing with consumer complaints), arbitration offices in the health system and in disputes over competition. In some of the above areas there have also been for some time established professional interest organisations (e.g. mediation over divorce, family disputes and victim compensation).

A study in 1990 showed that, in disputes under civil law, lawyers were already resolving outside the courts some 70% of all cases received, and it is estimated that 10-20% of potential court cases are avoided through the especially wide range of arbitration possibilities in civil law.[24] Despite these filters, about 1.6 million new civil cases annually come before the lower civil courts. In family law the figure is around 380,000, and in administrative law there are about 116,000 court cases (figures apply to the former West Germany, i.e. before re-unification). The fact that these figures are so high (at least when compared with the rest of Europe) can be traced back to the way in which the German legal structure still tends to look liberally on locus standi, rather than restricting the right to bring a court case. Blame for this is apportioned to, *inter alia*, the fact that the national system of legal education and training is still primarily oriented around a career as a judge, i.e. the conduct of court cases and legal decisions, and that the possibilities of preventing cases from coming to court through negotiation, compensation or arbitration are only taught to a negligibly small extent. This is in complete contrast to the US where, for example, such techniques are systematically taught at law schools.[25] These structural restrictions notwithstanding, the view has spread broadly through the German legal profession that negotiation, mediation and arbitration should be the natural forms of resolution for potential legal conflicts, and that formal court cases resulting in a legal judgement should present the exception, the last resort.

4. The Mediation Procedure in the District of Neuss
4.1 Introduction

In September 1991 the local council in the district of Neuss approved a waste management programme. The intention of this programme was to ensure reliable waste disposal as required by law in the state of North Rhine-Westphalia, and to put into practice the priority given in principle to the avoidance and recycling of waste over disposal. The remaining refuse was to be incinerated and incineration residue recycled or deposited in a landfill. The central components and planning data for this waste management programme were criticised, particularly by environmental associations and pressure groups, and also by the Green Party in the local council. The specific issues were:

- the full exploitation of all possibilities for avoiding and reducing house hold waste and waste from trade and commerce;
- the increase in the quotas of waste generated in the district from industry and commerce to be avoided and recycled;
- the use of all appropriate methods for separate collection and sorting and treatment of recyclable waste:
- the necessity, capacity, and ecological and health impacts of a waste incineration plant;
- the siting of new plants for incineration and landfill waste.

During the course of discussions, which sometimes involved vehement clashes dating back to long before the formal resolution taken by the local council on the waste management plan, the environmental mediation research group from the Wissenschaftszentrum Berlin für Sozialforschung (WZB, Social Science Research Center) and the local administration in Neuss persuaded all the main parties to the dispute to try to settle their differences through mediation. The WZB provided organisational and financial support to help set up and implement the procedure. It was able to draw on funding from the BMBF for this.[26]

The Neuss mediation procedure is selected as a detailed example for a number of reasons. It belongs to the still very small group of mediation procedures in Germany which were conducted throughout according to the classical model developed in the American literature.[27] Thus it included an intensive pre-negotiation phase where, with the help of the mediator, all relevant parties to the conflict carried out an analysis of the risks and opportunities involved in participation (in terms of BATNA, best available alternative to a negotiated agreement), there was absolute consensus among the participants on the choice of mediator, and virtually all stakeholders took part in the procedure. Moreover, with respect to the number of participants, the severity of the conflict, the legal and administrative complexity, the significance of the dispute for environmental and economic development in the region, and with regard to the planned investment volume and the economic interests thus associated, it was one of the most complex cases of mediation in Germany. The procedure also functioned as a "pioneer" in the territory of environmental mediation in Germany, which was then starting to be explored, and was a significant stimulus for political, legal and public debate on the advantages and disadvantages of mediation procedures, and on the necessary preconditions for their adequate application. Finally, it was and is the only mediation procedure in Germany (and, to the best of the author's knowledge, in Europe) to be observed and analysed from start to finish by a multidisciplinary research group. It has therefore made a contribution to the development of sociological methods for analysis and evaluation of mediation procedures.

4.2 Background Information on the District of Neuss

The district (*Kreis*) of Neuss is in the Lower Rhine region of the state (*Land*) of North Rhine-Westphalia. It is part of Germany's, and indeed Europe's, largest industrial conglomeration, the Rhine-Ruhr region, which is also Europe's most densely populated area (approximately 1,000 inhabitants per square kilometre). It currently has six household waste incineration plants, one incineration plant for hazardous waste (a further such plant is under construction), eleven household waste and nine hazardous waste landfills, and a number of special waste treatment plants.

With 425,000 inhabitants, the district of Neuss is the tenth largest district in Germany; it has a surface area of 576 sq km, comprising six towns and two municipalities. Its land use structure is mixed: it includes some highly industrialised areas as well as some mixed use areas and some rural agricultural areas; the profile of the district is characterised by large lignite-fired power stations and large expanses of open-cast lignite mines. This area has the highest "density of energy generation" and the largest uninterrupted deposits of lignite in Europe, and it has the greatest concentration of lignite-fired power stations in the world. Because of the industrial and energy generation structure and the population density, the pollution levels are at times way above the national average.

Under the *Waste Act* of North Rhine-Westphalia (para.5, LAbfG NW), the district of Neuss is a local authority with a disposal mandate for what is known in short as household and commercial waste, and is thus obliged by law to draw up and regularly revise a waste management programme. It was one of the first districts to do so in 1986.

The district of Neuss waste management programme of 1986 was revised in 1991 and further developed in the mediation procedure. The 1991 programme assumes that the total volume of waste will remain constant in the future. On the basis of this prognosis one more combined landfill (with areas for hazardous waste, and household and commercial waste) and an incineration plant for household waste are planned. These represented the most hotly disputed points in the mediation procedure. The responsible administrative department argued that the waste incineration plant was necessary, based primarily on the fact that forecasts of the volume and structure of waste, current disposal technology, and waste legislation at central government and state level put other disposal methods (in particular the biological-mechanical type) out of the question as single alternatives, from both an objective and a legal point of view (thus making them impossible to implement against the will of higher authorities).

4.3 Background to the Neuss Mediation Procedure

In December 1990 initial contacts were established between the WZB and the administrator responsible for the environment in the district of Neuss, and the following agreement was reached in February 1991: the district administration, as the local authority responsible for waste disposal, was prepared to participate in a mediation procedure on its waste management programme and to support the research interests of the WZB.[28] Thus, for the first time in the history of environmental policy in Germany, a public administration had decided in favour of a mediation procedure on a waste management programme. This means that a procedure had been selected with which there had been little experience in Germany: up to that time, only one other environmental mediation procedure had occurred: that over the leaking hazardous waste landfill in Münchehagen in Lower Saxony (mentioned above).

Following the agreement with the Neuss district administration, members of the WZB project team held intensive preliminary discussions with numerous groups who had an existing or potential interest in the districts waste management policy. During these discussions the project team informed the interest groups about the reasons for and aims of a mediation procedure (a procedure with which most of the parties to the discussion were not familiar). Parallel to this, a wide-ranging search for a mediator began. Finally, on the basis of these preliminary discussions, the WZB project team decided that the chances of implementing a successful mediation procedure were good. It remained the task of the potential mediator to review this assessment and decide whether to take the job.

At a public information meeting and discussion organised by the Neuss district administration to present its waste management concept, the mediation procedure and the provisional mediator were presented. Both the project and the mediator met with the broad approval of the participants.

In the ensuing period from September 1991 to the end of March 1992, the provisional mediator (who had not yet been formally appointed), Professor Georges M. Fülgraff,[29] held numerous preliminary, bilateral and multilateral discussions with a large number of potential participants. He began his round of discussions with the district administration. These discussions served to provide information about the purpose and form of the mediation procedure, and about the mediators own understanding of his task. They also explored to what extent there was scope for compromise and identified the central points of conflict.

As a result of preliminary discussions (concluded in the main by the end of January 1992), the mediator decided that there was sufficient scope for negotiation - just enough to justify a mediation procedure - even though the Neuss district council had already passed the waste management programme (which had been in preparation for some time) in September 1991, despite the Green Party's voting against it. The aim of the mediation procedure was specified as being to explore whether and how the waste management programme could be modified in such a way that it would enjoy the support of a broad consensus of the population, would benefit the environment and the people of the district of Neuss, and possibly compensate for local disadvantages. The relevant political bodies, represented by delegates in the mediation procedure, agreed to incorporate the results of the procedure into their decisions as much as possible.

4.4 Chronology of the Mediation Procedure

At the end of March 1992, the first full mediation meeting took place. Invited were representatives of all the groups who had shown an interest in participating in the procedure during preliminary discussions. Each group had the right to up to three representatives. This agreement was handled very flexibly, however, and it never became a point of contention. In all, nine full mediation meetings took place, some of them lasting an entire day, others only about four hours. The final meeting took place in August 1993.

In addition to the nine full mediation meetings, a number of smaller meetings also took place, some of them with the participation of the mediator. These smaller meetings can be subdivided into two main types: (1) special sessions that had been discussed and approved in the larger meetings, called to respond to the needs of particular groups (especially environmental organisations and pressure groups); (2) special sessions held at the request of individual groups without previous discussion in the larger circle of participants, usually called to prepare for larger meetings. In addition to these (as in any normal political process), there were further meetings between different groups with the aim, for instance, of co-ordinating their strategies within the mediation procedure.

4.5 How the Procedure Stands and Overview of the Results

The greatest differences of opinion amongst the participants concerned the objective necessity and the legal necessity for a waste incineration plant, its impact on the environment, the economic practicality of such a plant and its size. Questions concerning the siting of a waste incineration plant and landfill were also highly contentious. The procedure ended without a compromise acceptable to all the parties in the dispute on these issues.

Despite all the unresolved differences, it nevertheless proved possible to attain numerous agreements over objective issues, for instance, the deficits to be tackled in the field of commercial waste, more precise information on waste volumes, waste avoidance and waste recycling, improved access for environmental groups to the administrative departments responsible for waste management, and a tighter networking of environmental organisations and citizens initiatives represented in the district. Relationships between participants also improved - another positive result that can be ascribed to the mediation procedure. The level of data on waste has improved; among other things, waste flow recording is more sophisticated. At the end of the mediation procedure the administration drastically reduced its projected figures for residual waste volumes to be incinerated or landfilled - a source of considerable controversy before and during the procedure. Moreover, the fears, expressed by many groups before its outset, namely that the mediation procedure could serve to take critical environmental groups "for a ride" or "pull the wool over their eyes," were allayed.

Overall the result of the mediation procedure can be described as a contentious compromise. On the one hand, it contains extensive agreement on many specific points (some of them mentioned above) crucial to the waste management policy for the district of Neuss. On the other hand, as regards the main points of contention (waste incineration versus biological-mechanical waste treatment, and siting), there was only one course of action found within the formal procedure which might have gained majority support, and this was rejected by the environmental groups. The proposal, put forward by the district administration, was summarised as follows in a press release from the mediator:

"While in many areas, it proved possible for the various administrative departments, organisations and institutions to come closer together in their views, the technical solution for treatment of residual waste remained a disputed point. . . . The two opposing sides were irreconcilable to the bitter end: Should residual waste be incinerated, or treated biologically in a composting facility and then landfilled? The district administration has announced that it will table a motion at the council meeting on 29 September 1993 to set aside a site in Neurath for a waste incineration plant. This does not mean, however, that a decision has been taken to actually build a plant of this kind. No investment decision is planned before the end of 1995. Until then the search for the best solution will continue. It must be pointed out, however, that the district administration is thinking more in terms of new technologies along the lines of thermal treatment, while the environmental organisations and citizens' action groups still favour cold, i.e. biological-mechanical, methods. . . ."

On 29 September 1993, the Neuss district council (the highest parliamentary body in the district) made its decision on a waste management programme. With a clear majority, it adopted the environment committees draft resolution.

As the mediation procedure was drawing to a close, representatives of the environmental groups in particular began to express their dissatisfaction with important aspects of the outcome. The environmental groups then sent written comments, and held a press conference at which the Neuss district waste management policy was strongly criticised, especially the planned construction of a waste incineration plant. The environmentalists called instead for an immediate start in planning an alternative, biological-mechanical waste treatment plant. In addition they announced their intent to take legal and political action against any waste management policy based on incineration.

An independent voters group (UWG) was established across virtually all of the district. It intended to stand in the local elections to be held in October 1994. In the hot spots of the district waste management controversy, the UWG enjoyed strong support from members of the largest and most influential citizens action group, the Citizens Action Group Against Waste Incineration. Some time later, however, the district authorities decided not to build a waste incineration plant after all, because total waste volumes had dropped enormously!

4.6 Results of Research into the Neuss Procedure

Selection of participants

It is almost certain that no relevant group was ignored in the selection process. The decision not to allow the press uninterrupted access to the meetings did prove problematic. Two representatives of the regional press who had been covering environmental issues for many years criticised this decision, claiming that it was anti-democratic and at odds with the transparency principle of the mediation procedure itself. In all, two press conferences were held on the mediation procedure. It may be that more frequent press conferences could have realised the principle of transparency without foregoing the advantages of a no press rule.

All groups who had indicated some interest in the mediation procedure were invited to the first, constitutive, meeting. Approximately 60 individuals from about 30 organisations attended. In such large meetings, it is very difficult to facilitate a personal exchange of views. If everyone speaks out on a complicated point, time also becomes a problem. Spontaneity must therefore necessarily be suppressed in a tightly controlled, centralised chairing of the meeting. One advantage of this, however, may be that none of the groups involved in the dispute were summarily excluded. In pioneering procedures (often suspected at first of being manipulated, or at any rate more so than routine procedures) it is advisable to accept some loss of efficiency for the sake of the democratic principle of participation. In the further course of the Neuss mediation procedure the number of participants dropped of its own accord to around 40. It was also possible to ensure a potential for discussion by organising smaller, separate meetings to prepare for individual issues dealt with in the larger mediation sessions.

Equal treatment

The equal treatment of all parties is one of the fundamental requirements of a mediation. However, this principle soon collided with political and legal reality. For example, the mediator (and, prior to the convening of the mediation, the WZB research team) had to communicate more intensively with the Neuss district administration than with the other participants because in this case, without the co-operation of the district administration, mediation would probably not have been possible at all. On the other hand, the mediator had to take care not to allow himself to be drawn towards the interests of the district administration. Fortunately, he was able to make this (publicly) clear. Credible demonstration of the mediator's impartiality was considerably simplified by the fact that his salary and local office in Neuss were both paid for by the WZB.[30] Any allegation that the authorities were calling the tune would thus have been fairly difficult to substantiate.

Obstacles to participation

Mediation, as opposed to conventional procedures for conflict resolution, is characterised by the fact that it offers a wider circle of affected parties or those interested in environmental policy greater opportunities to exert an influence on decisions which affect the environment. As a rule, mediation costs a great deal in time and money, a fact that leads environmental or citizens action groups in particular rapidly to reach the limits of their capacity and organisational skills. In the tension resulting from this they, like others who are not officially participating or who have been excluded by vested economic interest, react particularly sensitively to processes and events within the mediation. They tend to perceive mediation as a procedure whose participatory characteristics are merely *apparent*.

On the other hand, mediation does not take place in a social and political vacuum; representatives at the procedure do indeed continue to use typical, functional means and strategies to bring their interests to the table, albeit in a more controlled way. In so doing, however, some groups have, by virtue of their greater resources and experience, considerable advantages over others. One of the central tasks of a mediator is therefore to redress the imbalance of power and relax the tensions which it causes. To do this, especially if some of the participants are skilled negotiators or possess a great deal of expertise or status, he needs considerable skills to facilitate negotiations, as well as a strong reputation, to enable him to be taken seriously as a management figure.

In a mediation, unlike in conventional procedures for conflict resolution, poor financial resources may mean fewer opportunities to exploit fully the improved possibilities for participation. In the Neuss mediation procedure, it was possible to counterbalance this to some extent by providing financial support through a special fund, set up by the WZB and administered by the mediator, who acted as trustee. This fund was used, for example, to pay for experts invited at the request of environmental organisations or to finance attendance at specialist conferences.

Responsibilities of the mediator

Scarce financial resources were not the only problem, perhaps not even the major problem, facing representatives of environmental groups at the Neuss mediation. They had to endure a great deal of pressure when conveying to their members the results of a procedure wherein they had agreed to compromise, and they had to try and persuade their members to commit themselves to the procedure voluntarily. Compared with those of the hierarchically structured organisations, the internal decision-making processes within environmental and citizens' action groups were considerably more time-consuming, less easy to predict and produced less stable results. The readiness for conflict among non-participating members of these groups is, as a rule, greater than their willingness to compromise. Their representatives therefore had to report back to them regularly and often throughout the mediation, in order to ensure that the compromises achieved during the procedure retained their "legitimacy" on the outside. This process of reporting back put a considerable extra strain on the delegates, presumably sometimes greater than the strain of the mediation procedure itself.

In view of the heavy demands placed on the environmental groups, one of the main tasks of the mediator was to scrutinise carefully the projects and the decision-makers, to determine whether there was sufficient scope for compromise to justify putting the environmental groups under so much pressure.[31] If a mediator does not, or if he or she lacks the necessary authority to do so, not only will the mediation procedure fail, it could also throw into question the whole philosophy regarding mediation. In the case of Neuss, the negative consequences for other mediation procedures in progress or being planned could have been especially far-reaching because in Germany these procedures were still somewhat rare at the time, and many individuals were suspicious of them.

Procedural rules

In the Neuss mediation procedure, the internal procedural rules (standing orders) were confined to a small number of assumptions, mostly formulated in general terms. The rules of order were closely based on the procedural rules of the Münchehagen mediation.

The participants agreed *inter alia* to a ruling that the internal workings of the procedure, particularly anything relating to other participants, should not be disclosed to anyone outside the procedure. Of course, there was a sizeable grey area here which, had the rules been interpreted more rigidly, could have triggered numerous secondary disputes. With the exception of two or three individual incidents, this was not the case.[32] Overall, the efforts made by participants to realise the spirit and substance of the self-imposed rules of order can be said to have been surprisingly strong (although such rules are, by legal standards, extremely vague).

In view of the somewhat rudimentary set of procedural rules, the negligibly small number of arguments over procedure was very surprising. This may be an indication of a tacit but powerful fundamental consensus between participants not to violate the spirit of the mediation for personal advantage - in other words not to exploit procedural rules strategically. The provisional conclusion here is that a few basic rules are generally sufficient for procedures of this kind. In particular, it would seem to be unnecessary to try to ensure a controlled development by imposing a straitjacket of detailed procedural rules which could strangle any attempt to achieve discursive continuity.

4.7 Participants Assessment of the Procedure

The survey of the participants' view and assessment of the mediation procedure was central to the research philosophy. It was carried out during and at the end of the procedure, and included written questionnaires. The participants were questioned about the procedure itself, the mediator and the issue the procedure addressed.

Results of the questionnaires during the mediation procedure

An initial glance at participants response patterns at the eight stages of the survey[33] reveals, strikingly enough, that their views remained relatively consistent, despite great variation between the individual meetings. In general, clear trends can scarcely be discerned, and even individual meetings did not seem to generate any characteristic evaluation structures. Individual participants seemed to have formed opinions on the issues raised in the questionnaires very rapidly in the first meetings. Opinions formed thus changed very little (systematically) over time.

It was important to participants that the solutions reached in the mediation procedures be lasting ones, and that they be brought about fairly, on the basis of mutual agreement. Participants were less concerned about public acceptance, ease of implementation and the speed with which a solution was found. In terms of content, maximum environmental compatibility was the overriding aim. Whether the results of the mediation procedure were economically feasible and compatible with existing law were considered less important.

As a whole, the participants in the procedure quite definitely saw themselves as representing specific interests and they were clear in their own minds about what they wanted. They did not, however, view other groups as opponents: they saw them rather as partners in a process of cooperation. Individuals were not so much concerned about persuading others as about understanding them and being open-minded. They interpreted the procedure more as a process of understanding than as a battle, and believed on the whole that a consensus, rather than a result that could be labelled as victory or defeat, would be reached.

Results of the final questionnaire (after conclusion of the mediation)[34]

Many of those questioned were of the opinion that the outcome of the mediation had been influenced by external factors: in particular they thought legal constraints (77%), regional politics (86%), and the interests of the waste disposal industry (59%) had had a significant impact. About half those questioned expressed the view that the mediation procedure had improved the waste management concept, particularly in the areas of waste avoidance and waste recycling; this was less the case, however, with respect to waste disposal. Overall, 26% of those questioned were satisfied with the outcome - 51% were not; 22% felt that the outcome was better than they had originally anticipated, while 32% thought it worse.

Of those questioned, 50% said that they had learned a considerable amount about the legal and technical aspects of waste disposal as well as about the actual waste situation in the district of Neuss. A majority (62%) felt that one important result of the mediation (compared with other effects) had been the establishment of a solid information base.

Would a different solution have ever been possible with respect to the highly contentious nature of the main issue (waste incineration)? More than half of those questioned could imagine agreeing to solutions quite different from those listed in the questionnaire; a good deal fewer, however, believed that other representatives of their group would do the same. Most individuals considered themselves to be more flexible than the other members of their group.[35]

Many individuals questioned saw their own group as being willing to compromise (i.e. they showed a readiness to make concessions against their initial positions) whereas only a few ascribed the same willingness to other groups. The tendency to see others as being less willing than oneself to give ground or compromise can also be an obstacle to mediation.

In terms, for instance, of frequency and duration in the meetings, or the structure of the mediation, the majority of respondents considered that the procedure had been run just right. Nevertheless, 60% would have liked to have seen further agreements on future co-operation. The majority (68%) believed that the mediation procedure had begun too late, and about half thought it had ended too soon.

Hardly any of the participants expected the implementation of the resolutions to be unproblematic. Of those questioned, 26% believed that those involved would adhere completely to the resolutions, but:

- 40% considered it meaningful to continue the mediation procedure during the implementation phase;

- 58% said, given a similar type of problem, they would participate in a mediation procedure again;

- 49% believed that mediation procedures would gain in importance;

About 50% of those questioned would recommend mediation to other local authorities faced with similar situations.

The overall picture painted by the data so far is, on the one hand, one of moderate scepticism towards the mediation procedure and its outcome. On the other hand, this picture has some positive aspects to it. This apparent ambivalence acquires a sharper profile in conjunction with responses to four questions on relative assessment of procedures. When participants were asked how the decision-making process would have gone without mediation, in other words decision-making through the usual political channels, the following picture emerged: with regard to all four points of the evaluation, practically no one held the opinion that standard political paths would have led to a better outcome or would have had more positive side-effects (cf. Table 1).

Table 1: Comparative evaluation of the success of the mediation procedure

Please estimate what would have happened if the mediation procedure had not been undertaken.

Without mediation	Likely	Equally likely	Unlikely
a more transparent decision making process	0%	21%	80%
a qualitatively better result	2%	43%	55%
a more consensual result	0%	23%	77%
a result more satisfactory to my group	0%	56%	44%

General conclusion

The outcome of the Neuss mediation procedure was received sceptically by a large proportion of participants. Increased transparency and a higher level of information were acknowledged as clearly visible effects. The flexibility of the mediation group was often systematically underestimated by the participants. Were each person to assume that others were as prepared to compromise as they believe themselves to be, the scope for negotiation might be greater. Those who viewed the outcome of the mediation with scepticism nevertheless did not blame the mediator, nor did they find fault with the way the procedure was designed. Mediation scores particularly high when it is compared to conventional forms of decision-making. At all levels of the assessment, mediation procedures are seen to have clear advantages.

4.8 Gravitational Force of Conventional Political Processes

Experiences gained in Neuss show clearly that mediation procedures can neither replace nor annul the normal political conflict-consensus process. In any case, against a backdrop of highly complex areas of conflict and numerous political networks with various interests in the waste management arena, and given that this web of interests extends far beyond the regional dimension, it would be highly unrealistic to expect mediation to play a very dominant role here.

Generally speaking, it was observed that all three phases of the mediation procedure in Neuss - the pre-mediation phase, the mediation procedure itself and the post-mediation phase - were heavily influenced by conventional political processes. Nevertheless, as a result of the Neuss mediation, some features of conventional political practice underwent qualitative change. This was particularly the case for the selection of participants in the mediation procedure. Here an attempt was made to mobilise any and all groups who could have had a potential interest (regardless of how small or remote). In this context, there was never any dispute about the legitimacy of participation by any group.

While the mediation was in progress, many political developments outside the district of Neuss had a significant impact. These included the passing of federal regulations and laws which in some respects brought radical change to federal German waste legislation. Political processes and constellations of interest within the district also had significant impacts on the mediation procedure.[36]

At the end of the mediation procedure, what one might call the traditional political modes of behaviour came into play again: recriminations and black-and-white descriptions of the situation. More emphasis was placed on differences than on agreement. What had been mutually achieved was either exaggerated by one camp or played down by another. Nevertheless, in the post-mediation phase the basic rules of order established during the mediation were adhered to voluntarily, even though they were not legally binding. For instance, confidentiality has not been violated there has been no "washing of dirty linen"' and no public revelation of strictly internal matters.

4.9 Conclusion

It was not possible to reach agreement on the most hotly disputed issue: that of whether the waste management programme should contain exclusively cold disposal technologies (e.g. biological-mechanical treatment plants) or whether the only possibility, in legal terms also, would be to construct an additional waste incineration plant. Nevertheless, as a result of the mediation procedure, it was possible to define more precisely, and thus limit, the field of conflict. Essential differences became explicit; and so decision-making within subsequent political processes and formal procedures has gained a sounder basis and became more conscious of important consequences.

To summarise, the researchers concluded that the procedure had, among others, the following positive effects:

- The information base was broadened for all concerned.
- The actions of the administration became transparent.
- The procedure generated a high degree of objectivity and professional competence and could be kept almost entirely free of personal biases.
- It was possible to resolve a large number of issues or points of contention by consensus.
- As to the fact that from the outset the issue of waste incineration was the most conflict-ridden, it was at least possible to achieve some form of compromise (i.e. modification of the original technical configuration).

5. Experiences with EDR: Results, Problems, and Advantages
5.1 A General Balance

EDR is spreading slowly, but steadily. In Europe, Germany is in the lead as regards moderated or mediated EDR procedures in multi-party conflicts.[37] The number of proponents in administration, business, political parties[38], and environmental groups is rising and, especially important within the legalistic culture of Germany, there is increasing support from legal professionals and their organisations. Experts in environmental law in particular consider EDR to be a useful extension of the existing dispute resolution system[39]. They also consider the adoption of EDR within the existing legal framework to be possible, and have already made proposals to this effect.[40] The same applies to political scientists. Furthermore, the respected independent Council of Environmental Advisors (SRU) has spoken out in favour of the systematic introduction of mediation and similar procedures into environmental policy institutions and the legal system.[41] The Federal Ministry for the Environment is also among its supporters, as are regional and state-level political institutions, such as the environment ministries of Lower Saxony, Schleswig-Holstein, Brandenburg and Berlin, to name but a few.

Compared with the situation about eight years ago, the attitudes of the important agency groups to EDR have been transformed. This is remarkable for Germany, if only because innovative procedures in the environmental field are normally subjected to a highly sceptical examination along fundamentalist lines. The abstract demand that new procedures be absolutely free of potential problems and able to solve every existing problem is often made. This kind of debate did take place, but it died down relatively quickly - perhaps also because this instrument has been more analysed by social scientists on the basis of empirical case studies than is otherwise usual.

But the fact that this assessment is so broadly positive is also remarkable because the success rate of the procedures to date is, at any rate at first sight, not spectacular. In a study[42] of 49 larger-scale procedures - mediations, procedures involving a moderator or facilitator, or those which were oriented towards consensus without the involvement of a neutral third person - five have broken down because no agreement could be reached on substantive problems or on the future course of the procedure. Eighteen procedures were still in progress, and as far as it is possible to tell, they are moving in a positive direction. Fourteen were concluded with an agreement which is (at least partially) being implemented. In three cases, agreements reached were not accepted by the institutions responsible for their implementation.[43]

However, it must be noted that, in the majority of procedures which concluded with an agreement, only a partial compromise was reached. In the subsequent implementation phase also, restrictions or modifications which were not approved by all participants have been made. Nor have expectations (which were in some cases extremely high) about the efficiency in terms of time and money of such procedures always been fulfilled.

Nonetheless, when one remembers that these procedures are still very much newcomers to the German environment policy field; that in the beginning there were almost no professional moderators; that the existing legal framework conditions are highly restrictive; that the shadow of past conflicts still covers the whole arena of environmental conflict; that the politico-administrative culture offers a sometimes disadvantageous basis for compromise-oriented negotiations involving citizens groups and environmental organisations; that the environment belongs among the most conflict-ridden areas of policy; and that, on top of this, a variety of cases were dealing with particularly contentious environmental issues (e.g. waste, chemical products), in this light, the results appear far more positive than when assessed from outside their context.

On the basis of practical experience up to now, and while recognising that not all of these points apply to specific cases, one can generally emphasise the following advantages of environmental mediation and similar procedures over conventional processes:

- Otherwise suppressed issues and aspects are introduced to the negotiations, which brings about a broadening of issues and options in the environmental policy framework.

- A decision-making process more adequate to society is created, taking into account the shift in values which has taken place particularly in industrialised countries; aspects which are not covered by law but are relevant to society and to the conflict, even diffuse concerns and insecurities, can be brought in.

- The transparency of the basis and goals of a decision is increased by increasing the quantity of factual information available.

- A communicative process more suited to the problem (a gain in rationality) is achieved, since the discussions do not take place in the political arena, which tends to promote over-dramatisation, and are not oriented around a final decision taken by the courts.

- There is a mutual stimulation of creative energy in overcoming or smoothing the ground between opposing positions and interests, working up to a ruling which is relatively advantageous to all participants,

- The decisions reached in the procedure are guaranteed greater stability during the subsequent implementation process, since they were developed on the basis of a broad-based transparent procedure of balancing interests.

- Direct public participation is extended and intensified through the active mobilisation of normally excluded interest groups or affected parties.

In the final analysis, there is no evidence that the issues have been or could be better resolved within formal procedures. In addition, a more comprehensive, long-term perspective indicates strongly that the procedures are initiating a social and political learning process, which is leading to a more broad-based consideration of environmental interconnectedness and to an increased ability to co-operate among the various agency groups. Judged against the new environmental policy challenges arising from the globalisation of environmental politics, and from the perspective of sustainable development, these have been positive developments. Cross-national studies on environmental policy have recently shown once again that flexible instruments, negotiated regulation, networking, and the capacity for co-operative problem solution are central preconditions for an innovative and effective environmental policy. Serious conflicts are often necessary to set things in motion within the environmental arena; however, seen from a long-term perspective it is obviously not litigious societies but rather a policy style of co-operation that leads to progress in environmental policy.

5.2 Problems

The following presents a brief overview of the problems arising most frequently in EDR practice. Leaving aside, the multi-faceted problem areas within legal and political theory already discussed.[44]

Feedback and ratification of agreement

The largest problem is the systematic linking of the EDR procedure to the outside world. In numerous cases, the delegates had problems seeking agreement from their respective organisations to the partial outcomes of the procedures. It has also emerged that only in a few cases was there an adequate flow of information to the organisations from their representatives, and their competence was equally often unclear. The citizens action groups, environmental organisations and their clientèle obviously experienced this problem most severely.

However, it could also be seen that, in questions of information transfer, serious mistakes were often made which might have been avoided. It can therefore be assumed that there will be improvements in the future, in particular by making it far clearer during the pre-mediation phases than has generally been the case how important systematic context feedback is, and clarifying necessary feedback in the rules of the mediation. It has also been rare for the mediator to pay systematic attention to whether feedback is taking place; and only in a few cases has the mediator taken an active role (e.g. shuttle diplomacy) in trying to reduce these context problems.

Finally, there are particularly legal problems for the public authorities in committing themselves over the implementation of any agreement reached. It would be possible to draw up civil contracts, but this is scarcely a practice in Germany, especially since dominant legal opinion rejects administrative contracts for reasons of dogma. For some time now, however, a re-think has been going on in legal circles, and such contracts are increasingly being discussed more positively. There have already been examples of private contracts concerning siting, to which public authorities were a party.

Training of mediators

There is in Germany no environmental mediator who has received a broad education in this specific area. Many mediators and moderators have learnt what they know from the literature. In many cases of EDR, it has been apparent that lack of professionalism and practical experience in the mediators has led to avoidable procedural difficulties. The situation has been improving. A few (but still only a few) training courses are on offer, and there are already about 20 people who have facilitated in several EDR cases, and thereby gained a high level of experience. In addition, there are now some 10 private organisations specialising in environmental mediation (and many other commercial organisations, in particular engineering firms and consultancies, but also law offices, now also offer to conduct EDR procedures). Furthermore, the first association of environmental mediators was established in 1996, and is now working on informational material and organising internal seminars. Also currently under discussion is the establishment of a publicly funded institution to offer, among other things, environmental mediation training.

Finance

Most EDR cases have been initiated by the local or state authorities. Funding often causes large problems in administrative law, as there are no regulations covering mediation procedures. Appropriate administrative guidelines could nonetheless be drawn up; there are at any rate no legal obstacles to this under existing law. However, the poor and still further deteriorating financial situation for public institutions is a great problem. In contrast to the US, there has to date been scarcely any German EDR funded by non-profit organisations, and procedures initiated by the business sector are still extremely infrequent.

The use of financial or material compensation in association with the settlement of environmental conflicts is taboo in Germany. A very few cases of financial compensation became public knowledge, and were discussed in the media in a spirit of overwhelming rejection; environmental organisations are particularly opposed to compensation. An environmental organisation which recently received a seven-figure donation from a company for abandoning a court action (which the organisation had in any case considered to be fairly hopeless) was severely criticised by its parent organisation. However, experts with practical experience consider it possible to increase the use of material compensation (e.g. funding for local authority and social institutions taking compensatory environmental action) in future, if this is clearly defined as a possible goal from the start of the procedure, if the appropriate regulations are unambiguous and if the process is conducted as transparently as possible.

Legal barriers

The existing legal situation places significant restrictions on the use of EDR procedures. It limits in particular the active participation and room for manoeuvre for representatives of the public authorities, and there only a very few possibilities for linking such procedures closely with formal decision-making and dispute resolution procedures. But this situation too has been improving for some years. In the first place, legal experts are increasingly being able to show that there are as yet unexploited possibilities, at least for limited use of EDR, on the basis of current law alone. Secondly, there are proposals from influential lawyers and legal organisations for strengthening such procedures in law, and thirdly, the representatives of public authorities, as numerous EDR cases to date have shown, have developed countless sophisticated ways and means of skirting around some of the restrictive legal barriers. At the same time, however, countless problems are still arising in practice, because there is still no regulation for EDR in environmental law.

Value conflicts

Cases involving "value conflicts" have proved to be the most difficult area for the application of EDR. They affect above all the issue of nuclear power and, to some extent, genetic engineering. Here, particularly within the environmental organisations, fundamentalist positions dominate, rejecting out of hand any participation in such procedures. Nevertheless, a gradual process of differentiation is developing here also. Whatever the case, there have already been several procedures on partial aspects of genetic technology where no agreements between all participants may have been reached, but where the debate was considered by a majority to have been highly objective and to have contributed to an increased rationality on the issue.[45] With respect also to nuclear power issues, possibilities for the use of EDR are emerging, now that some environmental organisations and environmental research institutions are talking about the present firm opposition to the storage of radioactive waste as being politically problematic (because then, among other things, the displacement of the problem, which is already taking place through the export of radioactive waste, for instance, is increased).

5.3 Lawyers and EDR

Lawyers play an important part in the so-called informal activities of environmental administrations, where oral or written agreements (which are not legally binding) or contracts are concluded on pollution control measures with private firms. Their function is essentially limited to checking strictly legal aspects, e.g. possible problems with existing law, or ensuring that no possibly undesirable and unintentional legal consequences result from the agreements. Occasionally, they play a role as mediators in siting decisions, permissions and enforcement activities. However, they form a clear minority among those who conduct or offer mediation procedures. As a rule, it is environmental or administrative lawyers who specialise in mediation. Sometimes they co-operate with experts in other disciplines (co-mediation) (e.g. environmental engineering or planning), but it is often the case that lawyers are called in as consultants to clarify specific legal questions arising in mediation procedures.

A fairly recent development has led to commercial lawyers specialising in mediation of commercial - including environmental - disputes. There are already professional organisations in this area. Thus the German Law Society (*Deutscher Anwaltverein*) has set up a committee on extra-judicial conflict resolution, offering information on, among other things, business mediators who can also take on environmental cases. Moreover the Society also has a working group on mediation, which is promoting the professionalisation of this area. Another organisation for mediators is the Federal Association for Mediation in Business and Employment (*Bundesverband Mediation in Wirtschaft und Arbeitswelt*), with 80 members. These organisations are very active, particularly in stimulating interest in mediation in business.

Until now there have been only very few cases of mediation in commercial environmental disputes; there are no statistics on this, and many cases are not publicised by the participants. The fact that there is so little mediation here is explained by a number of very different theories. Some legal scientists consider the transfer of alternative techniques developed in the US into the area of commercial disputes to be problematic. The techniques are judged to be typically American responses to specifically American problems. It is also argued that the justice system and arbitration function better (faster and more cheaply) in Germany than in the US.[46]

Most lawyers are nonetheless clearly of the opinion that even if the situation is better than in the US, there are still major problems which could be solved better through alternative techniques. They argue that adjudication in commercial disputes scarcely takes place and that arbitration functions poorly, especially in major cases of conflict. They see great interest in these alternative techniques among lawyers, also among companies which are informed about them. The main cause of their failure to spread widely is thought to be insufficient information and the lack of an attractive pioneer case. It is predicted that the use of such techniques in commercial disputes will soon begin and continue to increase.[47]

5.4 A Brief Résumé

In contrast to the US and Canada, Germany has so far had little experience with EDR procedures in areas of major environmental conflict, but there have been some very encouraging cases. The conditions for systematically building on practical and scientific experience are broadly favourable. Legal and political scientists are increasingly stressing the advantages of a "co-operative state" in the light of the transformations in society and business over recent years. Interest in mediation procedures is growing steadily and the procedures are gaining a foothold in practice. There are now several private institutions which use the term "mediation" in the name of their companies; other firms (particularly in the field of environmental planning and consultancies) are also increasingly offering mediation services, and an association of environmental mediators has been established. Competence in this area is clearly increasing. It is expected that legislation will soon be passed for reducing some of the existing legal restrictions on the use of EDR.

Despite the fact that there are still unresolved questions concerning this tool for settling environmental conflicts, and that it is still in its infancy in Europe, it may be argued, on the basis of practical experience to date, that alternative EDR procedures in general have a proven potential to enrich the existing set of tools available for settling environmental problems expediently. But it would be an exaggeration to claim that they can completely smooth the way in the field of environmental policy. There cannot be a universal panacea of this kind in a field as complex as environmental policy.

Bibliography

Bock, Bettina, *Umweltschutz im Spiegel von Verfassungsrecht und Verfassungsschutz.* Berlin: Duncker und Humblot 1990

Bohne, Eberhard, *Der informale Rechtsstaat.* Berlin Duncker and Humblot 1981

Bora, Alfons and Rainer Döbert, AKonkurrierende Rationalitäten. Politischer und technisch-wissenschaftlischer Diskurs im Rahmen einer Technikfolgeabschätzung von gentechnisch erzeugter Herbizidresistenz in Kulturpflanzen in *Soziale Welt* Nr. 44 (pp. 75-97) 1993

Breidenbach, Stephan, *Mediation-Struktur, Chancen und Risiken von Vermittlung in Konflikt.* Cologne: Otto-Schmidt-Verlag 1995

Bühring-Uhle, Christian, AAlternative Streitbbeilegung in Handelsstreitigkeiten in *Streitschlichtung. Rechtsvergleichende Beiträge zur außergerichtlichen Streitbeilegung.* Gottwald, Walter and Dieter Strempel (eds), Cologne: Bundesanzeiger 1995 (pp. 59-74)

Bulling, Manfred, AUmweltschutz und Wirtschaftsüberwachung in Verwaltungshandeln durch Verträge und Absprachen, Hermann Hill (ed), Baden-Baden: Nomos 1990 (pp. 147-157)

Claus, Frank, AÜberblick über alternative Verfahren der Konfliktmittlung - Neun Fragen zu den Perspektiven in Deutschland in *Alternative Konfliktregelungsverfahren bei der Planung und Implementierung großtechnischer Anlagen* WZB-Schriftenreihe FS II 96-301 Katharina Holzinger and Helmut Weidner (eds), Berlin: Social Science Research Center Berlin 1996 (pp. 53-62)

Daele, Wolfgang van den, AObjektives Wissen als politische Ressource: Experten und Gegenexperten in Diskurs in *Kommunikation und Entscheidung. Politische Funktionen öffentlicher Meinungsbildung und diskursiver Verfahren* Wolfgang van den Daele and Friedhelm Neidhart (eds), Berlin: edition sigma 1996 (pp. 297-326)

Fietkau, Hans-Joachim and Helmut Weidner (in collaboration with K. Holzinger, B. Lackmann, K. Pfingsten), *Umweltverhandeln* Berlin: edition sigma 1998 (in print)

Fülgraff, Georges M., ADas Mediationsverfahren zum Abfallwirtschaftskonzept der Kreises Neuss in *Mediation als politisches und soziales Prozess* Andreas Dally, Helmut Weidner and Hans-Joachim Fietkau (eds), Rehburg-Loccum: Evangelische Akademie Loccum 1994 (pp 33-61)

Funke, Rainer, ADie Sanierung des Norddeutschen Affinerie in Hamburg - Ein Beispiel kooperativen Verwaltungshandelns in *Verwaltungshandeln durch Verträge und Absprachen* Hermann Hill (ed), Baden-Baden: Nomos 1990 (pp. 179-192)

Funke, Rainer, AKonfliktbewältigung aus Anlaß von Genehmigungsverfahren in *Konfliktbewältigung durch Verhandlungen* Wolfgang Hoffmann-Riem and Eberhard Schmidt-Assmann (eds), Baden-Baden: Nomos 1990 (vol. 2 pp. 209-220)

Gottwald, Walther and Dieter Stempel (eds), *Streitschlichtung. Rechtsvergleichende Beiträge zur außergerichtlichen Streitbeilegung* Cologne: Bundesanzeiger 1995

Hill, Hermann (ed), *Verwaltungshandeln durch Verträge und Absprachen* Baden-Baden: Nomos 1990

Hoffmann-Riem, Wolfgang and Eberhard Schmidt-Assmann (eds), *Konfliktbewältigung durch Verhandlungen* (2 volumes) Baden-Baden: Nomos 1990

Holznagel, Bernd, *Konfliktlösung durch Verhandlungen* Baden-Baden: Nomos 1990

Jänicke, Martin and Helmut Weidner (eds), *National Environmental Policies. A Comparative Study of Capacity-Building* Berlin, Heidelberg, New York: Springer 1997

Kloepfer, Michael, AStatement zum Thema Der verhandlende Staat in *Alternative Konfliktregelungsverfahren bei der Planung und Implementierung großtechnischer Anlagen* Katharina Holzinger and Helmut Weidner (eds), WZB-Schriftenreihe FS II 96-301 Berlin: Social Science Research Center Berlin 1996 (pp. 184-186)

Lehmbruch, Gerhard, AThe International Framework of German Regulation in *The Politics of German Regulation* Kenneth Dyson (ed) Aldershot: Dartmouth 1992 (pp. 29-82)

MEDIATOR GmbH (ed), *Mediation in Umweltkonflikten. Verfahren kooperativer Problemlösungen in der BRD* Oldenburg: MEDIATOR GmbH 1996

Müller-Erwig, Katja, *Der Münchenhagen-Ausschuß. Eine qualitative Betrachtung der sozialen Prozesse in einem Mediationsverfahren, WZB-Schriftenreihe FS II 95-304* Berlin: Social Science Research Center Berlin 1995

Norton, Alan, International Handbook of Local and Regional Government. A Comparative Analysis of Advanced Democracies Aldershot: Edward Elgar 1994

Rose-Ackerman, Susan, ADemocracy and Environmental Policy: Reunified Germany as a Cautionary Tale in *Umweltpolitik und Staatsversagen. Festschrift für Martin Jänicke zum 60. Geburtstag* Lutz Metz and Helmut Weidner (eds), Berlin: edition sigma 1998 (in print)

Rose-Ackerman, Susan, Controlling Environmental Policy. The Limits of Public Law in Germany and the United States New Haven, London: Yal University Press 1995

Sander, Frank, AGerichtliche und außergerichtliche Streitbeilegung - Überblick über die Erfahrungen in den USA in Gottwald, Walther and Dieter Stempel (eds), Streitschlichtung. Rechtsvergleichende Beiträge zur außergerichtlichen Streitbeilegung Cologne: Bundesanzeiger 1995

Schmidt, Manfred G., ADie Politik des mittleren Weges. Besonderheiten der Staatstätigkeit in der Bundesrepublik Deutschland in *Politik und Zeitgeschichte* (supplement to the weekly Das Parlament) B9-10 1990, pp. 23-31

Schmitter, Philip and Gerhard Lehmbruch (eds), *Trends Towards Corporatist Intermediation* London: Sage 1979

SRU (Der Rat von Sachverständigen für Umweltfragen), Umweltgutachten 1996. Zur Umsetzung einer dauerhaft-umweltgerechten Entwicklung Stuttgart: Metzler-Poeschel 1996

Susskind, Lawrence and Jeffey Cruikshank, *Breaking the Impasse. Consensual Approaches to Resolving Public Disputes* New York: Basic Books 1987

Weidner, Helmut, AUmweltmediation: Entwicklungen und Erfahrungen im In- und Ausland in *Konfliktregelung in der offenen Büregergesellschaft* Peter H. Feindt, Wolfgang Gessenharter, Markus Birzer and Helmut Fröchling (eds), Dettelbach: J. H. Röll 1996 (pp 137-168)

Weidner, Helmut, AFreiwillige Kooperationen und alternative Konfliktregelungsverfahren in der Umweltpolitik. Auf dem Weg zum ökologisch erweiterten Neokorporatismus? in *Kommunikation und Entscheidung. Politische Funktionen öffentlicher Meinungsbildung und diskursiver Verfahren* Wolfgang van den Daele and Friedhelm Neidhart (eds), Berlin: edition sigma 1996 (pp. 195-231)

Wicke, Lutz, *Umweltökonomie. EIne praxisorientierte Einführung* (2nd ed.) Munich: Franz Vahlen 1989

NOTES

[1] cf. Jänicke & Weidner 1997

[2] The Green Party (then *Die Grünen*, now *Bündnis 90/Die Grünen*) is now firmly established within the political party and government system at all levels of the federal system of Germany. In 1979 it was first represented in a state parliament, in 1983 it entered the *Bundestag* (national parliament), and in the 1994 elections, it became the third largest party (with 7.3% of the popular vote) in the *Bundestag*. In some state governments it is, or was, a coalition partner.

[3] This is also reflected in an ideological concept of "the state": Germans in general and high-ranking governmental officials in particular (who often have a legal education) tend to distinguish between "the state" and "society", believing that the state is responsible for guiding, improving and protecting society, effectively taking care of it.
[4] cf. Norton 1994: 259.

[5] When compared with competitive pluralistic systems, the German system of political interest mediation is often characterised as a neocorporatist system, in which consensus on basic economic and social issues is pursued by the large business federations, trade unions and the government (cf. Schmitter & Lehmbruch 1979, Schmidt 1990, 1992).

[6] Norton 1994: 243; see also Lehmbruch 1992.

[7] Rose-Ackerman 1998: 3,5; cf. also 1995.

[8] BVerwGE55, 250 - *Voerde*

[9] BGHZ 92, 143 - *Kupol Furnace*.

[10] Bock 1990, 311.

[11] With government and industrial expenditure on the environment at DM 45 billion in 1992, Germany spends one of the highest proportions - among OECD members - of its GNP on the environment. The growth rate of the German eco-industry is above average and it is one of the worlds market leaders.

[12] cf. Helmut Weidner (1996), Umweltkooperation und alternative Konfliktregelungsverfahren in Deutschland. Zur Entstehung eines neuen Politiknetzwerkes (Co-operation on the Environment and Alternative Conflict

Management Procedures in Germany. The Development of a New Policy Network), WZB-Schriftenreihe FS II 96-302, Berlin: Wissenschaftszentrum Berlin für Sozialforschung. Contains numerous references to further literature on the subject.

[13] The co-operation principle was established officially in the 1970s, together with the precautionary and the "polluter pays" principle, as one of the three basic principles of government environmental policy.

[14] cf. Wicke 1989: 233 f .

[15] cf. Fietkau and Weidner 1998 in prep.

[16] cf. Müller-Erwig 1995.

[17] cf. Van den Daele 1996, Bora and Döbert 1993.

[18] cf. MEDIATOR 1996.

[19] cf. Claus 1996.

[20] cf. Bohne 1981.

[21] cf. Bulling 1990, Hill 1990.

[22] Funke 1990 (in Hill): 185.

[23] Funke 1990 (in Hoffmann-Riem et al): 220.

[24] cf. Gottwald and Strempel 1995.

[25] cf. Gottwald and Strempel 1995, Sander 1995.

[26] Since 1990, a group from the Standard-setting and Environment Research Unit in the *Wissenschaftszentrum Berlin für Sozialforschung* (Berlin Science Centre for Social Research) (WZB) has been conducting a broad-based research project, funded by the German Federal Ministry of Education, Science, Research and Technology (BMBF), on mediation procedures in the field of environmental protection. The main focus of the project was the mediation procedure in the district of Neuss. From the outset, this project was accompanied by parallel multi-disciplinary research conducted by a group composed of political scientists, psychologists and engineers.

[27] cf. Susskind/Cruikshank.

[28] The responsibility of the WZB, in turn, was to determine the chances for implementing a procedure of this kind. It would, if required, assume the organisational tasks, bear the direct costs, seek and finance a potential mediator for proposal to the disputing parties, and it would also set up a mediation office in the district of Neuss.

[29] Georges M. Fülgraff MD, born in 1933, specialises in pharmacology and toxicology. He is currently professor of public health at the Berlin Technical University (*Technische Universität Berlin*). Since 1974 he has served as president of the German Federal Office of Public Health (*Bundesgesundheitsamt*); from 1980 to 1982 he was permanent secretary in the German Federal Ministry of Public Health and for six years has been a member of the Council of Experts on Environmental Matters (*Sachverständigenrat für Umweltfragen*).

[30] This corresponds with the mediator's experience of the preliminary discussions: "The question of the financing of the mediation procedure played a part in discussions with other parties, and not just with the citizens' action groups. . . . The issue came up almost every time. This would seem to be an important point to consider for the further development of mediation procedures in Germany, since mediation, particularly if it is a commercial enterprise, is usually financed by the operators. This would make it very difficult to eliminate doubts as to the impartiality of the mediator. I believe therefore that, if mediation is to be widely used as an instrument of dispute resolution, it is vital to find methods of financing which avoid direct dependence on the operators or on any one party" (Fülgraff, 1994:38). In the meantime there are several examples of mediation-like procedures in Germany in which the financing of the mediator by the operators has not created an insuperable barrier to impartiality.

[31] Some participants were surprised by the abrupt end to the mediation procedure in Neuss. The mediator explained this as follows: "I felt that it was not justifiable to expect those participants who were not involved in a professional capacity to sacrifice any more free time and energy where no further scope for negotiation could be detected. New room for manoeuvre can only be created by the parties represented on the district council" (Fülgraff, 1994:61).

[32] Occasion when it was felt that the confidentiality rule had been violated were discussed among the participants in the mediation. An apology and explanation by the offender was usually sufficient to defuse the whole event.

[33] The participant were not asked to fill out questionnaires after the first meeting, as it was felt that this might overtax them at this early stage. Thus the sets in the database cover eight full meetings, although nine actually took place.

[34] Two months after the end of the mediation, a questionnaire was sent to 52 participants to enable them to make a more detailed final evaluation of the procedure. Of those questioned 45 (almost 90%) returned the questionnaires. Most evaluations were given on a 5-point scale, where respondents rated a statement from "true" (1) to "not true" (5). Reference made below to "agreement" corresponds to a score of 1 or 2, while "rejection" corresponds to a score of 4 or 5.

[35] Attributing a low degree of flexibility to others can lead to alternative solutions not being sought (or not sufficiently explored) during negotiation, and to premature demands for decision, entailing possible head-on confrontation. What was learnt from the survey is that individuals do not credit others with sufficient mental flexibility. It seems that it would be helpful in a procedure of this kind if participants could learn to base their beliefs on their own mental flexibility, that is, to consider others to be at least as flexible as themselves instead of judging them automatically to be more entrenched. Encouraging this behaviour might be a worthwhile function of the mediator.

[36] These included co-ordination processes between the traditional political parties, entanglements and links with other political issues (e.g. industrial policy), the state horticultural exhibition, the activities of district waste disposal companies and the activities of the monopolistic energy supply company. In the end, all these factors and events - within the district and outside it - affected the scope for negotiation within the mediation procedure itself.

[37] cf. Weidner 1996.

[38] This is especially interesting, since it is the political parties who should, as it is understood (and laid down in the constitution) in Germany, act as mediators between government and society. Their position was thus somewhat hesitant at first, not because they feared competition from mediation, but because it could have been interpreted as an admission on their part that they could no longer play this role of political mediator. Incidentally, representatives of political parties are often participants in EDR procedures in Germany.

[39] cf. the discussion in Hoffmann-Riem and Schmidt-Assmann 1990.

[40] cf. Kloepfer 1996.

[41] cf. SRU 1996.

[42] cf. MEDIATOR 1996.

[43] The available data did not permit a reliable assessment of the remaining procedures.

[44] But cf. discussion in Holzinger and Weidner 1996, Hoffmann-Riem and Schmidt-Assmann 1990, Holznagel 1990, and references in Weidner 1996 and Fietkau and Weidner 1998, in prep.

[45] See the scientific analysis of van den Daele 1996, Bora and Dübert 1993.

[46] cf. Bühring-Uhle 1995.

[47] This information is based on telephone interviews with members of the two organisations conducted in November and December 1997. cf. also Breidenbach 1995.

Chapter III
ENVIRONMENTAL CONSENSUS-BUILDING AND CONFLICT RESOLUTION IN THE UK

ENVIRONMENTAL CONSENSUS-BUILDING AND CONFLICT RESOLUTION IN THE UK

Hally Ingram
Assisted by Robin L Juni

1. Introduction

Finding lasting solutions to environmental problems is notoriously difficult in the UK, as in other countries, especially when there are many parties and issues involved. This chapter is about the growing use of collaborative process over the last five years to address environmental problems and sustainability, and about the lessons we in the UK have learnt as a result.

An increasing number of thoughtful decision-makers from government, industry and campaigning organisations in the UK are questioning the effectiveness of traditional, often adversarial processes, to address complex environmental problems. This has resulted in increasing levels of interest in how collaborative processes can be used to enhance or as an alternative to traditional processes.

In the UK, as in other countries, negotiation, co-operation and the building of agreements are part of everyday life. New in about the last six years has been the introduction of collaborative processes in situations where the dialogue is designed and managed by an independent facilitator and where many issues and parties are involved. Such situations often spring from the tensions inherent in the environmental and public policy arena.

Designed and facilitated collaborative processes are ways of helping people involved in a conflict or complex problem, where straightforward talking around a table has failed or is unlikely to succeed, to work together to find solutions they can all live with.

The introduction and development of collaborative processes in the UK have been greatly influenced by and benefited from experience in the US, which is described in the opening chapter of this work. However the UK has not duplicated the US approach: rather, we have learnt from their experiences and started to develop a collaborative approach to environmental decision-making that works in the British context.

As the US and the UK work within different political, cultural and legal frameworks it is only to be expected that there will be some differences in how the approach has developed. For example: (1) There is considerably less experience of using collaborative processes in the UK than in the US. Our approach is still in its infancy compared to the US where there is over fifteen years' experience and many more examples of consensus-building in practice. (2) Whereas practice in the US seems to have focused on resolving disputes rather than preventing them, experience to date in the UK suggests that it is used just as often to prevent conflict.

The terminology used in the UK to describe the approach is usually different from that of the US. "Environmental dispute resolution" is a term rarely used in the UK. It is too closely linked to "disputes" and does not reflect the large proportion of practice in the UK where the approach is as often used to prevent disputes. This chapter therefore uses the terms "collaborative processes" and "consensus-building" interchangeably. These terms are more commonly used and better reflective of UK experience.

There are a number of other terms used in the UK including: "mediation," "facilitation," "stakeholder dialogue", "community problem-solving" and "alternative dispute resolution" (or "ADR"). "Mediation" is the most familiar term in the UK outside environmental situations. It has been used for many years in a number of areas, notably neighbourhood and family disputes, areas described later in the chapter. "Facilitation" is also a more familiar term, though not often used in its full technical sense of designing and running multi-party problem-solving processes. Unlike mediators, facilitators rarely work with the parties separately. The range of these terms reflects the relative infancy of the approach in the UK, and the multitude of situations in which it can be applied.

It is clear that collaborative processes will become an increasingly popular approach to addressing environmental problems and sustainable development in the UK. Building on current experiences and understanding will be essential if we are to ensure that the approach is used appropriately and to full advantage in the future. This chapter reflects on the last five years of collaborative problem-solving in the UK.

2. Reasons for the Emergence of Collaborative Processes in the UK

Many factors have contributed directly to the growing interest and use of collaborative processes. These include the introduction of Local Agenda 21[1], the fear of escalating costs and the uncertainty associated with adversarial decision-making procedures and the fear of high profile environmental disputes resulting from direct action. Indirect factors, such as the increasing awareness within society of mediation in general (e.g. to resolve family, neighbour and commercial disputes), and a growing interest in strengthening local democracy, have meant that more people are exposed to collaborative processes and, as a result, are more open to its use in environmental settings.

These varied and seemingly unconnected factors are nudging more and more people to test collaborative processes as a means of addressing environmental problems and sustainability.

2.1 Problems with current procedures

Among the factors which have contributed to the emergence of environmental consensus-building in the UK is dissatisfacton with current procedures. In particular, traditional consultation and decision-making procedures (such as public inquiries, public meetings and consultation documents), often leave interested parties and the public not only dissatisfied with the final decision, but also frustrated by the process by which they were reached. In addition, traditional procedures do not always meet the needs of the officials who are leading them or of the elected representatives who have to deal with the outcome.

Time and money can be poured into adversarial processes, such as public inquiries and legal processes. Relationships can become damaged as parties only talk to each other in hostile environments where winning is their main concern. Parties can become paralysed by uncertainty because the final decision has been taken out of their hands and instead imposed by a third party, such as a judge or an inspector. Finally, the ultimate decisions do not "stick" where those who are responsible for their implementation are not committed to them.

The following quotation highlights how current procedures can anger and frustrate those involved and might even result in conflict: "Imagine for a moment that you wrote your opinion on a blackboard, and the next person grabbed an eraser and wrote his or her opinion instead. Not only do you have the impulse to erase the message, you'll write your message again, bigger, bolder, more strongly stated. If that's erased, you might be tempted to get out your pocket knife and carve your message in the board."[2]

D+ecision-makers in business, government and campaigning organisations are considering using collaborative processes in situations where they are likely to overcome many of the problems associated with adversarial procedures. In a collaborative process, relationships are valued, parties retain control of the process and the outcome, time and money are not wasted on fighting. Ultimately solutions are identified that everyone can "live with."

2.2 High-profile Environmental Conflicts.

Environmental conflicts in the UK have gained considerable media coverage over the last few years. Greenpeace successfully campaigned against the deep sea disposal of the Brent Spar[3]. At Newbury and Twyford Down, anti-road protesters camped out on the proposed sites of new trunk roads and attempted to stop bulldozers tearing up the land of proposed sites. Protesters often gain media coverage through using direct action, whether it is to stop the siting of a proposed airport runway or a road development scheme. This only affects a company's operations in the UK, but some companies are being challenged by pressure groups because of the perceived negative impacts of their activities and proposed developments overseas.

Such high profile conflicts and the fear of direct action are challenging decision-makers in government and industry to explore new ways to address stakeholder concerns and prevent disputes from arising in the future. Shell Expro, for example, decided to engage in dialogue with stakeholders following the Greenpeace campaign to stop the deep sea disposal of the Brent Spar and the resulting publicity in the summer of 1995.

2.3 Growing Awareness of Alternative Dispute Resolution (ADR)

The groundswell of activity in ADR generally has contributed to developments in processes for environmental consensus-building. Increasingly ADR is being recognised as an acceptable and mainstream way to resolve a dispute or make a good decision, thus providing a positive climate in which to develop collaborative processes in the environmental and public policy arena. ADR has also informed the development of skills and techniques used in environmental consensus-building.

ADR originated in the United States in the late 70s. It was introduced to the UK in the early 1980s. Thousands of people have benefited from ADR in the UK. It has helped ordinary people resolve neighbour, commercial, family and employment disputes without the expense, uncertainty or anxiety associated with litigation.

The proliferation of ADR has been most notable in the following three areas[4]

• *Divorce and separation* Since the early 1980s mediation has been used to resolve issues between divorcing couples, and in particular to help reduce the impact of divorce on the children. Since it was established in 1981 the National Family Mediation (NFM: formerly National Family Conciliation Council) has played a leading role in the development of family mediation.

NFM provides a range of services including selection, training and accreditation for mediators. Over sixty mediation services are affiliated to NFM. More recently the Family Mediators Association has played a key role in advancing the practice of mediation in this area.

• *Commercial and legal disputes.*[5] Commercial and legal mediation started in the late 1980s in the UK. The two major mediation providers and training bodies for legal and commercial disputes are the Centre for Dispute Resolution (CEDR) and the ADR Group. In the last few years these organisations have seen a significant increase in the number of cases going to mediation. ADR services are offered by a number of other organisations and individuals.

• *Neighbourhood disputes.* Neighbourhood mediation services have been helping people resolve disputes for many years, often in highly stressful situations. Since 1984 Mediation UK (formerly the Forum for Initiatives in Reparation and Mediation) has supported the work of neighbourhood mediation services by providing information, referral services, practical support, publicity and networking services. Mediation UK also promotes the idea and practice of mediation in other areas such as conflict resolution in schools, victim and offender mediation and elder mediation.

A common difference between cases where ADR is used in general and when it is applied to environmental problems is the increased number of issues and parties involved. As practice has developed, this has been reflected in the emergence of the differing skills and techniques required for working with multiple parties and issues. A number of these techniques are described later in this chapter.

A new development in ADR over the last couple of years has been the active support of the courts and the Master of the Rolls, Lord Woolf.[6]2 For example, the London County Court is, at the time of writing, piloting a mediation scheme (though it does not deal with environmental cases) intended to ease the heavy workload.[7] Mediation is offered to the parties in cases involving a relatively small claim (between £3,000 and £10,000). A single session with a trained mediator, usually lasts up to three hours. If the parties are then unable to reach an agreement their dispute is referred to the courts. Whether the pilot scheme continues, or new mediation schemes are set up, will be decided by the Lord Chancellor.

2.4 Developments in Community Participation[8]

The development of environmental consensus-building is also linking into government interest in strengthening local democracy, especially through the requirements of Local Agenda 21 for community participation and consensus-building. The following developments have influenced the interest and use of collaborative processes:

• *Local Agenda 21*. At the Earth Summit in Rio de Janeiro in 1992 the UK Government adopted the international agreement Agenda 21. This commitment to Agenda 21 by the UK Government has played a major role in the development of consensus-building processes in the UK.

The participation of communities is essential to fulfilling the objectives of Agenda 21. It is a central aim of Agenda 21 to broaden the range of people and organisations involved in decision-making and build a consensus with local people in the development of a Local Agenda 21. Many local authorities and communities in the UK have risen to this challenge. Many who have seen the benefits for Local Agenda 21 have gone on to use the approach to address other areas of local government, such as the development of local plans, traffic management schemes and biodiversity plans.

• *Growth in Participatory Processes*. Over the last twenty years participatory techniques have been used as a way to establish a positive relationship bet!ween a local authority and its community. They have also been fitted into a culture focused increasingly on partnership as a core way of working. However, some of these relatively new participatory techniques started to become discredited because (a) they involved using a number of entirely ad hoc techniques and (b) their actual medium of delivery was falling back into traditional modes of working, such as formal committees. Recently, however, community decision-makers have recognised that consensus-building provides a set of underlying principles, a clear structure and a range of techniques that ensure cumulative progress over a wide range of issues, while avoiding problems which previously discredited participatory techniques.

• *Land-use planning process*. There is a strong and successful tradition in the UK of land-use planning, well supported for over fifty years with a body of national legal precedent. Bishop suggests this is because of an interventionist governmental tradition in the UK, where emphasis is placed on ensuring that statutory processes cover issues often settled in other countries through the courts.

Land-use planning law, and the resulting detailed local practice, already contains some minor demands on developers and landowners in terms of consultation procedures. Recent years have witnessed a number of initiatives aimed at building a clearer and stronger set of participatory process requirements into the land-use planning process, for example where the siting of significant facilities is an issue. Environmental Assessment comes close to this but is in no way a collaborative process. While these participation requirements are aimed at the improved involvement of communities in decision-making, there is still a long way to go before they are consensus-building.

This increased interest from local authorities and communities in techniques for enhancing representative democracy has provided a positive context for the development and increased use of environmental consensus-building at the local level.

3. Experience with Collaborative Processes

The UK is at an exciting, innovative and experimental stage in the use of collaborative processes.

Over the last five years the demand for consensus-building in the environmental and public policy arena has grown dramatically. It is still, however, early days in British experience. An American mediator who has been involved in ADR for the last fifteen years recently described to the writer how administrative ADR in the USA is in its adolescent phase. If the US is adolescent, the UK must be trying to get through its first day at school!

3.1 Developments Over the Last Five Years

In the UK, consensus-building has been pioneered by Environmental Resolve, part of the Environment Council. The Environment Council was established in 1969 and is an independent charity dedicated to resolving environmental problems through promoting effective dialogue. In the last six years the Environment Council has played a leading role in the promotion, teaching, development and practice of consensus-building in the UK.

Following a conference in 1991 which introduced the concept of consensus-building to the UK, the Environment Council has been running introductory skills and awareness building workshops attended by people working in business, government and the voluntary sector. Over the last six years these courses have attracted over two hundred participants, many of whom have gone on to use collaborative processes in their own work.

As the awareness of collaborative processes has grown, through these courses and other awareness-raising activities among the Environment Council's members, the Council and other independent practitioners have received a growing number of requests to provide facilitation and mediation services in increasingly complex and contentious situations. Case studies are given throughout this chapter to highlight experience. Consensus-building activity has also increased because parties involved in a collaborative style of working often talk about their experiences of its advantages to colleagues and professional counterparts.

There is also a growing demand in business, government bodies and environment groups for in-house training to educate staff in the possibilities offered by collaborative processes and to equip them with the necessary mediation and facilitation skills. Also, as a result of the many requests from individuals who want to train in the field, the Environment Council has developed an intensive six-day training course in these skills for potential environmental facilitators.

Demand for the Environment Council's mediation and facilitation services has grown largely because they are provided within a respected institution, by a team of independent facilitators who have diverse experiences in the UK and abroad. The richness of the teams skills and experiences, both in consensus-building and the environmental field, has ensured the constant development and improvement of practice within the UK. The combination of these factors has encouraged the provision of high quality services and training, not only by the Environment Council, resulting in a greater awareness and usage of the approach in the UK.

3.2 Current Use of Collaborative Processes and Areas of Growth

At present consensus-building is most often being used by decision-makers for the first time. How it is used varies considerably from one situation to another. This makes it difficult to categorise situations where the approach is utilised most frequently.

Experience to date is most noticeable for the breadth and depth of examples, rather than frequent use in one area. Projects are being initiated at all levels (local, national and European) and by many sectors (business, government, the voluntary sector and lawyers). The process is being used to address any issue and is more often applied as a mechanism to prevent rather than resolve disputes.

3.2.1 Local Level

At the local and regional level, authorities are keen to test the approach, often because they are having to deal with the consequences of opposition or division within the community over a proposed plan or decision. Many local authorities, and statutory agencies with local responsibilities, are using the approach for the first time in a number of different situations such as traffic management plans, waste management plans, special area designations and air quality action plans. It is also clearly illustrated through Local Agenda 21 that local authorities have learnt the value of consensus-building with the community. The formulation of the Blackdown Hills management strategy is a unique example of local consensus-building in practice.

CASE STUDY: The Blackdown Hills Area of Outstanding National Beauty (AONB) Management Strategy[9]

Setting the scene

The Blackdown Hills in Devon and Somerset provide a classic picture of the pastoral English landscape. The area is a mosaic of semi-natural habitats of regional and national importance. The landscape is further enhanced by the many fifteenth and seventeenth century buildings.

The area was designated as an Area of Outstanding Natural Beauty (AONB) in June 1991. This AONB straddles two County Councils and four District Council boundaries. The proposed designation was not greeted with universal approval: for example, farmers were concerned that restrictive policies might hinder their work. From the earliest days of the designation process the communities of the Blackdown Hills had expressed a strong belief that the area was, and should remain, a "living landscape".

AONB management plans have a limited history of influencing actions on the ground. They are usually written by professional officers in some detail before being sent to the public for consultation. As a result they often fail to reflect the realities of local economics or are simply not relevant to local people.

In 1995 the Blackdown Hills Joint Advisory Committee decided it would be beneficial to involve the community in the development of the management plan, using a consensus-building approach. This was because of community concerns about the designation and the need to develop a plan that was "owned" by the community and in turn would deliver action on the ground.

The process

The community involvement programme, which was designed and managed by a team of independent facilitators, concentrated on seven distinct phases over a two-year period. Bringing in an outside independent facilitation team helped build local confidence in the process. The process was funded by the relevant local authorities, two government agencies and the European Life Fund.

In the beginning the various interested parties were briefed on the implications of working through a consensus process and sharing in the preparation of the management plan. The AONB project officers spent considerable time in the early stages explaining the process to the local community. They also reported each phase through parish newspapers and other forms of local communication.

Preparation was followed by a series of facilitated "round-table" open meetings held over a two-month period in 1995. These meetings identified issues that would need to be addressed in the development of the management plan. The work of each round-table was recorded verbatim and returned in a written report to the participants. Participants therefore knew they had been listened to accurately.

A Community Conference was held in autumn 1995. The reports from the round-tables provided a baseline of information for the management plan. The conference identified four main theme priorities and these became topic groups: agriculture and environment, access and movement, planning and development, community needs. Local people then decided who should participate in the topic groups.

During the autumn and early winter, the community-based topic groups met three times, and followed a similar plan. In February 1996 the results of the four topic groups were presented to the Joint Advisory Committee. These outlined recommendations for the management plan and further amplified them by identifying direct and practical action or other issues that would need to be considered in implementing the recommendations. In June 1996 a draft report of the strategy was circulated for wide public consultation over a three-month period. In October 1996 a second Community Conference was held to gain final feedback on the strategy and to reach a consensus on the action plan for 1997/98.

Overall the process took approximately two years. It is not however at an end as the Project Officers will continue to involve the community in the implementation and review of the strategy at Community Conferences.

The outcome

The Blackdown Hills Management Strategy was formally adopted in January 1997 and the final report was launched in February 1997. The early indication is that it will be accepted by all the relevant authorities as Supplementary Planning Guidance.

Since completion of the project, there are already ten strong community initiatives that address key issues raised in the Strategy.

Although it is hard to quantify, it is believed that there is no longer opposition to the AONB designation. There is local support both for the Strategy and the way in which it was developed, namely through an approach that did not impose decisions from outside, but generated solutions from within the community.

Over 120 people attended the Strategy launch on a Monday morning. It was noted that there was not the tension in the air which is usually linked to similar events, where members of the community are seen rushing to look at management plan documents with fear and trepidation over what they will find. Instead, those who attended the launch had been a part of the development process - it was their Strategy and they were pleased to have been a part of its development.

3.2.2 National Level

Decision-makers in business and government are testing collaborative processes on a national level. For example, the Highways Agency developed an Environmental Strategy with the involvement of many key stakeholders. This experience demonstrated how the approach can be usefully applied to issues of national significance, even when the parties have a history of hostility between them.

CASE STUDY: Highways Agency's Environmental Strategy[10]

Major road planning in the UK is an area fraught with conflict. It is not unfamiliar to see protesters chained to bulldozers or camping out at a site where a new road is planned.

In 1995, however, the development of an Environmental Strategy for the Highways Agency posed an opportunity to take a collaborative approach. The Agency decided it would benefit from involving stakeholders at the beginning of developing the strategy through interactive workshops. This process would involve members of the Agency working alongside those who had vehemently opposed them in the past. They felt the process would help inform the public and interest groups about how the Agency undertakes its work with regard to the environment.

Traditional consultation would have involved a small number of experts from within the Highways Agency drafting the strategy and circulating it to interested parties for comment. This was an approach that would not build broad-based ownership for either the process or the results, nor provide an opportunity for interested parties to develop any sense of mutual understanding.

The process

The collaborative process adopted instead involved working with both staff from inside the Highways Agency and external stakeholders. Internal workshops, which were managed by Highways Agency staff, introduced staff to the concept of sustainability and gained feedback on the issues that should be covered in the strategy.

In spring 1996 three workshops were independently facilitated to involve external stakeholders. Over forty organisations with an interest in trunk roads and the environment participated in the workshops, including: Friends of the Earth, Transport 2000, the Confederation of British Industry and the Automobile Association.

In each workshop participants started by considering what the Highways Agency did well, what it could do better and what it did not do at all but should do. This was an opportunity for stakeholders to vent their feelings and concerns about trunk road planning, whilst acknowledging what the Agency does well. In the afternoon the participants went on to identify and prioritise issues that need addressing in the Highways Agencys Environmental Strategy. Overall, participants reached broad agreement on a number of issues for the strategy.

In addition to the workshops, the Highways Agency used a questionnaire and one-to-one interviews to gain wider feedback from external stakeholders.

The outcome

The Highways Agencys Environmental Strategy was published in July 1996.The Highways Agency felt that the dialogue had been valuable and that the approach represented the right way of tackling difficult issues in the future.

Most of the participants felt the style of interaction had been very effective, though they could not yet judge the quality of the results. This would depend on how their suggestions were reflected in the implementation of the Strategy.

3.2.3 European Level

Facilitated stakeholder dialogues are also being encouraged and used to resolve problems that stretch beyond UK boundaries, such as the Brent Spar dialogue process (see below) and the development of policy within the European Union (EU).

There is considerable scope for the EU to use collaborative processes where the dialogue is designed and managed by independent facilitators, especially when straightforward talking around a table has failed or is unlikely to succeed. Current decision-making and consultation procedures could be enhanced by using a collaborative approach to address complex issues such as air pollution, hazardous substances or waste management.

Independent facilitators could be brought in to help run a key event or to design and manage a whole process, either formal or informal. For example, the Environment Council recently designed and facilitated a workshop attended by environmental NGOs from across Europe. The workshop helped NGOs consider whether they required a co-ordination structure as part of the standardisation process in Europe and what form a co-ordination structure should take. The process could also be used to assist Member States and key stakeholders in the development and implementation of EU policy. For example, an EU project concerning the implementation of the European waste management policies for health care waste was independently facilitated.

3.2.4 Dialogues Initiated by Business

Dialogues are being initiated by decision-makers in the private, public and voluntary sectors, though some of the most significant and high-profile projects in the UK have been initiated by business.

Growing media focus on crisis situations, or situations where highly contentious issues are emerging, has spurred businesses into using stakeholder dialogues. However, rather than a "knee-jerk" reaction which might involve a one-off mediation with a pressure group, businesses are carefully entering into medium to long-term dialogue processes to ensure that understanding and agreements are built over time with more permanent results. This is an area that will undoubtedly continue to grow.

The Advisory Committee on Business and the Environment, in its seventh progress report, is categorical in acknowledging the need for companies to engage in dialogue with stakeholders. It even recommends that "every company should develop clear guidelines for how and under what circumstances they could include dialogue with interested parties in the process of environmentally-sensitive decision-making. This recommendation has been supported by central government. "

CASE STUDY: Brent Spar Dialogue Process

The Brent Spar story captured the attention and imagination of the public throughout Europe. The events of the summer of 1995 created an unprecedented level of interest in its disposal.

The Brent Spar is or was a floating storage buoy. For nearly 20 years it was based in the Brent Oil Fields off Norway. Shell U.K. Exploration and Production (Shell Expro) is responsible for its decommissioning. When it went out of service Shell Expro had to make a recommendation to the UK Government on a disposal option through using the Best Practicable Environmental Option (BPEO) method of assessment. In 1994 Shell Expro made its recommendation of deep sea disposal, a solution based on thorough scientific analysis. There was limited consultation in making the decision as it was not expected to generate a high level of public interest. In 1995 the UK Government approved the company's recommendation.

At this point Greenpeace made the Brent Spar their campaign target and achieved wide media coverage of the controversy across Europe. Following the campaign, and the resulting public outcry, particularly in Germany, Shell Expro decided to halt the deep sea disposal plan and instead to consider new options.

This time Shell Expro wanted to be sure it made a widely acceptable decision. For this to happen it turned to the expertise of the Environment Councils team of facilitators to help design a process to ensure that it heard the opinions and concerns of a wide variety of stakeholders from across Europe.

The process

This process was designed and managed to ensure it effectively coincided with the technical decision-making process occurring in parallel within Shell Expro. The process aimed to take a more open and involving approach that would take account of a wide range of opinion in informing Shell's decision for the disposal of the Brent Spar.

Following telephone interviews with over fifty key stakeholders a launch seminar was held in November 1996. It was attended by over sixty people, including members of: Friends of the Earth Europe, Greenpeace UK and Germany, BP Exploration, the University of Aberdeen, Scottish Fishermans Federation, Institute for European Environmental Policy, The Institute of Marine Engineers and many more engineers, academics, environmentalists and consumer interests from around Europe.

Before the seminar Shell Expro invited tenders for the disposal of the Brent Spar. Thirty options, including a wind/wave energy generator and a coastal defence, were then presented to stakeholders at the seminar. The seminar aimed to present clear, concise information about the thirty proposed solutions to a largely non-technical audience, and then maximise the feedback opportunities for all participants. The facilitators independently set out to select a balanced audience from a range of interested parties.

Following the launch seminar, Shell Expro took all the participants comments, issues and suggestions and used them to inform its shortlisting process. Eleven proposals were shortlisted and the relevant contractors were invited to work up detailed proposals. The shortlisted proposals included: a training centre for personnel working offshore, a quay, a coastal defence structure and on-shore scrapping.

The dialogue process continued in 1997 in parallel with the technical decision-making process. A series of workshops was held in the UK, the Netherlands, Germany and Denmark to hear the concerns and views of stakeholders both within and outside the UK.

The outcome

The stakeholder dialogue and the technical evaluation were completed by the end of 1997. Shell heard many views, concerns and recommendations which helped inform its final recommendation to the UK Government on a disposal option for the Brent Spar. This recommendation, announced in January 1998 is to re-use the Brent Spar to build a new quay extension at Mekjarvik near Stavanger in Norway.

The Managing Director of Shell Expro said, "Our way forward launched in 1995 was to find a solution that on balance would be at least as good as, or better than, deep sea disposal; to work openly, and to gather a wide range of views and values to help inform our choice. We believe we have achieved what we set out to do."

Shell described in a press release the main lesson it had learnt. "We have learned that we must change the ways we identify and address issues, and interact with the societies we serve. Our way forward for Brent Spar has helped to promote a different approach in Shell to making decisions, and has stimulated us in developing new ways of being more open and accountable".

The Brent Spar dialogue process is a powerful example of effective stakeholder involvement helping a company in its decision-making process.

3.2.5 Dialogues Initiated by National Government

Central government bodies have been slow to initiate consensus-building processes. Some government bodies are starting to embrace the language of consensus-building, even if they do not yet fully understand the process. Over the last five years it has been more usual for businesses to initiate dialogues than central government. To date, government officials have tended to participate in processes or monitor them from a distance. As experience grows of collaborative processes there is increasing pressure for national government to initiative dialogues in appropriate situations. The current Labour Government is showing increasing interest in participative processes.

There are a few exceptions to this slow progress, for example ETSU (the Energy Technology Support Unit), on behalf of the Department of Trade and Industry has used the approach more than once. ETSU has commissioned the development of Good Practice Guidelines for the renewable energy industries and has supported an innovative study to test the feasibility of placing into the statutory planning system a consensus-building procedure for developing renewable energy schemes.

CASE STUDY: Good Practice Guidelines : Short Rotation Coppice for Energy Production[11]

Setting the scene

Renewable energy industries have come under increasing scrutiny over the last few years, most notably wind energy. Developers of wind energy did not expect plans to build wind generators to meet a lot of opposition, least of all from environmental groups. They were wrong. Conflict arose between communities and developers, and soon drew in environmental groups who were concerned about the potential impacts of this new industry. Developers were surprised and even a little hurt because they thought they were doing something environmentalists had been advocating for years.

Through this experience, they and other renewable energy developers became aware of the scrutiny under which this new green industry was operating and of the need for sensitivity in developing it. As a result, wind energy developers decided that formulating some good practice guidelines would help counteract their increasingly poor image by demonstrating their commitment to responsible and sensitive development. The guidelines were successfully produced with input from a broad range of stakeholders, including opposition groups.

The launch of the Guidelines for Wind Energy inspired those involved in supporting and developing Short Rotation Coppice (SRC) for energy production. SRC is an energy crop, usually willow or poplar, which is used to produce either heat and/or electricity. It is known generally as biomass. As yet, SRC is undeveloped, with only a few examples of energy production in the UK. With the support of government, environmentalists and academics, SRC developers decided that producing some similar good practice guidelines would help new projects to proceed in an appropriate and sensitive manner. In this way the industry as a whole could continue to expand while maintaining a reputation for responsibility and avoiding many of the conflicts associated with wind energy.

It was felt essential that the guidelines should be developed using a consensus-building approach, involving the ideas, expertise and support of those who would be using them, as well as of anyone who might be concerned about future developments.

The process

In 1995 Environmental Resolve was commissioned to produce good practice guidelines using consensus-building techniques. The project was funded by ETSU on behalf of the Department of Trade and Industry. A small steering group, including ETSU, British Biogen (a trade association), Friends of the Earth and Environmental Resolve were involved in designing and steering the process.

The guidelines were produced over an eight-month period. The process involved over forty-seven representatives from industry, environmentalists, planners and government bodies e.g. Royal Society for the Protection of Birds, the Game Conservancy Council, Friends of the Earth, the Forestry Commission.

This innovative approach, which was independently facilitated throughout, involved interviewing a wide range of stakeholders with an interest in the industry. Over thirty key stakeholders participated in the first workshop to define the audience and agree the basic framework for the guidelines. This was followed by a series of small sub-group meetings to draft the various sections of the document. The thirty key stakeholders then came back together for a final workshop to discuss, develop and finalize the final draft produced by the subgroups. Throughout the process draft material was written up by an editor, circulated and amended by agreement.

The outcome

The resulting Good Practice Guidelines: Short Rotation Coppice for Energy Production, were launched in November 1996 and were endorsed by over thirty key stakeholders involved in their development.

The process resulted in a wide degree of ownership for the Guidelines amongst the key stakeholders which in turn will help ensure that they are widely used and publicised.

It is believed that the Guidelines will play an important role in the development of an economically and environmentally sustainable renewable energy industry, that does not suffer from the conflicts and problems associated with the more well-established wind energy industry.

Since the development of these guidelines, similar guidelines have been produced for Anaerobic digestion of farm and food processing residues and Forestry residues for energy.

3.2.6   Dialogues Initiated by Local Government

Local authorities, in contrast with central government, are initiating a diverse range of consensus-building projects, described previously. Some of the most visible projects have been in the development of Local Agenda 21. These include Vision 21 in Gloucestershire.

CASE STUDY: Vision 21[12]

Setting the scene

Gloucestershires Local Agenda 21 process is an energetic and creative example of the use of participative processes and facilitation at the local level.

The aim was to involve as many people and as broad a cross-section of Gloucestershire society as possible, in working towards a future in which the quality of peoples lives (especially the most disadvantaged) is enhanced without damaging the environment. The project's focus was to achieve sustainable living in Gloucestershire by enabling individuals, organisations and communities to learn about sustainable living and to work together to achieve it by tackling issues of social, economic and environmental concerns.

The project started in 1993 with the launching of a magazine, and a conference bringing together local people to discuss a way forward for Local Agenda 21 in the area. The local authority called for a Local Agenda 21 to be drawn up for the area by 1996. In the early stages of the project the local authority decided the project would be best managed in the community by a local charity, rather than by external stakeholders or the local authority alone.

The process

The process was formally launched at a public event in April 1994. The event was effective in establishing eight autonomous working groups, and involving 160 people in establishing a two-year timetable and broad framework within which the groups could operate.

The Vision 21 process involved working groups, project groups and six-monthly conferences at weekends or in the evenings to enable the growing membership to drive forward their agenda. The six-monthly meetings were used to check on progress, share information and decide the way forward. A network of facilitators was an important part of Vision 21, developing examples and expertise in participatory techniques. A working council decided to establish a Vision 21 "not for profit" limited company and a charitable company.

After the launch many participative events and techniques were utilised to help realise a sustainable future for the area and its people. These included a time travel visioning exercise, with about 1,500 people ranging from ordinary teenagers to local elected politicians; a 'Global Footprint' conference which brought local practitioners together with overseas communities; an Information Bazaar at six-monthly meetings which kept local people informed about the sixty project groups through displays and guided tours. It is still doing this through developing and co-ordinating partnership projects.

Vision 21 identified 18 key stakeholders with whom it aimed to work closely, such as farmers, local authorities, families, and altogether involved about 1,000 people and organisations. In the future Vision 21 wants to involve thousands of more people.

The outcome

Many achievements and outcomes were identified in the research carried out at the University of Westminster, including:
- people embracing the partnership approach
- the development of an active network
- the development of a series of projects to explore sustainable living

- publications which provide an analysis of the current state of sustainability in the county, visions for the future, and examples of sustainable living/activities
- the radical nature of Vision 21 proposals, and the apparent willingness of decision-makers and organisations to embrace both them and the idea of sustainable development
- finding and tapping into a range of skills/ideas/enthusiasm within the area
- Vision 21 services being used to support action and to sort out conflicts e.g. County Structure Plan
- The effect Vision 21 has had on local authorities (officers have reported it has transformed their outlook and the way they work. One officer re ported it had had the greatest effect on the Council of any initiative he could remember, and he had been there 25 years).

3.2.7 Mediations Initiated by Lawyers

This is discussed by Christopher Napier in Chapter V below.

3.2.8 Investment in the Future and Prevention of Conflict

When collaborative processes were launched over six years ago it was anticipated that the approach would be used mainly to resolve environmental disputes. As interest grew, decision-makers quickly recognised the value of using the approach at the start to prevent a conflict, rather than waiting for a crisis to materialise.

In practice, it appears that collaborative processes are being used as often to prevent disputes, and as an investment in the future, as to resolve specific disputes. Many decision-makers in industry and government now recognise that in certain situations they can achieve more by working together collaboratively with stakeholders than they can by working separately. The possibility of engaging with a broad range of stakeholders becomes less daunting to decision-makers when they realise the potential benefits and understand the approach.

Some of the most innovative developments in collaborative problem-solving are taking place in situations where the approach is being used as a long-term investment and where conflict, or the prevention of conflict, is not an issue. For example, addressing the environmental sustainability of a company or business sector is an area of increasing significance, where businesses are recognising that investing in dialogue with stakeholders will reap benefits in the future.

CASE STUDY: Eastern Group plc Responds to the Challenge of Sustainability[13]

Setting the scene

In 1996 the energy company Eastern Group plc decided to define the nature of the challenge posed for it by sustainable development and to establish how best to respond to it. Addressing such a challenge could prove a major differentiating factor between the company and its competitors.

Eastern Group is one of the largest electricity generator, distributor and supplier companies in the UK. It had published an environment policy in 1992 and introduced an environmental management system (EMS) in 1994. It realised, however, that the challenge of sustainability meant going one step further to identify and manage the threats and opportunities beyond the current boundaries of the EMS. EMS enabled the company to '*do it right*' but the question posed by the environmental sustainability challenge was whether it was '*doing the right thing*'.

Eastern decided to use a dialogue process to establish what '*doing the right thing*' could be and how to move towards it. It would be important to involve senior managers from throughout the organisation to ensure a wide range of internal expertise and opinion. Managers also needed to listen to the views of outside experts concerned with the development and future of the energy sector. Eastern needed to know what its stakeholders expected of an environmentally sustainable energy company.

The process

The process was designed and managed by the Environment Council over a six-month period. It involved three key workshops:

(i) The first workshop for Eastern managers from across the company used a simple framework to discuss what corporate environmental sustainability might mean for the company. This involved identifying threats and opportunities that related to resources (such as available and preferred sink), innovation (such as changing energy sources) and values (such as approaches to dealing with people, for example over concerns about electric and magnetic fields).

(ii) The second workshop was attended by external stakeholders from government, environment and consumer groups, academics and businesses. Participants identified key sustainability issues for Eastern and suggested actions over a fifteen-year period.

(iii) Like the first, the last workshop was attended only by Eastern managers, and focused on turning the results generated in the previous workshops into quantifiable actions.

The Outcome

In the last workshop the following immediate goals and steps to maintain the momentum were identified:
  • continuing an ongoing dialogue with stakeholders about environmental sustainability
  • developing a sustainability vision for the company
  • beginning to build a service from renewable sources
  • developing indicators against which progress can be measured.

The process had been of great benefit to Eastern Group plc. The company had identified and prioritised corporate environmentally driven sustainability issues in partnership with knowledgeable outside parties. The Environment Business Unit leading the initiative within Eastern identified a number of additional benefits including: distributing ownership of the outcome amongst managers and preparing them for action, enabling the company to prepare effective strategic and operational responses, improving responsiveness to stakeholder concerns, and enhancing the companys reputation.

External parties had found their involvement useful, though they pointed out that any change based on their input would only be evident through the company's subsequent decisions and activities. The companys commitment to maintaining an ongoing dialogue with stakeholders will offer them an opportunity both to see the results of their involvement and to continue to influence the development of an environmentally sustainable energy company.

3.2.9 Effects of the Regulatory Framework on Consensus-building Efforts[14]

British regulatory officials have traditionally enjoyed wide discretion in policy implementation. In particular, British pollution control authorities have historically relied on informal negotiations with an industrial discharger and an agency to achieve broadly-stated environmental goals.[15] Until recently, this consensus-based style somewhat obviated the need for more formal consensus-building or dispute resolution efforts in the environmental field. However, as more individuals have sought a place at the table in taking environmental decisions, and EU directives have increased the specificity of British environmental regulations - so that compliance can be more readily monitored, both by government and by environmental activists, and the discretion of agency officials can be concomitantly reduced - the need for consensus-building in British environmental policy has become more acute.

With respect to EU influence in the enactment of increasingly specific British statutes, Brian Greenwood argues that "the United Kingdom really began to produce an environmental legislation with teeth only after its accession to the European Community."[16] While this sort of influence undoubtedly is a two-way street, adoption of many environmental directives by qualified majority voting in the EU Council of Ministers has contributed to rigorous environmental legislation enacted at EU level and applicable to the UK. Under the qualified majority voting system, each Member State is allocated between two and ten votes, depending on size, and a simple majority of favourable votes passes a measure. Thus, an individual State can be outvoted in the passage of an environmental directive, and the resulting "Europeanisation of environmental policy-making" has significantly affected national approaches in the field, including the negotiation-based approach favoured in the UK. [17]

In the most recent example of this effect, the EU Directive on Integrated Pollution Prevention and Control (IPPC)[18] may significantly influence British environmental regulations and provide more opportunities for effective utilisation of consensus-building processes. The existing British Integrated Pollution Control (IPC) regime, while reflecting a more arm's-length relationship between the regulatory agency and the individual discharger than has historically been the case,[19] regulates the potential releases to air, land and water of the approximately 2,000 *processes* deemed most likely to pollute the environment. By contrast, IPPC will require the regulation of 6,000-7,000 industrial *installations*, including significant portions of the metal and food industries that are not currently regulated under IPC.[20] In addition, rather than regulating impacts only to air, water, and land, IPPC will further address energy efficiency, raw material use, noise, waste minimisation, accident prevention and long-term site restoration requirements.[21] This substantially broader approach may well promote a comprehensive discussion of how a particular facility affects the area in which it is located, and a variety of stakeholders - including workers, local citizens and environmental groups, not to mention the industrial facility itself - may have opinions on the manner in which the Environment Agency implements IPPC at that facility. This sort of situation is ripe for the application of consensus-building techniques, since a large number of parties, often with sharply differing viewpoints, will seek to address a broad spectrum of issues.

Even where regulatory enforcement is being considered, Environment Agency policy should be flexible enough to support a consensus-building approach in appropriate situations. Formed in April 1996 from Her Majesty's Inspectorate of Pollution, the National Rivers Authority, and numerous Waste Regulation

Authorities, the Environment Agency continues to struggle with issues of institutional congruence, but has articulated four broad principles to guide its regulatory enforcement efforts: (1) *proportionality* in application, using standards of reasonableness to gauge Agency action; (2) *consistency* of approach among similar situations; (3) *targeting* of enforcement action on the most serious violations; and (4) *transparency* in regulatory operations.[22] The breadth of these guidelines provides substantial flexibility, and thus the principles should not impede the use of consensus-building processes at particular facilities. Indeed, both the proportionality and transparency principles support increased use of consensus-building techniques, because regulated entities, community members, and others involved in such a process can voice their concerns and better understand how those issues are affected by regulations applicable to a particular facility. In turn, having heard the concerns, the regulatory agency can better assess the reasonableness and appropriateness of its approach.

Finally, recent developments in judicial procedure may promote use of consensus-building efforts. As discussed above in Section 2.3, the July 1996 Woolf Report directly endorses consensus-building/dispute resolution techniques. In addition the Report encourages judges to take more responsibility for case management and seeks to make information for settlement available early in the judicial process.[23] Thus, in the judicial mechanism envisaged by the Report, a judge may hold a case management conference shortly after a matter has been filed, consult the parties during the conference about whether mediation, for example, might be effective in reaching resolution, then refer the matter to a mediator with the confidence that relevant information has been prepared and the parties are ready to engage in settlement discussions. Even if the mediation does not entirely reach resolution, the matters at issue may be significantly narrowed and subsequent judicial proceedings more focused: thus, even an "unsuccessful" mediation may contribute to judicial economy. Furthermore, where mediation can improve on the limited remedial solutions - generally money - available to courts, involved parties may be more satisfied with the results.

In sum, regulatory and institutional factors may significantly influence the use of consensus building processes in British environmental decisions. While neither a panacea for disputes nor a "magic bullet" for resolution, consensus-building efforts may have a substantial role in the future of British environmental regulation and should be fully integrated into discussions on these matters.

3.3 Characteristics of Situations that are Appropriate for Consensus-building

Getting stakeholders to work together in appropriate situations, where the process is carefully designed and managed, has proved an extremely powerful way of finding solutions to complex environmental problems. Yet it is not appropriate in every situation. Through experience in the UK and abroad, professional facilitators are starting to develop a clear understanding of the appropriate characteristics.

Situations where the application of the consensus-building processes would be particularly beneficial usually have one or more of the following character-istics[24]:

Numerous parties and issues.

These are the situations where a consensus-based approach makes immediate sense. An experienced negotiator from an international environmental NGO recently commented on how effective he had found a consensus-building work-shop. He described how astonished he was that so many people, with so many ideas and concerns, had been able to reach agreement by the end of one day. Collaborative processes use skills and techniques that enable numerous parties to work together effectively. The more people and issues involved, the less likely adversarial procedures are to produce results that all parties find acceptable. A key step in any collaborative process, and one of the hardest, is identifying all the relevant parties.

Implementation of the solution will only happen if all parties are committed to that solution.

Motivation for using a collaborative approach often arises from the fear that without it a decision or plan will not be implemented due to a lack of support from key stakeholders. Involving stakeholders early in the development of a plan will help ensure their commitment to the outcome.

Traditional procedures are likely to prove ineffective.

In certain situations, traditional consultation or decision-making procedures such as circulating a draft document for comment, holding a conventional pub-lic meeting, or holding a public inquiry are likely to prove problematic.

Public inquiries are adversarial processes where control over the outcome is taken away from the parties and vested in a third party who either makes a judgement or advises politicians who in turn make the decision. As yet it is uncommon for a collaborative process to be used instead of or as a precursor to a public inquiry, perhaps because it is usually considered only at time when par-ties have already invested considerable time and resources into winning a public inquiry. The Department of the Environment, however, is currently investigating the possibility of using mediation to resolve planning disputes as an alternative to local planning appeals.

Problems that can result from adversarial processes include a lack of ownership of the solution amongst affected parties, a limited opportunity for parties to hear and understand each others concerns in a constructive environment, and, in the case of the public inquiry, a loss of control.

Interested parties need to work together in the future.

Communities can easily become divided by contentious environmental problems. Collaborative processes aim to build relationships, unlike traditional processes. Investing in relationships not only helps in reaching agreement, it also ensures that communities do not remain divided and have a basis to work together more effectively in the future.

Absence of scientific data or disagreement on its analysis.

Adversarial processes encourage the parties to identify information or undertake research to support their own case - which is usually disputed by the other party. Collaborative processes encourage the parties to identify jointly where there is a lack of information and to decide together how best to obtain the information so that it is not disputed when it used in the decision-making process.

Parties hold different values and beliefs.

Parties involved in environmental disputes often have strongly held principles that do not fit comfortably in adversarial processes, where facts and figures are discussed, rather than values and feelings. Carefully designed process enable parties with strongly held views to express them in a way that enables other parties to listen to and acknowledge them, if not always to agree with them. The potential of dialogue in these areas has been recognised by a number of businesses, which are starting to use the approach to address contentious issues of national significance, e.g. the use of genetically modified organisms such as the soya bean.

The characteristics listed above, which are reflected throughout the case studies in the chapter, provide a starting point in the UK, based on current knowledge. As experience in collaborative processes grows, new characteristics will no doubt be identified.

3.4 Benefits of Consensus-building

The emergence of collaborative processes in the UK has reaped benefits similar to those enjoyed in the US where the approach is firmly established.

Although the UK is currently regarded as less litigious than the US, we may in some respects be heading in a similar direction. It is likely that the need to avoid the costs, delays and loss of control inherent in litigation and other adversarial procedures such as public inquiries will also influence our use of collaborative processes.

Anecdotal comments from stakeholders involved in a process and evaluation forms completed after workshops have been the main ways of identifying benefits. Evaluative research is required in the UK before a more complete picture can be provided of the strengths and weaknesses of current experiences. The following list gives the current state of understanding of the benefits in the UK:

- the costs, delays, loss of control, and anxiety associated with adversarial procedures are considerably reduced
- whereas in an adversarial process it is relatively easy for an interested party to say no to a proposed plan or decision, a collaborative process generates a wide sense of responsibility among parties to find a solution that they can all say 'yes' to and can all live with
- because parties generate mutually acceptable solutions that are not imposed by a third party, there is a wide sense of ownership for the solutions and commitment to their implementation;
- it is a process that can enhance participatory democracy without undermining the responsibilities of those in authority
- a shared understanding of the issues and possible ways forward develops among the parties, which results in parties building trust with one another, often most apparently towards the initiating body
- relationships are improved, which helps in the management of future complex problems
- through working collectively, parties develop better decisions, that they would not have reached by working in isolation.

Allen Hickling, an experienced independent facilitator, describes the importance of commitment. "The most perfect solution in the world is useless...unless those responsible for its implementation are committed to it. Such commitment cannot be bought or sold, neither can it be imposed or legislated. But it can be 'built'. It comes from a sense of ownership of the solution - from a feeling that there is consensus, and having been involved in the 'building' of it. Thus the way to making solutions work lies in the way in which those solutions are formulated."[25]

3.5 Challenges Facing the Development of Collaborative Processes in the UK

This relatively new approach to resolving environmental problems is facing a number of challenges and questions about its development and about occaisions when the process is being strained. For example, the relationship between collaborative processes, which are usually informal and voluntary, and representative democracy and statutory processes is not yet clearly defined - at present it is defined on a case-by-case basis. Whatever challenges face the use of collaborative processes it is important to remember that they are not a universal panacea and will not therefore be appropriate in every situation in the UK or in other countries.

The following section discusses a number of contemporary challenges.

Fear of loss of control

Many decision-makers, and often government officials, fear that through participating in a collaborative process they are losing control. Local councillors, who have been elected to represent local people, express concern that a collaborative process will undermine their authority and the democratic process. In practice decision-makers do not undermine their authority or responsibilities in a collaborative process. The process can in fact enhance local democratic process. Nevertheless this underlying concern needs to be overcome if more government bodies are to initiate collaborative processes.

This fear, which is also noticeable in the US, is often overcome through experiencing the process, which was reflected in the experience of a National Park Service official in the US: "Although it promotes listening to our critics and involving them in decision-making, negotiated rule-making does not suggest we abdicate our responsibility. It simply requires that we not let resource preservation become a way of eliminating input or ignoring solutions developed by others."[26]

The options are too limited

A collaborative approach may prove problematic in situations where the options are already severely limited. For example a consensus-building process has rarely been used in its full technical sense to reach agreement on the siting of a facility. This is in contrast with the US where the siting dispute was one of the first situations in which the approach was tested.

An example of this in the UK is motorway and trunk road planning. Where under current decision-making procedures, by the time the planning of a trunk road reaches public consultation, the options have been narrowed to approximately two routes for the road without any consideration, for example, of alternative transport modes. In these circumstances, generating options or packages of options is problematic. The Highways Agency has experimented with round-table meetings to explore issues relating to the siting of trunk roads, though these are not independently facilitated and for this reason are designed more like consultation exercises than consensus-building. Collaborative processes could be used to heal divisions within a community once a road had been sited, but could not be easily utilised in the current procedures adopted to site the road.

Growing awareness or confidence amongst decision-makers to try a new approach may well mean that it will not be long before stakeholder processes have been tried and tested in the siting of facilities. Such situations will need careful assessment by independent facilitators before deciding whether and/or how to proceed with a collaborative approach. It may mean that the approach is not used in its full technical sense to reach consensus, but as a means to develop recommendations and take into account stakeholder views.

Limited resources of Non Governmental Organisations (NGOs)

As the popularity of using collaborative processes increases, the participation of voluntary groups and campaigning organisations may become problematic. As more businesses want to involve the UKs leading NGOs in stakeholder dialogues the latters' limited resources in terms of personnel and funds may mean participation is not always possible. In some situations a *per diem* allowance to participants with limited resources is a cost-effective means of encouraging and enabling participation. However, it is likely this will only be part of the solution and many NGOs will make choices between which dialogues they participate in, based on where their involvement will have the greatest impact.

Clarity of purpose

There are many forms of collaborative process, ranging from a single meeting where the sole purpose is to hear concerns, to longer processes where the purpose is for the group to reach a consensus decision. A challenge faced in the UK is to ensure that organisations which initiate processes are clear from the outset why they are involving stakeholders. Problems can occur when stakeholders and the initiating body have different expectations as to why they are being brought together, or when an organisation has listened to the concerns of stakeholders but there is no willingness to change. Whether the purpose of the process is to reach agreement, develop recommendations, or exchange information and views, it must be clearly communicated to stakeholders from the outset.

Ensuring top level support

A collaborative process started without top level support creates a danger that any agreement reached may ultimately be blocked. In this situation, thorough preparation must be carried out by the initiating body before deciding to proceed with the process and involve external stakeholders. This may include using independently facilitated internal workshops involving senior staff to generate top level support and to develop an understanding for the process.

Statutory processes demand conventional consultation

In certain situations collaborative processes have to be a precursor to a traditional consultation process, such as the circulation of draft plans for wide public comment. Collaborative processes have still proved effective in these instances, but both processes need to be carefully planned together from the outset. The development of Hampshire County Council's Waste Management Strategy has successfully combined a consensus-building process with a wider consultation exercise.

CASE STUDY: Hampshire County Council's Waste Management Strategy

Setting the scene

Hampshire had a serious waste management problem. 40% of waste was incinerated. Four old incinerators were closed in 1996 because they could not meet new EU emission standards. Landfill was not a preferred alternative as insufficient sites were available.

The County Council proposed replacing old incinerators with one large waste-to-energy incinerator at Portsmouth, which would be able to meet all EU requirements. A service contract was let to a private sector consortium and a planning application lodged, but local opposition was too strong and it was finally abandoned. The Council then decided to try a consensus-building approach and employed an external consultant to provide facilitation services.

The process and outcome

Although Hampshire County Council did not abandon the principle of in-cineration, the starting point of the consensus-building approach was to go back to the beginning and examine with key stakeholders the causes of the problem.

The first stage was to build a partnership with the thirteen District Councils in the county (which are responsible for collecting waste). This led to the development of a draft outline integrated strategy addressing all elements of the waste hierarchy, from actions on waste minimisation to the use of energy recovery incineration.

Telephone interviews were held with a broad sector of the community. Following these, three advisory panels were set up to represent the interests of people over the county. These panels were used to test the outline waste strategy, including the potential role of the various elements of the hierarchy. The Council had to communicate the seriousness of the situation to the panels and in return to listen to what they had to say. It was also necessary to keep local people well informed about what was happening. The panels needed a lot of information and help in interpreting the information so they could understand the issues and make realistic recommendations. At the end one set of recommendations were taken on board by the County and District Councils and the strategy amended accordingly.

The consensus of the panels was that, for non-recycled waste, energy recovery incineration was one of the least favoured options, but better than exporting the waste to out-of-county sites. This was supported by the vast majority of those involved in the collaborative process.

The second stage involved testing the revised strategy against the opinions of the wider public to ensure that the proposals met the approval of the sleeping majority. This stage involved market research and facilitated focus groups to gain feedback. It resulted in a firming up of the strategy, with specific targets such as to recycle 25% of waste by the year 2000 and 40% in the longer term.

These two stages illustrate the possibility first of developing a strategy through consensus-building with key stakeholders, and secondly of testing the results with the wider public using innovative participatory techniques.

4. Practice of Collaborative Problem-solving in the UK

Consensus-building has developed rapidly in the UK over the last five years. The increasing number of practical projects, the varied skills and techniques, and the ever-developing knowledge and experiences of independent facilitators in the UK have contributed to this.

While an enormous amount has been learnt in the development of practice, for the purposes of highlighting current experience and reflecting on the last five years three key areas are covered below. These are the stages of the process, the facilitator and skills and techniques.

4.1 Stages of the Process

The following diagram has been developed to help trainee facilitators and potential users of consensus-building understand the stages of the process. It separates the stages for the participants and the stages for the facilitator.[27]

The stakeholder process:

• *Presentation.* Consensus-building begins for stakeholders with the presentation of the problem, the situation, to themselves and to each other. It may be presented by the facts of the situation, or by the announcement of new plans for a road or supermarket, for example, or of plans to review an existing situation, or as the result of pressure from campaigners.
• *Preparation.* The preparation stage for stakeholders involves research, forming alliances, developing arguments. This stage builds confidence for entering the consensus-building process.
• *Participation.* This is the stage when the stakeholders do the real work of consensus-building, by clarifying the issues, and exploring possible solutions.
• *Progression.* Progression is the stage at which ideas become real solutions. At the end of this stage the stakeholders begin to make commitments.
• *Performance.* Performance is putting commitments into action.

The facilitator process:

• *Enthuse.* The first task for facilitators is to stimulate stakeholders' enthusiasm for consensus-building, to sell the idea to them.
• *Enter.* Consensus-building usually begins for facilitators with an invitation to set up a process, but sometimes it is the facilitators themselves who begin it with presentations explaining consensus-building.
• *Engage.* Facilitators have to teach stakeholders how to use the process, and how to work with each other. Engage means helping stakeholders to identify the issues and ways to approach them.
• *Evolve.* At this state the facilitators help the stakeholders to develop their ideas into solutions.
• *Exit.* Facilitators must increasingly leave the stakeholders to do the work, but should not leave the process until they know stakeholders will carry out their commitments.

• *Enable.* Even after leaving the formal process, facilitators may still be needed to help stakeholders deal with later problems.

These broad stages apply to virtually any consensus-building process. The process is flexible and can therefore be designed to suit each situation. These stages apply whether there are two parties or multiple parties and whether the process is expected to last two months or two years. However, the skills and techniques which are used will vary, depending on the number of parties involved and the aims of the process.

The importance of preparation.

The flexibility of a consensus-building process is clearly one of its attractions, but flexibility should not be confused with a lack of structure. In fact, it is arguable that more thorough preparation goes into these relatively informal processes than into many conventional ones. Thorough preparation, ideally involving both the initiating body and the facilitator, is essential if such approaches are to work.

Preparation must include establishing the level of interaction required from the parties. The initiating body, with the facilitator, needs to establish whether the purpose is to exchange information and views, or to develop recommendations or to reach a consensus decision with the parties involved. Clarifying these kinds of expectations with participants at the beginning, and designing a process accordingly, will ensure there are no misunderstandings later on in the process.

For example, to try to engage a facilitator one week before a meeting, when the agenda is already set, but people are unclear about what they want to achieve, and do not know who will turn up, is an unworkable scenario. In such a situation, a facilitator must, in order to be effective, be given freedom and time to rebuild the agenda with the initiating body. Where there is conflict, merely putting people together in a room with no structured plan is likely to exacerbate the problem.

As experience and understanding of consensus-building grows, decisions-makers are beginning to understand the importance of thorough preparation and careful management of the process, and to recognise that it is not just a case of learning a few techniques.

4.2 The Facilitator

The facilitator designs and manages the process drawing on a range of skills and techniques. He/she is independent, and will not hold a position on the substantive content of the discussion, and must be so perceived by the parties. The management of the process is the only area where the facilitator makes decisions, in consultation with the participants. However it is generally helpful - but not essential - for the facilitator to know about, or be well briefed on, the organisations involved and the subject under discussion.

At present there are a handful of professional environmental facilitators based in the UK, many of whom are associated with Environmental Resolve, an undertaking of the Environment Council. The Council is, at the time of writing, the only UK organisation that provides training for individuals who want to learn environmental mediation and facilitation skills. The trend to date is that most participants go on to use the approach within their organisation, acting for example as Local Agenda 21 co-ordinators, rather than practising independently. Increasingly the ability to facilitate is being regarded as an important management tool and not just a skill of the independent professional facilitator.

There is currently no UK accreditation or recognised qualification for environmental facilitators, although qualifications do already exist in more established areas of mediation, such as neighbourhood and commercial mediation. While accreditation in environmental consensus-building will emerge if demand necessitates it, at present such a development is arguably premature as the approach is still in its infancy, and at a stage where practitioners are continuously learning and developing the process.

In-house versus independent facilitators

It is clear to the writer that in the UK context it is important to use an independent facilitator rather than an in-house facilitator, especially in these early stages when little experience of the setting up or management of collaborative processes exists, except among professionals.

For a number of reasons it seems problematic for an in-house person, such as a government official, to take the role of facilitator. For example, such a person is likely to be seen as party to the dispute or situation rather than independent. Participants may fear that a meeting facilitated by this person will be manipulated to achieve a predetermined outcome. If the initiating body (usually government or business) *is* seriously considering using an in-house facilitator - which may be the case if the organisation is seen as independent in the situation - it would be wise first to check both the facilitator's level of skill and experience, and his acceptability to the parties before proceeding.

There have been instances in a number of participatory processes, where people were referred to as facilitators when they had not been trained, were inexperienced and were parties to the situation rather than independent. This resulted in meetings being unproductive and parties becoming disillusioned with consensus-building as a whole - even though they had not experienced a professionally designed and managed process.

As experience develops in the UK it may, however, become easier to use trained facilitators from within an organisation because decision-makers will have a greater understanding of the overall process and will be able to judge when it is necessary involve an independent facilitator.

What happens when there are not adequate resources for a facilitator

Using experienced and skilled independent facilitators can be prohibitively expensive for local communities, especially when they have a limited understanding of the benefits and are therefore reluctant to invest in the process up front. In these instances such a service may not be feasible if the process is likely to be ongoing for a number of years, e.g. Local Agenda 21. Where there are resource limitations, external facilitators can sometimes be used for a short period, but to maximise this brief but invaluable input, the community must be equipped to continue with the process on its own. A number of innovative projects are currently underway where this is happening successfully.

Two local communities in England have recently developed networks of local facilitators to help manage local consensus-building processes. In one, Bedfordshire, a network has been set up by the Borough Council and County Council using a LETS (local exchange and trading system) system which is intended to enable the trading of time, skills and facilities where cash may be short. Everyone who becomes a member of the network receives facilitation training and joins an action learning group. One member of the network will call on the services of another member when an independent trained facilitator is needed. Members of the network have facilitated in many local situations, including Local Agenda 21, Biodiversity Action Plans and the development of Local Nature Reserves (described below).

In Stratford, the District Council has established a similar network of community facilitators, providing training and professional support. The network was established to help facilitate the District's Local Agenda 21 process, though the Council is also beginning to use members of the network to assist in other situations. An action research project, funded by the Local Government Management Board, is currently underway to ensure that other local authorities who want to develop facilitation skills in the community can benefit from the experiences and lessons of Bedford and Stratford.

CASE STUDY: Park Wood Local Nature Reserve, Bedford

Setting the scene

Brickhill allotments had been underused for some twenty years, to such an extent that by 1995 the majority of the site had been abandoned. Access was (and remains) open to the public and the usual problems of fly-tipping and undesirable activity were common. The site is bounded by garden fences, school playing fields and agricultural fields - a typical urban fringe location. A survey by the local wildlife trust in the spring of 1995 revealed a surprisingly diverse and interesting site.

This was good news except that, without intervention, the site would become little more than scrub and much of the diversity and interest would be lost. The site was owned by Bedford Borough Council, but there was no budget for any management. With this restriction the Council set three objectives to be pursued by the Council's ecologist (who was also a member of the community facilitators network): to manage the site to protect its ecological interest, to involve the community in looking after the site and to seek formal site protection as a Local Nature Reserve. Experience gained through Local Agenda 21 work suggested that people had to come first in this process.

The process

First, a leaflet was circulated to the public inviting them to join the Council's ecologist for an evening stroll and chat on the site. An informal atmosphere was maintained and the 20 residents who turned up were encouraged to recount their own experience of the place and its wildlife. By the end of the walk and talk the residents wanted to know what could be done and how they could help. It was agreed that another meeting was needed to discuss the sites future and that, before the meeting, the Council's ecologist would prepare an outline management plan for discussion.

At the next meeting, which was attended by 25 people, the plan was adopted and people volunteered to take part in practical work. The practical work went well and as a result it was decided that a further indoor meeting should be held to discuss the way forward.

The next meeting was critical. If anything was to happen in the long term it would have to be agreed now with sufficient enthusiasm to turn talk into more independent, community action. The Council's ecologist, who had managed the meetings to date, decided that the next meeting should be facilitated by a more independent person, so a colleague from the local community facilitator network was asked to fill the role.

The meeting was a great success. A name was agreed, along with a pro-gramme of work days for the coming year. Three people volunteered to act as co-ordinators for the group.

Outcome

The site is now formally designated a Local Nature Reserve. It continues to be managed by the community with minimal input from outside. In fact a local authority officer commented that the community is now driving the project faster than would have been dared by the Council. The group has won sponsor-ship for shared tools, two local schools are using the site for lessons and have built and erected bird nesting boxes on the site, and an environmental art project is planned for the future along with the planting of a community orchard.

Local residents now know each other and work-days are seen more as family, social occasions. The sites wildlife value has improved and, ultimately, a ne-glected problem area is now a valuable community and ecological resource.

In the words of a local authority officer, "There is no doubt that knowledge of consensus-building was central to the successful outcome of this project. From the start, the essential ingredients of honesty and openness were applied, everyone had an opportunity to shape the outcome, conflict was avoided, energy was positively focused on the commonly identified and desired results. The Council invested little more than patience and time - the pay-off has been sig-nificant."

4.3 Skills and Techniques

The consensus-building process and the related skills and techniques as used in the UK have been drawn from a wide range of experiences and training, gained by professional facilitators based in the UK and working both in the UK and abroad.

The two basic ingredients are mediation and facilitation.[28] In essence, media-tion skills are used to help resolve disputes where anger and emotions are run-ning high. Facilitation skills and techniques are used to help large groups of people reach consensus decisions. Using these skills and techniques within a carefully designed and managed process has created a highly effective way of helping both small or relatively large groups of people, often with conflicting views, to work together.

Listening, empathising and questioning are considered essential skills for a facilitator. It is not only essential for the facilitator to use these general skills, it is also important for the parties in a process to do so too. Acland and Hickling[29] describe them as follows:

- *listening*: active listening to indicate full attention and sensitivity to the emotional impact of what is being said.
- *empathising*: being able to see what the other person sees, hear what they hear, feel what they feel - and letting them know you are.
- *questioning*: asking the right person the right question in the right way at the right moment
- *body language*: using your body to communicate.

Facilitation techniques that aim to enable large groups of people to work together to develop joint plans and reach agreement have been developed over the last fifty years in the UK and abroad. Here are five examples of basic facilitation techniques that are increasingly being recognised as essential for environmental facilitators:

- *Metaplan*[30] Metaplan is a powerful way for a group to build a joint picture of its members' issues and concerns in a short period of time. It is based on the need to provide participants with instant flexible techniques for displaying the results of their work - as it happens. Here are two that are used widely:

The first is the use of relatively small pieces of paper or card, pinned or stuck to a wall or screen. The subject is chosen - issues, decisions, options, criteria, etc. - and each card has one item written on it. This process usually starts participants thinking quietly on their own. In order to sort out the mass of information which results, the cards can then be clustered, categorised, and put into levels or any other relationship as relevant. This technique is best in groups of 10 - 18, but can be adapted to work in groups up to 60.

The second technique involves the use of small, brightly coloured stickers to prioritise lists. It is often used to establish a short-list of the most urgent or important from a given list of items. A number of stickers - usually four or five - are given to each of the participants who then each place them against their own selection of items on the list. The participants sometimes perceive this as a sort of voting - which indeed it is. However, it should be made clear that this is not a decision-making system in which the majority rules. It is a way of trying to identify the common ground. This technique is fine for large groups, though it becomes unwieldy in groups of more than about 100. It is this technique which was used to define priority issues for the Highways Agencys Environmental Strategy discussed at **3.2.2** above.

• *Carousel.*[31] The Carousel has been developed as an efficient way to generate creativity among a large group of people in a way that ensures that all contribute and build on each other's ideas. It involves creating a number of sub-groups, giving each a task, and allotting to each a particular space as its home base. Once every group has completed its task, they all set off around the room to visit each other's home bases in turn - each leaving behind one person to explain how they have tackled their task and what they have achieved. This method of briefing people enables them to be more closely involved than would normally be the case in a large group. It also enables a number of tasks to be achieved at the same time, and where different factions have different perceptions, the physical act of visiting them can become a metaphor for understanding their points of view; people must - almost literally - stand in each others shoes. This technique was used in the Eastern Group meeting discussed at **3.2.8** above (which involved over thirty external parties) to generate a range of issues for the company to address.

• *Common-grounding.*[32] Common-grounding is used to develop consensus on the various solutions. The purpose is to identify any common ground which already exists amongst the participants, then gradually to enlarge on this and not focus on differences. An essential component of the technique is a visual presentation of the various solutions and the common ground on flip charts. Having identified where there is agreement the process then focuses on developing common ground in areas where there is nearly agreement. Those who are not in agreement are asked in what way any unacceptable option would have to be modified to make it acceptable. Often slight changes are all that is required. Everyone else is then asked whether they could live with that and if the outcome is positive, then the common ground is thereby extended.

• *Management of uncertainty.*[33] Uncertainty is always a factor in any complex situation, and the shared management and resolution of uncertainty is a step towards building a consensus. There are three types of uncertainty for this purpose: (1) There is uncertainty about the facts of a situation, where people can ask for more information, research, surveys and analysis. (2) There can be uncertainty about what values are involved, where people try to establish clearer objectives or policy guidance. (3) There is often uncertainty about related issues and decisions, usually decisions to be made later, or by others, which would affect the situation. People then need to ask for better co-ordination. One way to establish some consensus early in the process is to explore the shared uncertainties and how to reduce them. Often the hostility in a situation is caused by uncertainties, because hostility is often the product of fear, and fear is often the product of uncertainty. Working together to reduce the uncertainties can reduce the fears and hostilities they produce.

The combined application of these skills and techniques has proved a powerful and successful approach to address complex, multi-party environmental problems. As more people enter the field of consensus-building, new techniques, skills and styles of third party are starting to emerge, drawing on a wide range of the experiences of organisations such as Future Search, Round Tables, Open Space, Citizens Juries and Planning for Reach.[34]

5. Conclusions: Development Continues

In the last six years the use of consensus-building has increased dramatically. It is clear that the approach will continue to increase in popularity as a method of addressing environmental problems in the UK.

Current procedures for decision-making often hinder society's ability to resolve environmental problems effectively, and to address the challenge of sustainability. Many of the problems which are a by-product of adversarial procedures, such as decisions being contested, resources wasted and otherwise positive relationships destroyed, could be prevented through using collaborative processes in the appropriate situations. As a result, decision-makers are looking to the advantages and possibilities of collaborative approaches.

Many decision-makers are beginning to embrace the language of consensus-building even if they have not yet used it in practice. Phrases like "listening to stakeholders", "building consensus" and "working in partnership" resonate in government and business. For example, both the Environment Agency and the Scottish Environmental Protection Agency have set out clearly stated objectives to develop close relationships and partnerships with stakeholders.

A number of influential bodies have recently encouraged, if not mandated, collaborative approaches. In 1996 the United Nations published guidelines on "Public Participation in Environmental Decision-Making" which clearly state the importance of effective public involvement. These guidelines are likely to impact on the UK as well as other European Member States. A recent Parliamentary Select Committee encouraged the use of mediation to address disputes relating to tourism and the environment. The UK Advisory Committee on Business and the Environment has encouraged businesses to develop their own guidelines for engaging in dialogue with their stakeholders.

This increasing interest in collaborative processes will undoubtedly continue though the UK has some way to go before the approach becomes a mainstream tool for preventing or resolving environmental disputes. A number of our current procedures for decision-making will need to be reviewed, and changes pressed for accordingly, to allow for collaborative working. Government bodies and businesses will need to adapt to ensure that working with stakeholders is a mainstream activity, and not only thought of after a crisis has arisen, when its use may be problematic.

A few government bodies have recently initiated research in areas that could benefit from consensus-building. For example, the Department of the Environment recently circulated a consultation document about the possibility of using mediation to resolve planning disputes which, under existing procedures, would lead to an appeal. We have seen above how ETSU has supported innovative research into ways in which consensus-building procedures might be incorporated into renewable energy projects.

Further research, awareness raising, case examples, and institutional change to encourage and allow for the appropriate use of collaborative processes will be needed if the approach is to become mainstream. Further development of collaborative process in the UK is unlikely to happen overnight. It will have to rely on the creativity and foresight of practitioners, decision-makers and other stakeholders who are willing to test, question and together develop this relatively new approach to resolving environmental problems.

Bibliography

Acland, Andrew. *Resolving Disputes Without Going to Court. A Consumer Guide to Alternative Dispute Resolution.* Century Business Books. London. 1995.

Acland, Andrew. *A Sudden Outbreak of Common Sense. Managing Conflict Through Mediation.* Hutchinson Business Books. London. 1990.

Acland, Andrew and Allen Hickling. "Enabling Stakeholder Dialogue: training for facilitators, mediators and process managers." *Course Handbook* The Environment Council 1997.

Acland, Andrew and Allen Hickling *An Introduction to Building Consensus and Facilitation* Baltic Environmental Forum January 1996.

Advisory Committee on Business and the Environment. *Environmentally Sensitive Decision Making. Avoiding Crisis Management Situations.* Working Draft. 1996.

Advisory Committee on Business and the Environment. Seventh Progress Report to the President of the Board of Trade and the Secretary of State for the Environment. Department of the Environment. 1997.

Baines, John. *Beyond Compromise: Building Consensus in Environmental Planning and Decision-making.* The Environment Council. 1995.

Blackdown Hills Management Strategy 1997 - 2002. Produced for the Blackdown Hill Joint Advisory Committee by the Blackdown Hills Projects. January 1997.

Carroll, Eileen. "The Woolf Report on Access to Justice - CEDR Replies." *Resolutions.* Issue no.15. Published by Centre for Dispute Resolution. Winter 1996

Case study on building an environmentally sustainable business: Eastern Group plc. The Sustainable Business Forum/The Environment Council.

"County Court Mediation Scheme to go ahead." *Resolutions.* Issue no. 14 Published by Centre for Dispute Resolution. Spring 1996.

Creighton & Creighton. *Facilitation and Public Participation Training Manuals.* 1996.
Directive 96/61 (*Official Journal of the European Communities,* L257 (10 October 1996)), at 26.

Economic Commission for Europe. *Guidelines on Access to Environmental Information and Public Participation in Environmental Decision-Making.* United Nations New York and Geneva, 1996.

Environmental Strategy for England's Main Roads. Living with Roads. Highways Agency. 1996.

Friend, J.K. and A Hickling *Planning Under Pressure: the Strategic Choice Approach.* Second Edition. Butterworth-Heinemann. Oxford. 1997.

Good Practice Guidelines. Short Rotation Coppice for Energy Production. The development of an economically and environmentally sustainable industry. Funded by the Department of Trade and Industry through ETSU. November 1996.

Greenwood, Brian "Looking Ahead: Environmental Regulation — A Future?" , in *Environmental Regulation and Economic Growth* Alan E. Boyle, ed. Oxford: Clarendon Press (1994), at 127.

Hawkins, Keith *Rule and Discretion in Comparative Perspective: The Case of Social Regulation,* 50 Ohio State Law Journal (1989) 663, 666-68.

House of Commons. Environment Committee 4th Report. *The Environmental Impact of Leisure Activities.* Volume I. 12 July 1995.

Hyam Pippa and Jeff Bishop, *Planning By Consensus for Renewable Energy*. Environmental Resolve/ETSU. August 1996

Ingram, Hally. *Experience in the United States of using collaborative processes to resolve environmental problems: a briefing for central government and agencies in the United Kingdom*. March 1997.

"IPPC To Bring About Major Changes for UK Permitting Regime", *Environment Watch: Western Europe* (1 August 1997), at 17 (citing Environment Agency figures).

Leith, Martin. *The CLGI Guide to Creating Fast Change. How to use large group intervention methods and sabre interventions to create change that is fast, acceptable, strategic and transformational*. Published by CLFI. London. 1996.
Local Agenda 21 Case Studies. Case studies of work for local sustainability. Local Government Management Board/Environment Resource and Information Centre, University of Westminster. 1997. Case Study 18.

O'Riordan, Timothy & Andrew Jordan "Social Institutions and Climate Change", in *Politics of Climate Change: A European Perspective* London: Routledge Press 1996, at 84-85.

Planning Appeals. Consultation Paper. Department of the Environment. Planning Directorate. London. January 1997.

Report of the Copenhagen Seminar. Brent Spar Dialogue Process. Produced by The Environment Council. 1997.

Rowan-Robinson, Jeremy & Andrea Ross, *Enforcement of Environmental Regulation in Britain: Strengthening the Link*, Journal of Planning & Environment Law 200, 216 :March 1994.

Stewart, John. *Further Innovation in Democratic Practice*. Published by the Institute of Local Government Studies, The University of Birmingham.

The Environment Agency Enforcement Policy Statement, May 1996, para 12.

Woolf, Rt. Hon. Lord, Master of the Rolls, *Access to Justice* (Final Report) July 1996, at 5-7, 62-64 & 124.

NOTES

[1] At the Earth Summit in Rio de Janeiro in 1992 the UK Government adopted the international agreement Agenda 21. Local Agenda 21 is the process of building partnerships between local authorities and other sectors to develop and implement local policies for sustainable development. See Section 2.4 *infra.*
[2] See Creighton & Creighton, 1996.

[3] The Brent Spar Dialogue Process is described in Section 3.2.4 *post.*

[4] For further information about the growth of ADR in the UK and the organizations involved, see Acland, 1995, s.3:"Where to Find Your Mediator."

[5] See further the Chapter by Christopher Napier, *post.*

[6] The potential effect of the 1996 Woolf Report on consensus-building techniques is discussed in Section 3.2.9 *post.*

[7] See "County Court Mediation Scheme to Go Ahead." *Resolutions,* 1996.

[8] This section on developments in community participation has been informed by discussions with Jeff Bishop, one of the UKs leading environmental facilitators who has extensive experience of working with communities and local authorities.

[9] For further information, see *Blackdowns Hills Management Strategy 1997-2002.*

[10] For further information, see Environmental Strategy for England's Main Roads. Living with Roads, 1996.

[11] For further information, *See Good Practice Guidelines. Short Rotation Coppice for Energy Production,* November 1996.

[12] For further information, see Local Agenda 21 Case Studies. 1997, Case Study 18.

[13] For further information See Case Study on building an environmentally sustainable Business: Eastern Group plc.

[14] This section was contributed by Robin L. Juni.

[15] Hawkins, 1989.

[16] Greenwood, 1994.

[17] O'Riordan & Jordan, 1996.

[18] Directive 96/61.

[19] Rowan-Robinson & Ross, 1994.

[20] "IPPC To Bring About Major Changes for UK Permitting Regime," 1997.

[21] Id.

[22] The Environment Agency Enforcement Policy Statement , 1996.

[23] Woolf, 1996.

[24] See Acland, 1995.

[25] See Acland and Hickling, 1997.

[26] The National Park Service (NPS) used a collaborative approach to resolve a fifteen-year dispute on the Cape Cod National Seashore. The controversy involved off-road vehicles (ORV) and the management of the threatened piper plover (bird). ORV user groups felt strongly they should be able to drive along the entire beach when the plovers were not present and conversely environmental groups felt they should be banned altogether. A new approach was therefore needed and the NPS decided to use negotiated rule-making, a form of collaborative problem-solving using independent facilitators. For further information See Park Service, Volume 16, No 2. Spring 1996.

[27] See Acland and Hickling, 1996.

[28] Andrew Acland, Allen Hickling, Pippa Hyam and Jeff Bishop, well known facilitators and trainers in the UK and abroad, have been instrumental in ensuring that these two basic ingredients are combined and that the approach is taught, through the Environment Council's training courses, to a wide range of people working in the voluntary, private and public sectors. For further details on skills and techniques see Friend and Hickling, 1997.

[29] See Acland and Hickling, 1996 and Acland and Hickling 1997.

[30] Adapted from the Environment Councils one-day course materials, developed by Allen Hickling.

[31] Also see *id.*

[32] Adapted from Friend and Hickling, 1997.

[33] See Acland and Hickling, 1996.

[34] For further information see Stewart.

Chapter IV
THE PRACTICE OF COOPERATIVE ENVIRONMENTAL CONFLICT RESOLUTION IN DEVELOPING COUNTRIES

The Practice of Cooperative Environmental Conflict Resolution in Developing Countries

Dr. Christopher W. Moore

1. Introduction

During the last twenty five years, environmental problems have increased tremendously at all levels - local, regional, national and international. Multiple factors have contributed to pressures and strains on the environment: rapidly escalating competition for resources, struggles over water quantity and quality, air pollution, population growth, urbanisation, problems with waste management, declining wilderness areas, over-harvesting or unbalanced regulation of animal and plant species, and declines in biological diversity.

As environmental problems have developed, new trends have emerged in environmental ethics and environmental management. In almost every part of the world, concerned citizens and governments have mobilized to address environmental problems, and an ethic of environmental stewardship has developed. Today in most countries at least one public interest group or non-governmental organisation (NGO) acts as an advocate for the environment or for people who are dependent upon the sustainability of a specific resource.

Concurrently, local, national, regional and international governments and organisations are seeking ways to mitigate and regulate adverse impacts on the environment, become good stewards of natural resources, and at the same time achieve sustainable development and meet the needs of their citizens. Many governments have created Ministries for the Environment; passed legislation that establishes environmental impact assessment procedures; developed monitoring, enforcement, and compliance mechanisms; trained their staffs; and started a host of other initiatives to address environmental problems.

One component of the emerging environmental ethic and the institutionalisation of environmental management has been the development of public participation and environmental dispute resolution (EDR) approaches. These new social technologies have enabled government agencies, citizens, public interest groups and the private sector to work together to respond to environmental issues and strive for collaborative and mutually acceptable solutions.

This chapter provides an overview of trends in public participation and environmental dispute resolution as they are evolving and being practised in developing countries. Specifically, the chapter will define, analyse, and describe:

how public participation and EDR are viewed and defined in developing countries; how the practice of public participation and EDR has evolved; motivating factors for its use; some areas of application and future pathways for development of the field; trends of professional development; and obstacles and opportunities to further development.

There is tremendous diversity in the ways that EDR is being practised around the world. This chapter will identify general trends common to a number of regions, and illustrate these trends with selected cases. While CDR Associates, the writer's firm, has firsthand knowledge of the development of EDR in roughly a dozen countries in Africa, Asia, Central and Eastern Europe, Latin America and the Oceana-Pacific region, and has conducted research or discussed these issues with other practitioners, governmental officials and NGOs in numerous other nations, the firm s_knowledge of existing practice is far from complete. This general overview of international EDR is intended to help readers and others working in the field in developing countries to implement more effective ways of protecting the natural environment, create and maintain sustainable development, and resolve the inevitable conflicts that arise when trying to achieve these goals. It is also hoped that this overview will spur others to conduct more extensive research into this growing discipline.

2. Environmental Dispute Resolution (EDR): Contexts and Definitions

EDR occurs in specific cultural, historical, institutional and environmental contexts, and has emerged in both developed and developing countries as tailored responses to specific problems that citizens, public interest groups, the private sector and governments encounter as they interact. People from specific cultures exhibit significant diversity in how they define conflict, identify what triggers or demands a response, determine who is seen as being responsible for addressing or improving a situation, decide upon what procedures are used to manage and/or resolve a dispute, and define what constitutes acceptable outcomes. In addition to these local variables, influences from outside a specific culture or nation - such as knowledge, trends, cultural borrowings, and political/ economic or social constraints - affect how environmental conflicts are played out and addressed.

Before examining how these types of disputes are being handled in developing countries, it is important to define what is meant by environmental conflict and describe the range of procedures that fall under the rubric of EDR. (For the remainder of this chapter, the words dispute and conflict will be used interchangeably.)

Environmental disputes are tensions, disagreements, altercations, debates, competitions, contests, conflicts, or fights over some element of the natural environment. These disputes commonly occur over air, water, land, minerals, plant and animal species, waste management, and development issues. Environmental disputes may involve different visions, philosophies or religious teachings about the meaning, purpose or correct use of the environment; competition over resource allocation; or disagreements about how nature should be managed (or not managed). Environmental disputes are often over what should happen, how, when and where. Conflicts of this type are often further fuelled by relationship problems between the parties, differences over data and information, competing interests, structural and resource constraints, and value differences.[1]

Environmental Dispute Resolution, or *EDR,* includes a range of voluntary and less voluntary approaches and procedures which are initiated to address, manage, and resolve conflicts over the purpose, use, and management of some aspect of the natural environment. Many of these procedures are similar to those used to resolve a wide range of other social issues such as interpersonal, neighborhood, commercial, civil, and other disputes, while others are used almost exclusively in the environmental arena.

EDR is practised widely in many cultures and countries. Many applications have been implemented on an ad hoc, or as needed, basis. However, there have also been initiatives to institutionalise the use of EDR procedures and to create dispute resolution systems.[2] Most of these systems include both voluntary and compulsory elements.

While compulsory decision-making assistance, such as bureaucratic or judicial decision, is an important approach that should be included in any EDR system, such procedures are not the major focus of this chapter. For the most part, the emphasis will be on unassisted, voluntary, and collaborative approaches that are being created and implemented in the developing world to build social consensus on issues in question. For the remainder of this chapter the term EDR will be used to refer to these voluntary procedures.

3. A Continuum of EDR Approaches and Procedures

How, in general, have governments, citizens and the private sector gone about the business of managing and resolving conflicts to achieve desired environmental objectives? In general, governments, which have had the major role in defining decision making or dispute resolution procedures, have employed either command decision making, consultation or co-operation as primary approaches, with major emphasis on the command approach. (See Figure I: Continuum of Decision Making and Conflict Management Approaches.) However, trends in many parts of the globe appear to be shifting significantly toward the consultative and co-operative end of the spectrum for both pragmatic and philosophical reasons.

FIGURE I: A CONTINUUM OF DECISION-MAKING AND CONFLICT MANAGEMENT APPROACHES

COMMAND DECISION-MAKING«CONSULTATION«COOPERATION

3.1 Command Decision-making

This is the process with which most governments, their personnel and citizens are most familiar. As participants in bureaucratic organisations with traditions of top-down decision-making and authoritative technical expertise, government officials are aware of how decisions have been made in the past and at present. An environmental issue, possibly at the local level, emerges, and its disposition is referred up the chain of command within the concerned and involved organisations. Finally, an authoritative decision-maker issues a decree outlining the dispensation of the issue or dispute.

The command system and process of decision-making and dispute resolution works well when the knowledge, expertise and the authority of the decision-maker are respected and accepted by affected parties; no one party or agency must bear more than his share of the burden of costs or changes (or in a manner considered to be unfair or inequitable); the decision-maker can enforce his will regardless of the wishes of affected parties; and relatively few people know or are concerned about the problem.

These conditions are becoming more and more rare in disputes involving environmental or sustainable development issues. These issues are contentious. More members of the public know about the issues and want to be involved in determining their outcome. The knowledge and authority of decision-makers is no longer sacrosanct, as information is more widely available and more people have developed expertise or discovered contradictory information. In addition, the ability of many agencies to make command decisions and enforce them against public will has declined because power and authority have become more diffused. In order to implement a specific outcome or resolution the affected or concerned parties must co-ordinate and co-operate with each other. Such co-ordination is especially important for negotiating environmental issues of international concern, where no one party has unilateral authority or resources to resolve complex issues.

For all of the above reasons, command decision-making is not working as well today as it may have in the past. This situation has prompted many government officials and affected parties to move along the continuum to more consultative approaches to problem solving and dispute resolution. This dynamic is demonstrated by Ministries of the Environment which have received mandates from executives or parliaments to create broad policies and to *co-ordinate* decision-making agencies in charge of development or natural resource issues. These environmental ministries often lack strong regulatory or enforcement mandates and capabilities, and their relatively weak structural positions within governments almost requires them to use consultative or co-operative approaches to achieve their goals.

3.2 Consultative Decision Making

This is motivated by pragmatic needs to obtain wider input into decision making, so that broader support can be garnered and actions can be taken in a timely, efficient, and cost-effective manner. Consultative decision-making is also commonly called public participation or public involvement.

Consultative-decision making does not require elected or appointed decision-makers to give up their mandated authority for making final decisions. It does ask these decision-makers to engage concerned and affected parties by a) providing them with information about social, economic, political, technical and environmental aspects of environmental or developmental problems; and b) soliciting information from them about their interests and potentially acceptable solutions before making a decision.

As mentioned before, governments and other stakeholders initiate consultative decision making for both pragmatic and philosophical reasons. The pragmatic benefits of consultative processes include:

• A broader understanding, on the part of decision-maker(s), about concerned parties issues and interests;
• Greater dissemination of information and wider two-way public education and understanding about the diverse interests that have to be addressed and satisfied in an acceptable solution;
• Greater opportunities for the involved public to provide input as to preferred policy, regulatory, or site-specific options that might best meet their needs and satisfy their interests;
• The ability to generate a range of possible solutions to a problem from which the decision-maker can select;
• Mechanisms for building support for a proposed option; and

• Opportunities to expand ownership of the substantive outcome, due to participation in a fair and open process, even if the final solution is not identical with any single party s preferred alternative.

3.3 Cooperative Decision-making and Dispute Resolution

This expands upon the consultative procedure and public involvement approaches described above. Co-operative procedures may be conducted in an unassisted manner, whereby which parties directly engage in cooperative problem-solving or negotiations; or may be assisted by a third party process advisor, coach, trainer, facilitator, or mediator. They may also be enhanced by advisory substantive assistance, in the form of knowledgeable input from a mutually respected authority on the issue in question. In either assisted or unassisted co-operative decision making, the involved parties generally develop recommendations that they either forward to a formal decision-maker or agency for consideration, approval, and implementation; or the parties themselves approve and implement the settlement.

Figure II below presents a Continuum of Decision-making and Conflict Management Procedures and Roles, showing a variety of forms of unassisted and assisted decision-making and dispute resolution processes and roles that have been found to be effective in addressing and resolving environmental controversies.[3] On the left are unassisted procedures such as information and exchange meetings, joint problem-solving, and unassisted negotiations. Moving to the right are procedures with third party assistance to establish and promote more positive relationships, improve the process for co-operative problem-solving and negotiations, and increase the acceptability and quality of information used to make decisions.

Figure A Continuum of Dispute Resolution Procedures and Roles

COOPERATIVE DECISION MAKING	THIRD PARTY ASSISTANCE WITH NEGOTIATIONS OR COOPERATIVE PROBLEM SOLVING			THIRD PARTY ADVICE	THIRD PARTY DECISION	
Parties are Unassisted	Relationship Building Assistance	Procedural Assistance	Substantive Assistance	Specific Non-Binding Advice	Binding Decision	Democratic Group Processes
I. Informal Talk/Discussions	VII. Introductions (Introducers)	XVI. Coaching (Process Consultant)	XXV. Testimony (witness)	XXXIII. Advice from Respected Friend, Associate, Leader or Elder (advisor)	XXXVII. Binding Arbitration	XLV. Structured Facilitated Conciliation Meetings
II. Conciliation	VIII. Convening (convener)	XVII. Training (Trainer/	XXVI. Expert Opinion (expert)		XXXVIII. Med-Arb (Conducted by the same person)	XLVI. Negotiated Economic Development Forums
III. Information Exchange Meetings	IX. Message Carrying (Messenger)	XVIII. Educator)	XXVII. Data Collection (data collector)	XXXIV. Non-Binding Arbitration (Arbitrator)		XLVII. Democratic (adversarial and consensual) Decision-Making Procedures and Structures (committees, Legislatures)
IV. Co-operative/Collabor-ative Problem Solving	X. Protocol Advice (protocol officer)	XIX. Facilitation (facilitator)	XXVIII. Fact Finding (fact finder)		XXXIX. Mediation [b] Then Arbitration (Conducted by two separate interme-di-aries)	
V. Negotiations	XI. Counselling (therapist/counsellor)	XX. Mediation (mediator)	XXIX. Advisory Mediation (advisory mediator)	XXXV. Summary Jury Trial (judge/jury)		
VI. Rituals that Result in Decisions	XII. Conciliation (conciliator)	XXI. Brokering (broker)	XXX. Disputes Panel	XXXVI. Council Meeting (councilors)	XL. Disputes Panels/ Councils	
	XIII. Third Party Consultation (relationship consultant)	XXII. Middleman	XXXI. Mini-Trial		XLI. Private	
	XIV. Spiritual Advisor (religious leader)	XXIII. Ombudsperson	XXXII. Settlement Conference (judge/magi strate/heari ng officer)			
	XV. Team Building/ Partnering (Process Consultant)	XXIV. Chairperson				

4. History and Applications of EDR in the Developing World

Environmental conflicts are not new to the developing world. People in these societies have disputed over hunting grounds, fisheries, use of water and land, urbanisation and environmental degradation almost since the beginning of time. Each of these societies and cultures have developed procedures to address, manage, and resolve environmental disputes. These included dialogues, argumentation, negotiations, contests, mock battles, mediation or arbitration by elders, mechanical or ritual procedures for arriving at a decision, or more formal judicial procedures. With the coming of the colonial period, many developing countries, both those which were directly colonised and those indirectly influenced by colonial models, experienced a revolution in how disputes in general, and environmental problems in particular were handled. Colonial powers often replaced local or indigenous dispute resolution approaches and procedures, except in arenas which were not deemed politically important, with administrative or judicial procedures based on European models. For the most part, these models relied upon third party decision-makers, often colonial officials, who collected data or testimony on a case and dispute, and made a binding decision. On occasion there were appeal processes which parties could use if they were not satisfied with the disposition of the case by the third party.

As colonial influence expanded, many developing regions looked toward Europe as the model for progressive political and economic development. Many existing or future nations began to modify their dispute resolution approaches and procedures and adopted western models of conflict management. Where alternative voluntary consensus-based models did exist, they began to decline, become marginalized, or to disappear. (It is important to note that similar trends in the decline and use of non-judicial, voluntary, and consensual procedures also occurred in Europe and North America, where the judicial system began to dominate and displace competing dispute resolution approaches and systems located in communities, churches, guilds, co-fraternities, and voluntary organisations.)

At the time of the emergence of the present-day environmental movement, and the increase of governmental efforts to address natural resource problems, it is safe to say that most cultures, societies, and nations relied on top-down, third party, command decision-making to address these problems at least when they were of significance to those in power. But some characteristics of environmental disputes themselves and world trends regarding public participation and democratisation have made it difficult for many command decision-making models to reconcile differences and find fair and mutually acceptable solutions to public disputes over the environment.

In general, environmental conflicts differ from many two-party conflicts. (See Figure III: Characteristics of Environmental Disputes.) A number of these differences make environmental disputes more difficult to resolve by an administrative or judicial either/or decision-making procedure.

FIGURE III: CHARACTERISTICS OF ENVIRONMENTAL DISPUTES

1. Involvement of Multiple and Diverse Parties
2. Diverse Perceived or Actual Incompatible Interested Between or Among Parties
3. Differing Appraisals of the Situation by Diverse Parties
4. Contrasting Sources, Amounts and Forms of Power, and Leverage Among Parties
5. Lack of Relationships Among Involved Parties or History of Problematic Relationships
6. Divergent Expectations On the Part of the Parties Regarding Who Should be Involved in the Resolution Process and How
7. Confusion Over the Appropriate Forum for Resolving Issues
8. Unequal Levels of Knowledge and Expertise
9. Different Levels of Knowledge, Skills in, and Support for Cooperative Problem-Solving Techniques
10. Lack of an Identified and Respected Convener Who Can Bring Parties Together, Facilitate Communications and Problem Solving, and Assist People to Reach Mutually Acceptable Agreements.

In addition to differences in the characteristics of environmental disputes themselves, there have been significant changes in both global and national consciousness and values regarding the participation of citizens in decisions which affect their lives. Developed nations with histories of democratic participation have undergone, during the last hundred years, a revolution in expectations of who, how, when, where, and how often citizens can expect to participate in making public decisions. Enlargement of the franchise, growth of more open political parties, and widening opportunities for citizens to vote or participate in committees addressing public issues, have expanded the vision, expectations, and opportunities for involvement in democratic deliberation. Far from being confined to Western European or European-rooted nations, these values and expectations have spread around the world[4].

Democratising trends and increased public participation in developing countries often first appeared in societies colonised by nations which had more democratic systems of deliberation and decision making at home. Contradictions between participation levels in the colonial power and in the colonies often spurred independence struggles which culminated with the independence of most nations in the 1960s and 70s. But political independence did not necessarily guarantee public participation in domestic issues in newly autonomous states.

A second major wave of democratisation and increased public participation emerged in North America and many countries in Western Europe in the 1960s and 70s. One of the arenas in which this occurred was the environment. Laws were passed in a number of developed countries that protected the environment, established new institutions to address natural resource problems, provided legal grounds for enforcement of environmental regulations, and mandated public participation in the decision-making process. But public participation was not initially equated with direct involvement in deliberations concerning the resolution of environmental conflicts; it was primarily considered to be either written or oral input to decision-makers, or feedback at public meetings. Increasing participation to include actual involvement in decision-making was to emerge later as issues became more complex, administrative procedures increasingly cumbersome, outcomes more unpredictable, and costs of judicial decisions increasingly prohibitive.

Once again, environmental and political trends in developed nations influenced developing countries. As had occurred in North America and Europe, developing nations began to create new Ministries for the Environment, environmental impact assessment laws, regulations, procedures and mechanisms, and began to adopt more formal approaches to seeking ways of addressing environmental issues and conflicts. Initially, most decision-making procedures adopted were administratively or judicially based and command and control in nature. Often the source of decision-making authority on environmental issues remained outside the new ministries and was lodged within existing ministries of local affairs, mining, forestry, or with the military. But other trends would soon begin to open up the concentration of authority previously held by these agencies, and expand wider public participation.

The late 1960s and 70s saw the emergence of another major force for the environment: NGOs as environmental advocates. Starting with developed countries, by the early 1990s almost every nation had either local or internationally affiliated groups of citizens, farmers, students, academics or the intelligentsia who were generally advocates both for the environment and for greater participation in public decisions.

Domestic concerns for the environment and broader participation in decision making were also affected by changes in attitude in the international community. Until the last half of the 1980s, environmental issues were often seen "as local or regional concerns, extraneous to economic growth, matters of health, aesthetics, and perhaps ethics. After it, they assumed a global dimension, beginning to be seen as intrinsic to economic growth or decline, and to be recognized as significant determinants of nations prosperity, governability and security."[5] The publishing of the United Nations report on the Commission on Environment and Development, *Our Common Future*, 1987 (commonly known as the Brundtland Report) defined environmental degradation as a survival issue and introduced the concept of sustainable development to a broader public. Other international activities, such as the UN s Conference on the environment held in Rio de Janeiro in 1992, also expanded environmental visions and expectations. The linkage of the environment to development, and the need for local co-operation and buy-in to implement sustainable development projects, led many international donors and lenders to incorporate public participation, and some form of dispute resolution, as components in their initiatives.

5. Motivators and Perceived Advantages for Using EDR

Trends, such as those described above, have had significant impacts on the application and use of environmental dispute resolution procedures in both developed and developing countries. There is extensive literature in developed countries describing these trends as well as other motivators.[6] Additional factors in developing countries, beyond those mentioned above, include high costs of administrative and judicial procedures, unpredictable outcomes, long time delays before settlement, lost opportunity costs, damaged relationships and difficulty in implementing command decisions.

The impetus for finding new and effective ways of managing and resolving environmental disputes in developing countries, while frequently similar to motivators in developed countries, may also be different. These differences are often related to cultural and historical factors; different institutional arrangements; diverse psychocultural orientations toward conflict, appropriate resolution procedures, and perceptions of desirable outcomes; and best alternatives to negotiated agreements , or BATNA of the parties.[7] Some parties are motivated to use EDR for positive reasons or to attain benefits, while others are motivated by negative costs or to avoid costs or risks. Some of the factors that are influencing the use of EDR in developing countries include:

• Strong cultural values and beliefs held by many people in the government, business and community sectors that consensus-based processes are more culturally appropriate and acceptable than adversarial procedures. (This belief may be based in historical tradition or precedent, or may be based on widely held social goals for harmony or myths.)
• Broad social values to preserve and/or re-establish harmony at the local, regional and state levels. (These beliefs may be based on a cosmology in which specific actions are desirable or required and need to be enacted in order for the universe and social relations to be kept in balance. These values are commonly found in more traditional societies, and in many cultures in Asia, Africa and the Oceana-Pacific region.)

• Broad social commitments to protect and preserve individual face, and institutional reputation. (This is especially important in cultures that are strongly influenced by avoidance of public shame, rather than private, individual guilt.)

• Strong desires to avoid adverse press or publicity, both for economic and credibility reasons. (Threats of adverse publicity in many developing countries often have more impact on a recalcitrant party than the risk of a lawsuit or administrative decision.)

• Perceived susceptibility, or actual experience by involved parties, of governmental personnel or agencies and/or the judiciary to illegal or unethical political or economic pressures, i.e. threats or corruption, that adversely impact the outcome of a dispute.

• A weak regulatory environment and limited administrative or judicial enforcement authority/capabilities, which inhibit governmental agencies from compelling compliance to environmental regulations and laws.

• Cumbersome, unpredictable and costly (time and money) bureaucratic and judicial decision making.

• The potential for public dissatisfaction and unrest over environmental issues that can escalate and spread to other social issues, thus weakening control of those in power.

• Clear and compelling needs on the part of local governments to find effective and efficient ways to handle nuisance disputes.

• Greater community expectations and demand for participation in the resolution of public disputes;

• Strong beliefs, by advocacy and public interest groups, that they will have more influence over the process and fairness of the outcome of a dispute if there are direct negotiations, than they will through either a bureaucratic or judicial forum or process.

• External pressures by international public interest groups, governments, and/or multi-national corporations subject to corporate codes of responsibility.

• Expectations, conditions and demands of international leaders and donors.

6. The Development of Practice and Institutional Arrangements for EDR

EDR has been practised in many countries on an ad hoc basis. However, many countries are now moving to institutionalize its use. To date there is no one universal development path, or common process for the creation of institutional arrangements to provide EDR services across cultures, either in developed or developing countries. There are, however, some central agencies or organisations that frequently play catalytic roles in the development of these procedures and agencies, and some activities that are often used to promote institutionalization.

Entities that are most likely to take the lead in this area are domestic NGOs and universities as catalysts, champions, educators, and networkers; international professional conflict management firms and development agencies as vision builders, model providers, trainers, and systems designers; and domestic governmental agencies as market creators, implementers, conveners, and system co-ordinators. It should also be noted that specific professions have also played leading roles in the introduction and use of EDR in developing countries. As the process of addressing environmental issues often results in conflict, and issues are often framed as legal disputes, it is not surprising that lawyers are frequently involved. In many developing countries, where law is one of the most common courses of study, professionals trained in the law are often in positions in both governmental and non-governmental organisations to advocate or make decisions about procedures to address environmental conflicts. Lawyers have clearly played the leading role in drafting legislation and model procedures for dispute resolution. Lawyers have also acted as advocate/participants in EDR processes, and have been engaged as intermediaries.

Other professions and vocations that have played major roles in the introduction and use of EDR procedures in developing countries are planners, scientists, government bureaucrats, university faculty, and community organizers. Individuals from these backgrounds have often played roles as organisational administrators, educators and intermediaries.

6.1 Domestic NGOs and Universities

In a significant number of the developing countries where the use of voluntary EDR has grown, NGOs and universities have played a major role. They have promoted the concept within government agencies, persuaded citizen advocacy groups to participate in co-operative problem-solving initiatives, and leveraged the involvement of the private sector either through coercion or persuasion. Some of the NGOs that have played this catalytic role are advocacy groups (consumer, environmental, human rights, etc.), while others have been more impartial research or educational organisations working on environmental issues. In a number of countries, staff for these NGOs have been lawyers. In several instances, the catalyst NGOs have specifically established themselves as independent dispute resolution organisations, with either a broad focus on co-operative dispute resolution or with a specific environmental emphasis. In other cases, EDR services have been added to the functions of an existing group. Often these NGOs are led by a charismatic and visionary individual who has been exposed to alternative dispute resolution principles and methods.

Universities, too, have played a critical catalytic role in educating governmental personnel, advocacy groups, and the public about the uses, advantages, and procedures of EDR. Universities have sponsored seminars, courses and conferences to

promote new ideas, prepared skilled graduate students who can advocate and participate in EDR initiatives, and provide institutional homes for conflict management
centers. Generally, law, public policy, and environmental sciences and planning
faculties have taken the lead as EDR promoters.

6.2 International Professional Conflict Management Practitioners and Firms

A second group of agencies which have been major catalysts in EDR promotion
and institutionalisation in developing countries are professional conflict management practitioners and firms from developed nations. These entities whose services
are usually contracted for by international development organizations, government
agencies, NGOs or universities have provided a range of assistance and services to
individuals and groups exploring the introduction of participatory conflict management procedures. Some of these services have included: situation assessments or
institutional conflict audits, consultation on strategy design for the resolution of
specific conflicts, intermediary assistance (facilitation or mediation), conflict management training (negotiation, facilitation, mediation, convening), dispute resolution system design, and administrative support for operating dispute resolution
systems.

6.3 International Non-Governmental and Governmental Development Agencies and Foundations

These entities have performed a critical role in directly promoting and funding
EDR activities (consultation, training, dispute systems design, and interventions) in
developing countries, funding consultations by international professional conflict
managers, or requiring public participation and EDR as part of their own or funded
development projects. These organisations have also provided a very valuable networking function by supporting individual and group study travel tours on EDR,
and hosting international conferences on EDR.

International governmental organisations that have made significant contribu-
tions to promote the field, either directly or indirectly, have been the US Agency for
International Development (USAID), the Canadian International Development
Agency (CIDA), the German Gesellschaft für Technische Zussammenarbeit
(GTZ), and the World Bank.

Among the non-governmental promoters of the field, the Asia Foundation
(TAF) and a handful of North American, European and Australian private
foundations have been significant. TAF has directly supported projects in Indonesia, Sri Lanka, and the Philippines, and has sponsored numerous international exchanges, study tours and conferences on the subject of EDR. In the US,

the Ford Foundation, the Hewlett Foundation, the Mott Foundation, and Pew Charitable Trusts have been leaders in supporting EDR through direct operating funds to NGOs, or support for targeted projects. In Europe and Australia, the German Marshall Fund and the Winston Churchill Foundation have funded a number of international consultations, study tours, and visitor exchanges.

6.4 Governmental Organisations in Developing Countries

In many developing countries the direct involvement of the government in EDR is *the* critical factor that determines whether more participatory and collaborative procedures take hold or are institutionalised or not. However, the role and functions performed by governments and governmental agencies in this area are very diverse.

The roles and functions of governmental agencies in EDR generally depends upon historical precedents and norms for the government to provide conflict management services; citizen expectations regarding the appropriate role of government in resolving disputes; the relationship of political to civil society; the presence of multiple and often potentially competing agencies that can assist in the resolution of disputes; the freedom and acceptability of non-governmental conflict management organisations to develop and provide services; and the level of openness or chaos in the society.

In a significant number of countries, the judiciary has been unable to perform a satisfactory role as an environmental dispute resolver. Because of limited judicial technical expertise on environmental issues, cost, extended time periods to obtain a decision, lack of clear applicable law, fear of precedents, parties wishes for privacy, unpredictability of outcome, unwillingness of other agencies to delegate authority to judges, parties fear of corruption, and so forth, many governmental agencies, public interest groups and businesses have been reluctant to take their cases to court.

Difficulties with judicial procedures and outcomes have often encouraged parties to seek EDR assistance from other executive or administrative structures. Frequently, EDR initiatives or services have been located in new governmental agencies or environmental ministries mandated to address and protect the environment, a national planning agency, an existing ministry authorized to manage a specific resource or local governments that are the recipients of a large number of citizen complaints.

Where new agencies or environmental ministries have been created, they have rarely been given adequate authority to impact directly or forcefully on environmental decision making. Power struggles between governments and the private sector, competition for influence and authority between existing resource-specific agencies and ministries, or unclear governmental policies and priorities concerning the relationship between environmental protection and economic development, often result in new agencies having only co-ordination functions to work out agreements concerning environmental issues with the public, private parties and other ministries or agencies. They often have limited or no authority to make binding policy or regulatory decisions, or compel compliance with environmental laws or agency rules. These constraints have encouraged many new environmental agencies to promote and initiate collaborative EDR procedures as pragmatic means for them to achieve their mandate, protect the environment, and gain more political influence.

The impetus for local governments to pursue co-operative EDR factors might best be called the headache factor . Local governments often become involved in environmental issues because of problematic and difficult nuisance disputes, or because there is intense competition between contending local groups over development issues or natural resource use. Increasingly, as citizen groups have mobilised, and have had greater expectations for input and/or participation in decisions, governmental agencies have sought ways to lower levels of conflict and reach agreements that will be more satisfactory to all of their constituents. This trend has been true not only in more democratic regimes, but also in those where there are few democratic traditions. (It should be noted that in Eastern Europe and the former Soviet Union, environmental problems were some of the first issues around which the population mobilised for greater democratic participation.) In still other countries and cultures, where a high priority is placed upon harmony and smooth interpersonal relationships, governments have pursued EDR as a means of re-establishing community peace (as well as of staying in power).

Promotion and use of EDR by governmental agencies at national, regional and local levels have taken a variety of forms:

•Ministries of the Environment have sponsored conferences to educate parties about EDR principles and procedures. They have also solicited the co-operation of and networked with stronger ministries or local governments, which often have environmental mandates and regulatory or enforcement authority, to broaden support for EDR concepts and procedures.
• Ministries of the Environment and the legal departments of other agencies have also been leaders in drafting policies and regulations which support and promote the use of EDR. By including EDR procedures in executive decisions or legislation, agencies have found that there is a greater likelihood that EDR procedures will be used.

• Ministries of the Environment and local governments have also acted as conflict assessors, conveners, and sponsors of EDR initiatives, to determine which dispute resolution procedures are appropriate and to bring contending parties together for joint problem-solving and negotiations. In many cases these agencies are the only bodies that have the legitimacy, functional responsibility, credibility, and on occasion clout, to encourage joint co-operation between conflicting parties.

• Ministries of the Environment and other agencies have also played central roles as data providers or have conducted technical data assessment. Frequently, parties to environmental disputes, especially citizens or public interest groups, have limited access to requisite technical information, and/or do not have the resources to conduct scientific analysis of contested information. Ministries of the Environment, either through internal laboratories or contracted services, have in the past provided parties with relevant technical information to promote wise decision making.

• Ministries of the Environment, other national agencies, and local governments have also provided or secured the services of intermediaries facilitators and/or mediators. Government agencies have appointed intermediaries from inside the involved agency, obtained the assistance of personnel from another concerned but not directly involved governmental entity, or secured the services of external impartials to assist in the resolution of disputes. (The first model, that of an internal agency intermediary, has on occasion posed some ethical problems, especially where the intermediary was expected to be impartial and neutral.) In many conflicts, where the government itself is a central party to the dispute, and is frequently mandated to be an advocate for a broader or specific public interest, it is often difficult for its agents to play a totally impartial intermediary role. In other disputes and cultures, where the government is expected to act as a fair but possibly a partial mediator, government personnel have been highly successful as intermediaries.

• Ministries of the Environment and local government are often witnesses, implementers, monitors and enforcers of environmental decisions. This role is often critical in assuring that consensual decisions are executed and compliance achieved.

• Ministries of the Environment have also provided an institutional base and personnel to train internal staff in co-operative advocacy and dispute resolution skills and procedures, to educate intermediaries, and prepare parties to resolve disputes more effectively. External contracts for these services have also been arranged by these agencies.

• Finally, other national and local government agencies, most notably ministries of justice and municipal governments, have provided a base or home for more general dispute resolution services mediation and arbitration which address local environmental issues. Examples of these services are the Barangay Justice System in the Philippines and the Sri Lankan Mediation Boards.[8] Both services provide impartial intermediaries, who provide citizens with low cost resolution of community-based environmental issues.

7. Some Institutional Models of EDR Programmes and Service Providers

There is not a single ideal or right institutional model for the provision of appropriate dispute resolution or EDR services. There are a number of programmes, governmental and non-governmental, in different countries, that indicate the range of possible alternative structures and processes. These models differ according to where services are based (i.e. their institutional home), their mandate/authority, degree of autonomy/independence from involved parties, sources of staff/intermediaries, services provided, procedures for dispute resolution provided and sources of funding. Figure IV: Institutional Models for EDR Programmes and Services describes several models that have been developed in various parts of the world.

8. Possible Activities and Roles in Institutional Development

There is not one routine path or set of sequential activities that individuals, NGOs or governmental agencies in developing countries have used to introduce or institutionalize EDR principles and procedures. Generally promoters of EDR have used a combination of activities, some found to be successful in other countries and others developed specifically for their culture, to educate and gain support and participation from important parties.

As mentioned before, several of the major actors in introducing and institutionalising EDR are NGOs, universities, and governmental agencies. Generally, the stronger the central government, and the less there is a tradition of democratic participation, the more governments play a primary role (although non-governmental organisations may play a significant role as catalysts). This has been the case in countries such as China, Indonesia, Japan, Korea, the Philippines, Turkey and several Middle Eastern countries.

In situations where the central government's role is not as strong (or has been weakened by political crisis), or where there is a vacuum of power, or where there is a dynamic of decentralisation of authority, or where civil societies institutions are stronger, the impetus for EDR development has come from outside the government. This has been the case in many countries in post-Communist Eastern Europe and in South Africa.

Listed below are some of the activities (and related strategies) that governmental agencies, NGOs, universities and advocacy groups have used to promote the use of

Figure IV: Institutional Models for EDR Programmes and Services					
INSTITUTIO NAL BASE OR SPONSOR	**MANDATE/ SCOPE OF WORK**	**SERVICES PROVIDED/ SOUGHT**	**SOURCE/ CONFIGURATION OF INTERMEDIARIES**	**PROCESS VARIATIONS**	**SOURCE OF FUNDING**
Indonesian Ministry for Environment ∏ Environmental Impact Management Agency	Mediation of water pollution and other environmental conflicts on an ad hoc/as needed basis	Mediation of water pollution and other environment- al conflicts	Internal agency staff and external mediators selected by parties	Process oriented and evaluative mediation	Government funded
Korean Ministry of Environment ∏ Environmental Dispute Resolution Committee	1) Adjudica- tion brought by claimants, 2) disputes crossing local govt. boundaries, and 3) cases referred by local committees to central committee	Advisory mediation with advisory options	Members of national committee nominated by the president for term of three years. Local committees appointed by local govt. Independence guaranteed. Panel consists of three member. Supported by permanent agency staff.	Orientation toward evaluating the case with advisory opinion. Award becomes final if not contested by one of the parties in 60 days.	Government funded
South African National, Provincial and Local Government Agencies	Open mandate on an as needed basis	Mediation	Provided by external independent mediators whose services are contracted for by govt. agencies	Process oriented mediation	Government or private sector funded
Sri Lankan Ministry of Justice ∏ Mediation Boards	Mediate minor civil and criminal disputes, some of which are environmental cases	Mediation	Provided by local panels of volunteer mediators. Potential panel members are first identified by an independent national commission, and then selected by the parties to the dispute	Process oriented mediation	Government funded
Philippines Barangay Justice System	Mediate or arbitrate minor civil disputes, some of which	Mediation and arbitration	Provided by local panels of volunteer mediators. Potential panel members are identified by local	Process and evaluatory mediation, first by the Barangay Captain, and if	Local government

Bulgarian National Center for Negotiation and Conflict Resolution (an NGO)	Build cooperation between various communities in Bulgaria, and resolve public disputes, some of which are environmental	Conciliation, communication and trust building workshops, training, meeting facilitation, and mediation	Independent facilitators and mediators who work as individuals, in teams or as members of panels or commissions	Process oriented facilitation and mediation	Funded through private foundations and grants from international government donors
Futuro Latin Americano (an NGO)	Build consensus decisions on sustainable development issues	Facilitation and mediation	Independent mediators, often notable former Latin American government officials or business leaders	Process oriented mediation with the option of advice	Grants from private foundations, international donors and fees for service

EDR:

- *Past unsatisfactorily litigated or administratively decided cases*, whose outcome is not accepted or positively perceived by parties or the public, have often provided an impetus for parties to pursue in the future alternative procedures for managing their differences.

- *Press campaigns and adverse publicity* have also motivated parties to pursue EDR. In many countries the threat of adverse publicity, with potential adverse impacts on sales or production, the loss of face, or shame, have been stronger motivators for EDR than a threat of going to court. This has especially been the case in Asian developing countries, where a positive public image is highly desirable or where avoidance of public shame is a strong motivator.

- *Threats of, or actual, non-violent campaigns*, such as boycotts, conducted by citizen or advocacy groups have also promoted the use of EDR. Lack of access to, or lack of credibility of, institutional structures for dispute resolution often push parties to extra-parliamentary action and ultimately to negotiated non-judicial settlements.

- *Judicial deadlock, time delays, unpredictability and corruption* often motivate parties to use EDR. In a number of situations, environmental NGOs have indicated that they believe they have much more control over the outcome of a dispute, and have a greater chance of getting a positive implementable result, when using direct or mediated negotiations, than when they turn cases over to judges or administrators who may be subject to political or economic pressures or bribery.

- *Ad hoc use of EDR* is probably the most common way that parties in developing countries begin to use collaborative processes. This means that a case develops and someone, usually from an NGO or a government agency, suggests trying a voluntary EDR procedure. Success in one or more cases often induces parties to try procedures again, and has also encouraged the development of institutionalised means to channel future conflicts to EDR.

- *Targeting and experimentally trying out EDR on a series of potentially successful interventions* has been another strategy used by EDR promoters to educate potential parties and build a successful track record for the process. Start-up pilot projects that are experimental in nature and limited in scope are often less threatening to parties and agencies then making a full commitment to use or institutionalise EDR.

• *Research projects* on the practice and past use of EDR have been used to learn about how dispute resolution has been used in a specific context, describe cultural patterns of disputing, further institutional learning, and to promote the use of EDR procedures. This approach has been especially useful in cultures which value objective studies and the opinions of experts before trying or institutionalising a new decision-making process. An example of this approach was a study commissioned by the Indonesian Ministry for the Environment on six mediated cases concerning water pollution.

• *General Educational Conferences* on collaborative dispute resolution approaches, in general, and EDR methods in particular, have been used to promote the use of EDR. Meetings have been held at national levels, but probably more significantly, at regional or international levels, where cross-fertilisation of ideas between countries in similar situations have occurred. Examples of past conferences are the Asia-Pacific Organization for Mediation which led meetings in Asia in the 1980s, the Asia Foundation's (TAF) series of All-Asia Environmental Law Conferences and the Conflict Resolution in the Asia Pacific Region Conference (1994) (sponsored by TAF, the Asia Pacific Research Association and the Research and Education for Peace Unit at the Universiti Sains Malaysia), and a series of meetings of the European Conference on Peacemaking and Conflict Resolution (which have been held in Turkey and Bulgaria).

• *Expanding upon or borrowing from other existing cultural dispute resolution systems or procedures* has been another way that developing countries have developed EDR models and institutions. For example, Indonesians in developing their own models have begun to incorporate elements of *musyawarah*, an indigenous consensus-building process that is also used to manage and resolve differences.[9] In the Philippines, government agencies have taken models and learning successfully developed in the Barangay Justice System, a nation-wide Philippine government mediation and arbitration programme, and are applying them to the resolution of agricultural and land disputes.

• *Model EDR seminars*, often conducted by conflict management experts from abroad, have been used to raise awareness about EDR procedures, and build support for their use. These seminars have often focused on collaborative interest-based-negotiation procedures, or intermediary skills and procedures. Ministries and other agencies with environmental mandates in Bulgaria, Hungary, Morocco, Poland, Russia, South Africa, Tunisia, Turkey, and the West Bank/Gaza have implemented this approach as a way of educating potential parties about EDR approaches and procedures.

• *International visits and study abroad programmes* have provided many people from developing countries with opportunities to learn new approaches, procedures and practises used in other countries. Visits need not be exclusively to countries in North America, Australia, or Europe where EDR is more institutionalised. An example of this type of activity was a 1995 exchange between Asians and environmental conflict management practitioners in the US. Sponsored by the Asia Foundation, the exchange engaged participants in a one month intensive study tour in the US and Indonesia that enhanced their understanding of various cultural approaches to practicing and institutionalising EDR. This Exchange helped to spawn a new informal Asian network of EDR supporters and practitioners.

• *Model legislative and regulation development* is often an important step toward the use of EDR and its institutionalization. This has been especially true in countries where governmental endorsement or sanction is critical before a new approach or procedure can be introduced. Legislation or regulation, has often legitimized EDR procedures and encouraged mandated use. An example of this approach was the work of the Environmental Evaluation Unit of the University of Cape Town, South Africa, which prepared draft legislation, that was ultimately approved, concerning environmental impact assessment procedures, which paved the way for broader public participation and the use of EDR approaches.

• *Agency dispute system design and capacity building* has engaged agency personnel in design-focused workshops to revamp existing procedures or develop new systems for resolving environmental disputes (Dispute Systems Design, 1996). These processes and workshops are often facilitated by a conflict management professional with expertise in dispute systems design and institutional capacity building. This approach has been used in Indonesia, the Philippines, and Sri Lanka by a variety of governmental agencies.

• *User education and capacity building,* like the model seminars described above, these activities focused on preparing potential users of EDR approaches to participate effectively in specific processes. These seminars, unlike model programmes, have often been targeted to prepare parties as effective advocates in specific disputes. An example of this type of intervention was CDR Associates' training work with the Palestinian National Negotiation Teeam, working on environmental and water issues in the Middle East peace talks.

9. Arenas of Applications: Appropriate Issues for EDR

As in developed countries, EDR has been successfully applied in a number of developing countries to resolve a wide range of disputes over water development, allocation and use; air quality; land use; development; habitat and species protection and management; irrigation systems operation; forest management;

Figure V: SAMPLE APPLICATIONS OF EDR

Figure V: SAMPLE APPLICATIONS OF EDR					
COUNTRY	**CATEGORY OF PROBLEM/ DISPUTE**	**ISSUE/ CONFLICT**	**PARTIES**	**FORM OF EDR**	**OUTCOME**
Egypt (World Bank Participation Sourcebook, 1995)	Planning	Conflict over sustainable animal husbandry and agricultural projects in an isolated region of Egypt	National government, local village team, World Bank advisor	Facilitated planning process (Process oriented facilitation)	Consensual plan supported by multiple Bedouin communities
Indonesia (Soetrisno, 1995)	Regulatory enforcement/ compliance	Water pollution of fishponds and rice fields of Tapak village	National and international NGOs, local government, the national Environmental Impact Management Agency, and the involved company	Mediated by the mayor of Semarang, a nearby city (Process and evaluative mediation)	A consensual agreement on environmental restoration and compensation for affected parties
South Africa (Fowkes, 1995)	Site specific development issues	Proposed marina expansion at Kalk Bay and issues around change of use (commercial vs. recreational use)	Cape Town city Council's Town Planning Branch, Council, provincial officials, local residents, fishermen, visiting recreationalists	Facilitated public involvement process by an independent consultant team (Process oriented facilitation)	Consensual agreement on planned development
Tunisia (Baouendi, 1995)	Public policy dialogue	Comprehensive strategy for managing growth and development in the western area of greater Tunis	Municipalities, Ministry of Housing, Ministry of Agriculture, citizens, and industries	Facilitated public policy dialogue by independent consultants (Process oriented facilitation)	Recommend-ations forwarded to appropriate government agencies regarding components of a growth management and development plan
Peoples Republic of China (Tao Bie, 1975)	Regulatory enforcement/ compliance	Noise emissions from Harbin Steel Rolling Mill and impacts on a local community that developed around the plant	Harbin Steel Rolling Mill, Harbin Municipal Government, local citizens, Municipal Bank, Tax Bureau, Land Bureau, Municipal Police Office, Commercial Service Bureau, and the Education Bureau	Administrative mediation by municipal government staff (Process and evaluative mediation)	Consensual agreement by all parties to move the local community to a location away from the mill and compensation of community members for the move
Thailand (Songsam-pham, 1996)	Land use and forest management	Violent conflict between two families concerning use of forest land	Leaders and elders of two families, the district officer, the governor of the province, local teachers, and a respected Buddhist priest	Convened by the Governor and mediated by the Buddhist priest	Termination of violence and agreement on the use of the land
Korea (Jae Hyun Yoo, 1996)	Site-specific species and habitat protection	Conflict over impacts of prospective logging operations of the Hyundai Resources Development Corporation in Siberia, on the habitat of the Siberian Tiger	Hyundai Resources Development Corporation, international and Korean environmental groups, and the Citizens Coalition for Economic Justice (CCEJ) (an NGO)	CCEJ acted as the interested intermediary and mediated a settlement	Agreement to terminate logging operations in the disputed habitat area
Bolivia (Menedez-Ortiz, 1995)	Policy dialogue	Preserving both the banana and shrimp industry from disease and water pollution	Bolivia's Department of Fish and Game, Eastern Ecological Association, the State University, Association of Agricultural Engineers, and the Minister of Sustainable Development	Facilitated by an independent conflict management firm	Mult-sectoral agreement on a sustainable development management plan for the region, to be enacted through participatory mechanisms

mining; transportation development, personal injury, and a range of other issues. Specifically, EDR has been used to address permitting and compliance/
enforcement issues; regulation development; policy questions; regional or inter-
state problems; and international development projects. Figure V: Sample Applications of EDR provides examples of some of these applications.

10. Development of EDR Service Providers and Professionals

As EDR projects and programmes have become institutionalised, both users
and providers of conflict management services have been faced with the problem of how to secure the services of knowledgeable and effective intermediaries. This problem includes such questions as: who are the intermediaries? how are
they selected? how are they trained? how are cadres of intermediaries created so
that the parties have a choice? and how are intermediaries' skills honed, quality
of performance assured, and incorruptibility guaranteed?

Who is to be the Intermediary? and Types of Interventions Provided

Unlike many developed countries, where intermediaries in environmental issues are usually independent, trusted, impartial individuals who are not parties
to the dispute, providers of intermediary services in developing countries may be of
a number of types. Five possible types of intermediaries can be identified:[10]

• Social network mediators are usually part of the disputing parties network
of friends, associates or colleagues, who may not be impartial, but can provide valuable intermediary functions.
• Benevolent mediators are usually informal or formal authority figures
elders, church officials, politicians, wealthy or influential individuals who
while having no formal authority to decide an issue, have considerable influence on the parties because of their person or position.
• Administrative or managerial mediators, are usually people with institutional positions, who may be a party to a dispute or may actually have authority to make a binding decision. Governmental officials most frequently oc-
cupy this role. Because government is frequently in between disputing parties, its agents may be called upon by the parties or may initiate intermediary
involvement themselves.
• Vested interest mediators are individuals or groups who have specific interests in the outcome of the dispute and have the ability to reward or coerce
parties to agree. Community strongmen, politicians, and powerful external
parties, such as governments of other nations, have often played this type of
intermediary role.
• The independent impartial/neutral mediator has already been described
above.

In developing countries, informal and non-institutionalised EDR is often carried out by social network, benevolent or vested-interest mediators. More formal and institutionalized mediation is usually provided by either administrative or independent mediators. There has been significant debate among leaders in governmental agencies and parties in a number of developing countries regarding the appropriateness, or desirability, of intermediaries being drawn from inside an agency directly involved in an environmental dispute, whether they can provide fair and impartial services, and whether impartiality is necessary or even desirable. In many nations where the state is seen as a father figure provider, advisor, final arbiter of decisions, and enforcer many people do not expect governmental agents to take a neutral view toward disputes. Parties often accept the multi-faceted role of an internal agency mediator as an advocate for the broader public interest and for the interest of the specific agency (and perhaps even an advocate for his own interest). At the same time parties can also accept officials as intermediaries who can provide advice, help seek consensual agreements, and if necessary reach decisions. While some parties may want impartiality from an intermediary, others want the government agent to tell them what is right and what to do.

Governmental agencies too, especially in highly centralized states or ones with limited democracy, are often reluctant to grant independent mediators a role in EDR, even if the intermediaries have no formal authority to compel a settlement. Agencies often want to keep political control of the ultimate decisions, and the public s perception that they are both the final arbiter of decisions and the source of all resulting benefits. (Government agencies also often believe that they are the only body knowledgeable enough, and with the necessary clout, to help parties make a decision.)

The view from the other side of this question is similar to that commonly found in developed countries that parties will best be served by an independent, trusted and impartial intermediary, and that government s role and interests will best be met by having its agents act as a party and advocate for the public interest rather than as an intermediary. Clearly, there are not any final answers on this debate. Some countries are pursuing developing independent intermediaries, at a minimum for cases where the government s interests are very clear or strong and are very different from those of other parties. Other countries and agencies are developing internal governmental intermediary capacities, but trying different methods to separate the intermediary role from the decision-making function. (One way that this has been done, in several countries is to have the intermediary come from a government agency, but not one that is directly involved in the dispute in question.)

Designation or Selection of the Intermediary Closely related to the source of intermediaries and their relationship to parties is the question whether parties have a choice in selecting who will assist them. Here too, there is a wide range of practice. In some countries, such as Sri Lanka or the Philippines, where community-level environmental disputes are handled by local boards, parties do have a choice in selecting or approving who will participate on their specific dispute resolution panel. In other countries, the choice of the mediator is the prerogative of the assigning agency, albeit in some cases with the final approval of the parties.

Quality Assurance An important factor in obtaining high quality intermediaries, whether external or internal to governmental agencies, is to guarantee that they have adequate training in an acceptable philosophy, approach, and procedure of dispute resolution or mediation, and that they have an understanding of the ethics of intervention. Training helps increase the number of voluntary settlements, and promotes ethical behavior on the part of intermediaries.

As many developing countries do not have the experience, skills and resources to develop specialized training programmes in co-operative dispute resolution, many potential personnel and systems developers have sought the assistance of professional conflict management firms from abroad to assist in the design of the system, conduct a cultural conflict audit to determine existing cultural approaches that help successfully resolve conflicts, conduct training programmes and develop training-for-trainers seminars to build agency and national capacity for ongoing conflict management education. Training programmes generally cover conflict management philosophy and approaches, conflict resolution strategy design, convening methodologies, party and intermediary dispute resolution procedures, methods of avoiding and overcoming impasses, communications skills, and ethical issues. Also, most successful training programmes have extensive clinical components, where participants practise intermediary or other conflict management procedures and skills and receive feedback on their performance from professional conflict managers. It should be noted that a number of countries have also developed customized training programmes in conflict management for people who will administer the system, for parties in successful advocacy skills, and for intermediaries.

Professional Associations and Development As the field of dispute resolution has matured, there has been a growth of associations and conferences formed or conducted to provide ongoing education and networking between administrators, practitioners and potential users. Most of these conferences focus on dispute resolution in general, but many of them have environmental sections or topics on the agendas. A number of the international and regional conferences have already been listed above. In addition to these meetings, many people from developing countries also attend the meetings of the Society of Professionals in Dispute Resolution, the North American Conference on Peacemaking and Conflict Resolution, and Interaction Canada which are held in North America on an annual or bi-annual basis, or other conferences in the developed world such as that held by national dispute resolution associations in Britain, France, Australia and New Zealand.

In addition to regional associations and conferences, a number of developing countries have initiated national gatherings or organisations. Examples of these include the South African Association of Conflict Intervention and the Asociación Argentina de Arbitraje y Mediación.

Development of Ethics and Standards of Best Practice Many of the professional conflict management associations in North America, Australia and South Africa have been exploring the development of ethical qualifications and performance standards. Associations and organisations in Britain, Ireland, Germany, and France are also in this process. It is expected that similar trends will eventually occur in developing countries, although to date they have not been a major focus.

Assuring the fairness of a dispute resolution process and, where appropriate, the impartiality of the intermediary has been of particular concern for many government agencies and NGOs which provide EDR services. Achieving this goal is especially critical in countries where there has been a low level of trust in elected or appointed decision makers, or where there has been a history of administrative or judicial corruption. Approaches implemented to prevent or inhibit the possibility of undue political or economic influence on procedures or intermediaries include: training programmes for interveners that include ethics modules in which impartial behavior is stressed and participants explore the boundaries between cultural norms of gift giving and bribery; having a body of respected individuals identify a large panel of potential trustworthy intermediaries, from which involved parties may select their intervener; use of three-person mediation panels instead of a solo mediator, on the assumption that several people will be harder to unfairly influence than a lone individual; and designating case supervisors and quality control feedback mechanisms.

11. Further Development of Environmental Dispute Resolution: Issues, Obstacles, Opportunities, and Trends

As the field of EDR grows and matures in the developing world, and innovations and applications increase, a number of issues have emerged that will need to be addressed.

11.1 Developing Culturally Appropriate Dispute Resolution Approaches and Procedures

As various countries and cultures have begun initiating new procedures for resolving environmental disputes, there has been a tendency to adopt models, approaches and procedures from other countries. This has often occurred without careful consideration as to whether these are a good cultural fit for the situations, issues, and people that they are supposed to serve. A number of dispute resolution practitioners have raised concerns about whether the North American Model of dispute resolution is appropriate for diverse cultures and whether it should be exported for use in situations and cultures which are extremely different from the one for which it was designed.[11]

Some of the questions that have been raised are:

• How well do co-operative dispute resolution approaches work in settings where there is not a strong legal system that enables parties to bargain in the shadow of the law, and use legal frameworks as models for settlement?

• How well do EDR procedures work in highly adversarial situations or cultures, which seem to be orientated more toward win-lose than toward co0operative procedures or outcomes?

• How do these procedures work in cultures where the normative negotiation process is bargaining over positions rather than jointly seeking to satisfy interests?

• How well do collaborative procedures work in highly stratified societies, where it is both unusual and difficult for people from different backgrounds, rank, and classes to talk frankly and as equals?

• How well do direct dealing face-to-face procedures work in cultures which are much less direct, and where members rely extensively on intermediaries to manage differences?

• What should be the balance bewteen procedural assistance and evaluative assistance, i.e. advive or strong opinions, provided by intermediaries, and how should these differences in procedure be adjusted for cultures which value and expect different forms of third-party assistance?

• How can the fairness, and impartiality, where appropriate, of intermediaries be assured in societies where decision-making authority and intermediary roles are combined?

• How can co-operative processes be used in cultures which place such a high value on maintaining smooth interpersonal relationships and avoiding conflict, that procedures may be used to cover up or mask conflicts, manipilate publics, sacrifice partcipants rights, or create unfair outcomes?

• How can governments in relatively undemocratic societies be the major sponsors of dispute resolution initiatives, and not manipulate, co-opt or corrupt the procedures?

There are no easy answers to the above questions. A procedural approach to begin to address them, is to conduct (a) a careful situation assessment of the conflicts to be addressed, which includes consulting involved parties, and analysing the institutional structural arrangement which influences both procedures and outcomes, and (b) a detailed cultural analysis of the national, ethnic, and institutional cultures and approaches to handling and resolving prospective participants conflicts. The latter can be implemented using an analysis framework that identifies common cultural patterns concerning parties orientations toward and comfort with conflict, competition and cooperation; the importance and ways of building relationships; negotiation styles and patterns; communication preferences and styles; orientation toward time; venue and use of space preferences; culture-specific dispute resolution structures or procedures; and orientations toward third parties. [12]

11.2 The Problem of Resolving Disputes in a Weak or Under-defined Legal/Regulatory Environment

To date, most developing countries have relatively underdeveloped legal and regulatory systems to address environmental issues. While many have created environmental agencies and developed broad policies, they are only starting to define specific regulations and consequences for non-compliance. Weak legislation, regulations and limited institutional authority can make it more difficult for governmental agencies to convene parties, initiate a process, provide a relatively predictable BATNA for participants if agreements cannot be developed, or implement and monitor agreements that have been reached.

When environmental disputes are sent to court, judges often have little knowledge of environmental issues or laws, and may have few legal parameters to guide their decision making. In addition, lawsuits are often long and expensive: costs that many citizens and public interest groups cannot afford.

Finally, in many developing countries, the existence of corruption in both their administrative agencies and the courts makes the presence of existing laws irrelevant to the final outcome of a case. Parties with complaints often believe that dispensation of their dispute is more likely to be determined by a well-placed bribe, than a fair adjudicated decision. This makes them reluctant to trust or use existing institutional processes for dispute resolution.

The above problems pose both opportunities and barriers to the initiation of EDR. Parties with few viable administrative or judicial options may be more open to trying direct or mediated negotiations. Also, the lack of specific legal or regulatory parameters may provide parties with greater opportunities for creative and customised problem solving. However, absence of these standards and criteria can make it more difficult to build a compelling case and to reach agreements that can be implemented and enforced.

11.3 Resistance by Potential Parties

Potential parties in developing countries are, on occasion, not open to using EDR. Their reluctance is based upon a number of interests and concerns.

Government agencies often resist using EDR because they fear losing control or giving up the right to make a final decision, which they believe is their prerogative. They may also be reluctant because of: the lack of a common view of the dispute within the agency; competition with other agencies regarding who has the authority to decide issues in question; or lack of resources personnel, technical, or financial to implement an EDR process.

Businesses have identified a number of reasons for reluctance to participate in EDR procedures. These include: satisfaction with existing governmental and judicial decision-making procedures which parties believe they can positively influence, either directly or indirectly; a belief that the delays and financial costs of non-EDR approaches can be used to parties' advantage when contesting an issue with public interest groups; a belief that laws and regulations do not exist, or will not be enforced, under the current system; and minimal consequences for non-compliance. (This latter perception is often reversed when adverse publicity or citizen campaigns or direct action come into play.)

Citizens and public interest groups are often resistant to using EDR because they expect the administrative and judicial system to work, want the government to make wise and fair decisions (in their favor) and do not want an existing command-based decision-making process replaced with another system. They also want to use the judicial system to create legal precedents that might be applied to similar cases in the future - an outcome that is harder to achieve through voluntary settlements which address a specific dispute. NGOs are often reluctant to negotiate, at least early in the development of a dispute, because they want to use the conflict to achieve organizing and public mobilization goals.

Implementing EDR generally means developing strategies to overcome some of these resistance points. Often, a general strategy needs to be developed for each broad group of actors, as well as targeted strategies to engage participants in specific disputes.

11.4 Lack of Resource on the Part of Government Agencies and Public Interest Groups

A final barrier to the implementation of EDR procedures in developing countries is the lack of resources financial, personnel, procedural skills, and technical knowledge to implement new approaches. The impetus to try more participatory EDR most frequently comes from weaker and generally poorly-funded government institutions ministries of environment and local government or NGOs. Government agencies often lack the funds to conduct research, develop culturally appropriate dispute resolution procedures, train staff in the principles and approaches, and administer EDR programmes. NGOs often lack funding either to start independent EDR services, or to participate as fully knowledgeable and empowered parties. For EDR initiatives to work, start-up funding either from the national government, international donors, or the private sector is needed, as well as technical assistance from consultants knowledgeable in EDR.

In addition to financial assistance to governmental agencies and dispute resolution NGOs providing EDR services, funding is needed by advocacy groups. As in developed countries, public interest groups have found that participation in voluntary dispute resolution procedures can be both time consuming and difficult if they do not have adequate resources to collect, analyse and understand technical data, and to support their representatives at the negotiating table. For EDR procedures to be accessed effectively and used by a wide audience, means need to be developed to support and provide resources for citizen and public interest group participation. Sources of resources, either financial or in kind, developed in some developed countries have included financial assistance from: foundations (grants), government agencies (designated funds allocated to assist public interest groups), the private sector (general funds that are or are not tied to a specific dispute, which are often administered by an independent or intermediary NGO), and financial assistance from national environmental groups to local citizens' groups for use on specific cases or projects. Similar models need to be explored in developing countries.

12. Conclusion

EDR is clearly a growing field in the developing world. Initiated primarily by government agencies, NGOs, universities and advocacy groups, these voluntary and cooperative approaches and procedures have already had significant success in addressing and resolving a wide range of environmental disputes in the areas of planning, permitting, enforcement/compliance, the creation of regulations, policy development and the resolution of site-specific disputes.

Inducements to use EDR procedures have come not only from failures of institutional, judicial and administrative structures adequately to address and resolve environmental problems, but also from psychocultural factors and historical cultural practises which support cooperative dispute resolution initiatives.

While there is not a single path or route for the creation of EDR interventions, projects, institutions and systems in developing countries, there have been a number of activities that have been found to promote greater awareness and use. These activities have not only resulted in the implementation of voluntary EDR procedures to resolve specific cases, but have also been used to create new dispute resolution systems and conflict management services provided by either governmental agencies or non-governmental entities both in the public and private sectors.

In introducing EDR in developing countries, proponents have to overcome a number of barriers including: a weak legal and regulatory environment; environmental agencies with limited authority; competition between governmental agencies; resistance by parties to shift from direct action, political lobbying, or economic pay-offs to cooperative problem solving; and lack of resources to implement or participate in EDR. Despite significant barriers, there has been substantial growth and use of EDR around the world.

Bibliography

Auerbach, J. Justice. *Without Law: Resolving Disputes Without Lawyers.* New York: Oxford University Press, 1983.

Bacow, Lawrence, and Michael Wheeler. *Environmental Dispute Resolution.* New York: Plenum, 1984.

Bie, Tao. "A Negotiated Settlement of a Pollution Dispute Through Administrative Mediation." *Lessons Learned in Environmental Mediation.* Geneva: International Academy of the Environment, 1997.

Baouendi, Abdelkader. "Land-Use Planning in the Western Area of Greater Tunis." *Lessons Learned in Environmental Mediation.* Geneva: International Academy of the Environment, 1997.

Bingham, Gail. *Resolving Environmental Disputes: A Decade of Experience.* Washington, D.C.: Conservation Law Foundation, 1986.

Carpenter, Susan, and W.J.D. Kennedy. *Managing Public Disputes.* San Francisco, California: Jossey-Bass Inc. Publishers, 1988.

Diamond, Larry, and Marc Plattner. *The Global Resurgence of Democracy.* London: Johns Hopkins Press, 1993.

CDR Associates (ed.), *Dispute Systems Design,* Boulder, Colorado: CDR Associates, 1996.

Fisher, Roger, and William Ury. *Getting to Yes.* Boston, Massachusetts: Houghton Mifflin, 1981.

Fowkes, Sandra. "First Foray into Public Involvement: Upgrading of Kalk Bay Harbor and Environs." *Lessons Learned in Environmental Mediation.* Geneva: International Academy of the Environment, 1997.

Herat, P. B. *Community-Based Dispute Resolution in Sri Lanka.* Forum (National Institute of Dispute Resolution), Winter 1993.

Huntington, Samuel. *The Third Wave: Democratization in the Late Twentieth Century.* London, United Kingdom: University of Oklahoma Press, 1991.

Jae, Hyun Yoo. "Saving the Siberian Ecosystem from Hundai's Logging Operations." In *Constructive Conflict Management: Asia-Pacific Approaches.* Fred Jandt and Paul Pedersen (eds.), London, United Kingdom: Sage Publications, 1996.

Lederach, John Paul. *Preparing for Peace: Conflict Transformation Across Cultures.* New York: Syracuse University Press, 1995.

Lederach, John Paul. *Mediation in North America: An examination of the profession's cultural assumptions.* Paper presented at the National Conference on Peacemaking and Conflict Resolution, Denver, Colorado, 1985.

Mathews, Jessica (ed.). *Preserving the Global Environment: The challenges of shared leadership.* New York: W. W. Norton, 1991.

"Matruh Resource Management Project." *World Bank Participation Sourcebook.* Washington, D. C., 1995.

Meeks, Gordon. *Managing Environmental and Public Policy Conflicts.* Denver, Colorado: National Conference of State Legislatures, 1985.

Melendez-Ortiz, Ricardo. "That Taura Sundrome (Equador) and the Rivers of Chane and Pirai (Bolivia): Case Studies in Conflict Management for Sustainable Development." *Lessons Learned in Environmental Mediation.* Geneva: International Academy of the Environment, 1997.

Moore, Christopher W. The *Mediation Process: Practical Strategies for Resolving Conflict.* San Francisco, California: Jossey-Bass Inc. Publishers, 2nd Edition, 1996.

Moore, Christopher W. and Mas Achmad Santosa. "Developing Appropriate Conflict Management Procedures in Indonesia." *Cultural Survival,* 1995, 19(3), pp. 23-29.

Moore, Christopher W. "Some Structural Variables that Influence Problem Solving and Negotiation." Boulder, Colorado: CDR Associates, 1992.

Moore, Christopher W. and Jerome Delli Priscoli. *Executive Seminar on Alternative Dispute Resolution.* Ft. Belvoir, Virginia: U.S. Army Corps of Engineers, 1989.

Our Common Future. United Nations Report, 1987.

Salem, Paul. "A Critique of Western Conflict Resolution from a Non-Western Perspective.@ *Negotiation Journal,* Vol. 9, No. 4, October 1993, pp. 361-369.

Soetrisno, S. *Cooperative Settlement of the Tapak Case in Semarang Municipality Through Mediation Forum.* Semarang Municipality, Indonesia: 1995.

Songsamphan, Chalidaporn. "Vendetta and Buddhist Mediator in Southern Thailand." in *Constructive Conflict Management: Asia-Pacific Approaches.* Fred Jandt and Paul Pedersen (eds.), London: Sage Publications, 1996.

Sullivan, Timothy. *Resolving Development Disputes through Negotiations.* New York: Plenum, 1984.

Susskind, Lawrence and Patrick Field. *Dealing with an Angry Public.* New York: Free Press, 1996.

Susskind, Lawrence and Jeffrey Cruikshank. *Breaking the Impasse.* New York: Basic Books, 1987.

Tadiar, Alfredo. *Effective Dispute Settlement*. Manila, the Philippines: privately published, 1990.

Ury, William, Jeanne Brett, and Stephen Goldberg. *Getting Disputes Resolved: Designing Systems to Cut the Costs of Conflict*. San Francisco: Jossey-Bass Inc. Publishers, 1988.

Von-Benda-Beckman, Keebet. *The Broken Stairways to Consensus: Village justice and state courts of Mjnangkabau*. Cinnaminson, New Jersey: Foris Publications, 1984.

NOTES

[1] Moore 1996.

[2] Ury, Brett, and Goldberg 1988; CDR Associates 1996.

[3] Moore and Delli Priscoli 1989.

[4] Diamond and Plattner 1993; and Huntington 1991.

[5] Mathews, pp. 15-16, 1991.

[6] Bacow and Wheeler 1984; Bingham, 1986; Carpenter and Kennedy, 1988; Meeks, 1985; Moore and Delli Priscoli 1989; Sullivan 1984; Susskind and Field 1996; Susskind and Cruikshank 1987.

[7] Fisher and Ury 1981.

[8] Tadiar 1990; and P.B. Herat 1993.

[9] Moore and Santosa 1995.

[10] Moore 1996.

[11] Lederach 1985; Lederach 1995; Moore and Santosa 1995; and Salem 1993. See also: Susskind and Secunda, Chapter 1, Section 10, *supra*.

[12] (Moore, 1992).

Chapter V
THE PRACTICE OF MEDIATION IN COMMERCIAL ENVIRONMENTAL DISPUTES

THE PRACTICE OF MEDIATION IN COMMERCIAL ENVIRONMENTAL DISPUTES

By Christopher Napier

When are mediation techniques suitable?

In commercial disputes the real issue, so often, is money: in particular, how much, if any, will pass from one party to another in compensation for a breach of contract or tortious injury. This is equally true of environmental commercial disputes which tend, in one form or another, to revolve around the cost of regulatory compliance or remediation of contaminated land, the amount of compensation for harm caused to people or the environment, or related liability issues.

Mediation and facilitation techniques are appropriate for resolution of many of these environmental disputes. The main motivations for their use are:

• speedy resolution of the dispute without the need for Court procedures or a trial
• avoidance of the risk of losing outright which comes with a Court trial
• the variety of possible outcomes (including outcomes which could not be ordered by a Court)
• confidentiality
• informality, and
• maintenance of good business relations between the disputing parties.

It is now the policy of a number of US and UK corporations to use mediation in preference to formal litigation or arbitration for resolving environmental (and other) disputes in appropriate cases.

Mediation techniques are particularly suitable for resolving contractual disputes. And the extensive use, in the sale of businesses, of contractual warranties and indemnities relating to contamination of land, and relating to compliance of industrial plant and equipment with environmental laws and regulatory requirements, is generating an increasing number of contractual disputes over environmental matters.

Contracts are usually limited to a small number of parties, but tortious environmental disputes often involve several parties for example, large groups of people living close to an industrial plant. Provided the parties are not too numerous these multi-party dispute situations can be suitable for resolution by process of mediation. Where the numbers are large, then collaborative and consensus-building processes may still offer an alternative to a court trial.

There is increasing interest and experience in the US of the use of mediation to resolve disputes over governmental regulation of environmental issues, and there exists the potential for development within the regulatory processes of other countries. The mediation process offers opportunity for the regulatory body to achieve greater environmental gains than through the ordinary regulatory process.

Good judges in the UK have shown themselves highly competent to resolve the complex and differing scientific evidence given by expert witnesses which is so often at the core of environmental disputes, notably evidence as to the effect of particular substances on people and the environment, and as to the cause of incidents in industrial plant. Nevertheless, corporations may well prefer trying to resolve the technical elements of a dispute using their respective technical staff, assisted by a neutral mediator. This process can sometimes be further helped if the mediator or a co-mediator is an expert in the relevant field, although there will generally be other facets to the dispute less appropriate for a technically qualified neutral. Similarly a lawyer may attract more confidence as the mediator or a co-mediator where legal issues are a significant element of an environmental dispute.

Where the subject matter of the dispute is sensitive because airing it in public will affect reputation, or will attract other claims, the regulators, or the media, then the privacy of resolution by way of a mediation will carry attractions. However, often in environmental disputes it will be as much in one party's interests to attract publicity as it is in the other party's interest to minimise it.

The crucial point is that in many cases there is little to be lost and much to be gained by a commercial party participating in a mediation in an attempt to resolve an environmental dispute. The process is entirely voluntary and confidential. The mediator is neutral but yet brings an added dynamic to an attempt to find a settlement of the dispute. If the end result is not to the liking of either party the offered settlement can be rejected and the dispute taken to Court. Also, the whole mediation process is intended to be "without prejudice", so that it cannot be referred to in subsequent Court proceedings in a way which is adverse to a party's legal position. The parties therefore have control of the outcome throughout the mediation process, and are not disadvantaged within the legal process.

There is, of course, the risk that the cost of employing the mediator, and related legal and administration costs, will be wasted if the mediation should fail and the dispute then has to go on to Court. However, this risk is a low one as typically more than 80% of commercial mediations result in resolution of the dispute and, even if the process should fail, the parties will in the mediation have set out their cases to each other in the sort of detail which will tend to reduce the issues which need to be tried, and accordingly cut down the expense of the trial.

But not all environmental disputes are suitable for resolution by mediation or facilitation. Environmental disputes are often technically and legally complex, containing serious underlying environmental concerns and public policy considerations. Often they give rise to novel issues of fact or law, and so generate significant uncertainty. The substance of the action may affect a vital corporate interest (such as a major product), or the amount at stake may be very significant in relation to the financial strength of the company - for example, where potentially a large number of people or area of land has been affected. It may be crucial for a corporation to ensure that its factual, legal and scientific case is heard in public, and prevails in a legally binding forum as a precedent for further cases (if it wins). Indeed, the corporation's insurers may insist on it. These disputes may be better resolved in Court.

Equally, environmental interest groups bringing cases in their own right, or supporting cases being brought by individuals, will often have an overriding interest in a public hearing before the media and in obtaining a legally binding judgment for use in other cases. Such disputes need adjudication on tested factual evidence and legal rights, and clear rights of appeal, not a neutral mediator with no power to make any form of decision on these matters.

Then there is the advantage of Court proceedings, at least within the litigation system of the UK and US, of access to documentation of the other party through the process of discovery, and of the ability to cross-examine the other party's witnesses. This may be essential to success where a defendant corporation has all the knowledge of relevant emissions from its site, how they came about, and their likely effect on the local environment. In most cases such knowledge will only emerge by a process of compulsion within the Court process.

Certainly, reduced legal costs will flow from the elimination or reduction of Court process, but this aspect should not be over-emphasised as in any event most Court actions are settled without the need for the most expensive part of the legal process, the trial. Also, almost whatever the dispute, and however suitable for mediation, legal rights cannot be ignored. They are the background to any out-of-Court process of dispute resolution, as the parties' legal positions are the positions they must pursue in Court if the process fails. Each party will, therefore, acquire in advance of mediation a good understanding of the strength of its legal position, and some feeling for that of the other parties. In most commercial cases such understanding will require the collection and processing of facts and documentation, and their analysis in terms of legal rights, which are classic lawyer roles.

Parties will be well advised to have legal advice immediately to hand in the mediation if they are to evaluate properly the degrees of risk associated with the various possible solutions which will come forward in the course of a mediation. For this reason most mediators will ask the parties to ensure that their lawyers are fully involved in the process. The parties will also need legal advice on the agreement which sets up the mediation, and the final agreement of settlement. Preparation for the mediation itself will often involve legal assistance. The roles for legal advisors in the mediation of a commercial dispute are therefore clear and essential, and will carry significant cost.

In many cases legal proceedings commenced before an attempt to resolve a dispute by mediation can assist the mediation process because the written pleadings required in the legal proceedings should identify and clarify the issues between the parties; and the fact that the route to resolution of the dispute by the Court is already well advanced can help to "focus the minds" of the parties quite considerably on achieving a successful result in the mediation but, again, additional legal costs will be involved.

2. The Mediation Agreement

After the parties have agreed in principle to try and resolve their dispute through mediation, the first steps will be to agree on a mediator and on the detailed terms of the agreement to mediate. Choice of mediator may be a troublesome issue in environmental disputes as it is often the case that one party will see the strength of its case as, say, legal, and other parties see theirs as factual, or technical, and each party is looking for a mediator with a background to reflect its perceived strength.

One route is to leave the choice of mediator to an appropriate institution (such as Environment Council in the UK). In multiparty situations this will often be the only realistic way of appointing a mediator. However, appointment by an institution does remove from the parties a degree of participation in the choice of mediator, which can be helpful in building confidence in the process and so assist in a successful result. Thus, a common mechanism is for the choice to be made from a list of recommended mediators put forward by an institution, or from a list of acceptable mediators put forward by one of the parties. Another possibility is to appoint a mediator for his/her skills in the mediation process to work together with an expert in the relevant technical area.

Mediation agreements which are as simple as possible in the circumstances are to be preferred, but at the same time all relevant issues need to be dealt with. Some institutions (such as CEDR in the UK) have model forms of agreement, which may be used as they stand or as the basis of an individually tailored agreement. There are no hard and fast rules as to what provisions must be in a mediation agreement, but the main areas generally covered are the procedure leading up to the mediation, conduct of the mediation, confidentiality of material, inadmissibility of documents and oral statements in subsequent Court proceedings, mediators' fees and expenses, and the law and jurisdiction of the agreement. It is general practice for the mediator to be a party to the agreement so as to ensure its terms are acceptable to him. The usual agreement is that the mediator's fees and expenses will be split between the parties, whatever the outcome, but it is not unknown for one party to pay the share of another party in order to persuade it to come into the process, or where the other party cannot afford to pay.

The mediator's role is essentially one of absolute impartiality, to provide the process designed to assist the parties to reach an agreement to resolve the dispute. But to be most effective in understanding the parties' interests and needs, in reality testing, in developing options and in steering the parties towards a solution, the mediator needs to develop a real understanding of the substance of the dispute. Recognising this, the parties may want the mediator to be more openly involved in the content of the dispute and to express his/her own views (often then called a moderating role), or even produce a formal non-binding opinion at some stage. If so, these elements may be covered in the mediation agreement.

3. The Pre-mediation Procedure

The usual practice is for the parties to have at least one meeting with the mediator before the mediation itself, at which he will express his views as to how the mediation will be conducted and his expectations of the parties. The parties will respond with their views. In this way the groundrules for the mediation process will be set. Whilst the conventional mediator's role is one of absolute impartiality, the process will be assisted if the mediator can establish respect and even a degree of authority. This meeting is a first occasion for the mediator to achieve this.

Generally it will be agreed that the parties will prepare in advance written summaries of their case and bundles of relevant documents, for exchange several days before the mediation, with copies to the mediator. This helps the parties to focus their thoughts, and to take any additional legal advice needed, as well as briefing the mediator and (hopefully) narrowing the issues between the parties. However, in order to prevent summaries of case becoming an occasion for greater entrenchment of positions, mediators will generally impress on the parties that written summaries of case should be brief, and only a very limited number of essential documents included in the bundles.

If legal proceedings are already in existence the mediator will generally be provided with copies of the pleadings. If there are expert's reports or witness statements in existence, it may be appropriate for the mediator to see these, but not if the effect of providing them to the mediator will only be to entrench the positions of the parties.

4. The Mediation Process

The mediator will make an opening statement setting out the principles of the process, the role of the mediator, and the basis upon which the parties have agreed to attend. It is usual for mediators to emphasis their neutrality.

Generally, each party will then make an opening statement. In principle, this is made to the other parties and not to the mediator. It is expected that each of the parties will describe from its perspective the history of the dispute and the current state of it, will set out the essence of its case and overall approach to settlement, and will describe its business needs. The opening statement is also an opportunity to get emotive matters "off one's chest" in front of the other parties and an outside party (the mediator) - thereby clearing the way for a reasoned agreement - and allows the mediator to form a view on the initial attitudes of the parties. Responses may then be permitted in order to clarify opening statements, issues between the parties, and areas of agreement. The mediator will generally have questions designed to achieve these objectives.

In practice the statements and responses are taken also as an opportunity to restate respective positions. Mediators are nervous of this if it means the parties thereby become more adversarial and potentially less flexible in their responses to proposals for settlement. On the other hand parties can feel deprived if they are denied the opportunity to state their best factual and legal positions in front of the other parties and the mediator; and a statement of positions does have the merit of ensuring everyone hears those initial positions and issues, and hears the emphasis which can be put on particular aspects of them in an oral presentation, but which cannot easily be appreciated from a written summary of case.

In the case of a corporate party, the preference is for the presenter to be the senior business person present. Where legal issues have an important role in the dispute then it may be appropriate for the lawyers to the parties to make a presentation, and some parties feel more comfortable leaving the whole of the opening presentation to their legal advisors.

The procedure will thereafter be under the control of the mediator, and each mediation is unique. Nevertheless, most mediations of commercial disputes involve the mediator meeting in succession each party alone (often known as "caucus" meetings), with regular plenary sessions at appropriate moments, such as at the end of each day, to summarise progress and allow the parties to improve their relationship. Group meetings of some of the parties in a multi-party dispute, meetings between the lawyers to the parties, or between technical staff, are other possibilities. A particular objective of the mediator will be to keep up the momentum of the discussions.

The mediator should:

- establish the underlying interests and needs of the individual parties, and how these might be accommodated within possible solutions,
- encourage the parties to take an objective and dispassionate view of the issues and to recognise the needs and interests of the other parties,
- reframe and clarify issues and views,
- seek common ground which might be the basis of a consensus solution
- build trust and defuse emotions, and
- establish each party's "bottom line".

The caucus meetings give the opportunity for these and other difficult matters to be discussed with the mediator in circumstances of strict confidence, as the usual ground rule is that the mediator will pass nothing on to another party without express consent.

The mediator will help the parties to craft realistic solutions which would bring real and tangible benefits to all parties to the dispute and, in practice, will often bring forward ideas for solutions - although where these come from the parties themselves they will have the best chance of being the basis of a lasting resolution of the dispute. The mediator will seek reactions and probe established positions by a process of questioning ("reality testing") designed to help parties reduce the issues, adjust their perspectives and perceptions, and see their positions more realistically against the risks and costs of the alternative route to resolution of the dispute if the mediation should fail, which is usually formal litigation. Reduced uncertainty, cost and management time will almost always be attractive to commercial organisations if the terms on which it can be obtained are acceptable. It is in the area of reality testing that use of a technically or legally qualified mediator or co-mediator can have considerable impact, notably in environmental disputes.

Experience shows that a crucial element in achieving a successful outcome in commercial disputes is for those representing a corporation at the mediation to have sufficient authority to commit the corporation to any reasonable solution, however unexpected at the outset. Where the corporation is large this may be hard to put in place, as the tendency of those who are outside the process but responsible for the relevant budget is to seek to control the worst outcome by putting a limit, often an unrealistically low one, on what the company's representatives may agree by way of settlement without reference back to the company. This is understandable, and some limit of authority to the representatives may have to be accepted, but then the result may well be a reference back towards the end of a mediation, with loss of the chance of resolution because those consulted have not been subject to any of the rethinking engendered by the mediation process and will tend to be constrained by the corporation's pre-mediation position. Some mediators will not start a mediation until they have appropriate assurance that the senior representative of a corporation present does have power to agree any reasonable settlement. In any event, the means of obtaining instructions must be clear at the outset of the mediation process.

Once the mediation has started it will not be easy to gather new facts or data, or new scientific evidence, or carry out legal research. Nor will it be easy to test offered solutions against budgetary projections or profitability forecasts. Indeed the pressure from the mediator will be not to complicate matters and break the flow of the mediation by seeking to bring in newly gathered information. Therefore, as well as preparing summaries of cases and opening statements, the parties need to prepare in advance detailed responses to the various facts, issues and assumptions on which they are likely to be tested by the mediator (or the other parties) in the course of the mediation. They also need to explore in advance the limits of acceptable outcome scenarios. If not well prepared a party risks ending up making an agreement without really understanding the effect on its business - something which may be regretted later. On the other hand good preparation in this way tends to assist achievement of a truly successful and lasting outcome to the mediation process.

5. Failure to agree

In some cases parties are unable to reach agreement within the mediation process, in which event they may agree that there is no point in continuing, or one party will withdraw, and the mediation will come to an end. Alternatively, mediators can use the power which the mediation agreement usually gives them to terminate the process if they decide that continuing the mediation is unlikely to result in a settlement.

Occasionally, but rarely, the parties will, as a last attempt to reach an agreement within the mediation process, ask the mediator to produce what he or she considers are appropriate terms of settlement in the circumstances as they then appear to the mediator. The parties will then consider those terms, essentially on a "take it or leave it" basis.

6. The Settlement Agreement

If legal advisors are present, and the agreed terms of settlement are straightforward, then a legally binding agreement can be signed before the parties depart from the mediation process. However, if the terms of agreement are more complex, parties often prefer to initial a document setting out only the main principles of the agreement before departing, and to leave their lawyers to draft a detailed written agreement thereafter. This has the benefit of producing a more considered wording of the written agreement, and so a stronger agreement in legal terms. There may also be consequential documents to draft in order to implement the settlement.

On the other hand, difficult parts of the agreement may become less attractive as time passes and dispute arise as to the agreed principles. In this event the mediator, with the consent of the parties, will often be given power to decide the precise meaning of the agreed principles in a way which is effectively binding on the parties.

The result of signature by the parties to a final written settlement agreement is that the agreement replaces the dispute in most cases. The only legal action which can then be brought is to enforce the terms of the written agreement. Alternatively, it can be expressly provided that the agreement will lapse if not fully complied with, so that the original dispute will revive. However, this latter approach leaves doubts as to whether the dispute is truly resolved, so that it can continue to colour the relationship between the parties, and can give rise to serious difficulties if lapse of the agreement occurs after partial compliance.

In cases where legal proceedings are in existence, it may be possible to make the main terms of the written agreement directly enforceable by the Court by incorporating them in a Court order terminating the proceedings.

7. Case Study

One of the benefits of the mediation process in commercial environmental disputes is that it is a strictly confidential. Accordingly, specific cases rarely become widely known outside the parties involved. However, the story of one case of a commercial environmental conflict which showed itself as classically suitable for resolution by way of mediation is available from the writer's personal involvement.

In the early 1990s a large US corporation purchased a manufacturing business in the UK, from a UK corporation which had other business interests and no longer wished to be involved in industrial manufacturing. UK environmental law was in a period of substantial change at the time, and it was clear to both the US and UK corporations that substantial expenditure would be required over a period of time to bring the relevant manufacturing plant into compliance with forthcoming environmental regulatory requirements. However, as those requirements were not yet formulated in any detail, the amount of such expenditure was impossible to estimate with any degree of certainty.

Accordingly, the UK corporation entered into an Environmental Indemnity Deed by which it agreed to indemnify the US corporation for all costs and expenses incurred by the US corporation, after purchase of the plant, in achieving compliance with environmental laws and regulations becoming applicable to the manufacturing business within a period of five years. This was at the insistence of the US corporation if the transaction was to proceed, but in the interests also of the UK corporation as the price paid for the manufacturing business was as a consequence largely unaffected by the unquantifiable and prospective expense of achieving compliance. The Deed was part of a series of complex agreements covering the purchase of the business.

When some years later the US corporation came to claim on the indemnity deed for the actual costs and expense of achieving compliance with what were by then firm regulatory requirements, disputes arose as to which environmental laws and regulations were covered by the indemnity deed, as to whether an appropriate technical route to achieving compliance had been selected, and as to the amount of costs and expenses incurred in achieving compliance. Discussions between the parties failed to resolve the issues. Litigation proceedings were commenced in the UK Courts by the US corporation to recover what was a significant sum of money. The documents produced in the Court proceedings demonstrated a fundamental difference between the parties as to the legal meaning of the indemnity deed.

However, it was to the advantage of both parties to settle the matter if possible, and so obviate the need for long drawn out and technically complex litigation. This allowed them to agree that the matter would be committed to mediation on an entirely confidential and "without prejudice" basis. A special mediation agreement to meet the circumstances was prepared, built up from the basic CEDR Model Mediation Agreement. Complex statements of facts and summaries of case were prepared by the lawyers and exchanged between the parties.

After three days of intensive mediation process, which involved opening statements, plenary sessions, caucuses, sessions between the parties' technical staff, the preparation of numerous schedules designed to narrow the issues, reality testing of the parties by the mediator, and careful consideration by the parties of their best alternative to a negotiated agreement (BATNA) prompted by the mediator, the parties assisted by their lawyers not only reached agreement on the amount to be paid under the indemnity deed in respect of the particular compliance costs subject to the ligation proceedings, but did so in the context of a global agreement settling also much wider compliance issues and costs which had held out the prospect of substantial future litigation. Both parties were pleased with this "win-win" outcome.

The basic principles of the settlement were recorded by the mediator and initialled by the parties before closure of the mediation session. The detailed agreement was drawn up subsequently by the lawyers to the parties and, although complex, without the need for any reference to the mediator on the principles agreed. Once complete and signed by the parties, the legal proceedings were formally discontinued by order of the Court.

8. Conclusion

Whilst it is clear that not all commercial environmental disputes are appropriate for resolution by process of mediation or facilitation, there are many that are. Mediation and facilitation techniques are sophisticated and powerful, and have been shown to be capable of helping the parties to resolve the complex situations which arise in the environmental arena, provided the parties come to the process fully prepared, in the right frame of mind, and with sufficient authority. These facts are now reflected in the rise in the number of such disputes being submitted to mediation process in the USA, and the growth of mediation in the UK.

ANNEXES

Annex 1 - Susskind Chapter

NORTHERN OXFORD COUNTY COALITION
Draft Ground Rules

I Mission and Goals

The Northern Oxford County Coalition has been established to improve the quality of life in the valley by protecting and promoting public health and enhancing air quality. The goals of the NOCC are:

1.   To bring together as many individuals and groups with a stake in air quality in the region as possible to work together in an open and collaborative manner;

2.   To document current levels of air quality and the state of public health in the valley;

3.   To inform and educate the members of the coalition, and then the public-at-large, about current and projected future air quality in the valley and its relationship to the public health of the residents of the valley;

4.   To identify, explore, and recommend specific actions that government and local stakeholders might take to reduce risks in the valley associated with current or expected air quality; and,

5.   To recommend monitoring strategies, if appropriate, to provide continuous information regarding the changing nature of air quality and public health in the valley.

6.   To improve the overall image of the valley through the actions above.

II Representation

The Northern Oxford County Coalition began meeting on February 2, 1994. At its April 4, 1995 meeting, participants discussed whether additional individuals or groups should be added to the NOCC. The Consensus Building Institute (CBI) offered to prepare a stakeholder analysis based on in-person and phone interviews with everyone who had attended a NOCC meeting as well as other people who NOCC participants recommended. The main purpose of the analysis was to identify the range of "stakeholder groups" with specific concerns about air quality in the valley, and to assess whether there was a need to add people to the NOCC to ensure that all stakeholder groups are fully represented.

Role of Alternates

Each of the eight stakeholder groups can select one or more alternates to participate in NOCC meetings when one of the representatives from that stakeholder group cannot attend. If a member is absent from a meeting, then the alternate for that stakeholder group will be invited to sit at the table and participate in the discussion. When alternates take a seat at the table, they should identify the member they are replacing.

Alternates will be on the NOCC mailing list and will receive copies of all meeting summaries, reports, handouts, and other documents necessary to keep them informed so that they will be ready to step in at any time. They are encouraged to attend all NOCC meetings in order to keep informed about the progress of the coalition's deliberations. Alternates can participate actively on all subcommittees.

V.   Role of Other Members of the Public

Meetings of the NOCC are open to the public. Interested citizens are invited and encouraged to attend. Observers will be seated separately from the members and alternates. They will be asked not to interrupt the discussion taking place at the table, unless there is time set aside for observers to offer their views on issues under discussion.

VI Communication and Decision Making

The purpose of the NOCC is to share information, discuss concerns and viewpoints, and build consensus. There will be no formal votes taken during NOCC meetings. Instead, members of the group will aim to reach agreements that meet the interests of all the participating stakeholder groups. Any consensus achieved on a specific issue will be tentative pending an agreement on all the issues being considered by the NOCC. A member's absence will be considered equivalent to not dissenting.

In order to facilitate an open and collaborative discussion, all members and alternates will be asked to follow the following rules:

  • Only one person will speak at a time, and no one will interrupt when another person is speaking.

  • Each person will express his or her own views rather than speaking for others at the table.

• No one will make personal attacks. · Each person will stay on track with the agenda.

• Each person will refrain from dominating the discussion, in order to ensure that everyone at the table has an opportunity to speak.

Pratt Ground Rules
December 20, 1996

If a person feels the group is not abiding by the groundrules, the person should notify the facilitators of his or her concern.

Members are expected to communicate concerns, interests and ideas openly and to make the reasons for their disagreements clear. In the event that a member is unable to speak about a concern directly to another member, he or she can contact the facilitators by phone (or in person). The facilitators will serve as a channel for these concerns. Upon request, all information or views shared during conversations with the facilitators will be kept confidential.

VII Role of Facilitators

Facilitation will be provided by Patrick Field and Sarah McKearnan of the Consensus Building Institute. Professor Lawrence Susskind will provide supplementary training and advice on the design of the workplan and any joint fact-finding process the NOCC decides to undertake. The facilitators will help to:

1) formulate the agenda for all meetings of the NOCC and its subcommittees, and facilitate discussion at full NOCC meetings;

2) summarize points of agreement and disagreement and communicate these to the NOCC in the form of written meeting summaries;

3) assist in building consensus among participants;

4) serve as a confidential communication channel for members, alternates or observers who wish to express views but do not feel comfortable addressing the full NOCC;

5) advocate for a fair process and remain nonpartisan with respect to the outcome of the NOCC's deliberations;

6) ensure compliance with all the above listed ground rules; and

7) draft summary reports, if appropriate, for review and approval by NOCC members.

The facilitation team can be reached at

Consensus Building Institute 131 Mount Auburn Street Cambridge, MA 02138 1-800- 433-3043

VIII. subcommittees

Ground Rules December 20, 1996 Page 4

Subcommittees will be established by the NOCC to engage in more in depth discussion on specific issues, to carry out tasks described in the work plan, and to perform administrative functions that are best left to a small subset of NOCC members. These subcommittees will meet between meetings of the full NOCC and will report back to coalition members about the results of their work.

Outreach

All meetings of the NOCC will be open to the media.

The facilitators will assist NOCC members in identifying ways of keeping residents of the towns of Rumford, Mexico, Peru and Dixfield informed about the NOCC's work. It may be possible to have meetings of the NOCC videotaped and later broadcast by a local cable channel. The facilitators will also distribute all meeting summaries and other documents prepared for coalition members to any members of the public who want to receive them. A database of such interested citizens will be maintained at CBI, and members of the NOCC are encouraged to add additional names to it at any time.

NOCC members and alternates are free to make statements to the press regarding their own concerns or reactions to NOCC meetings, but should at all times refrain from attributing statements or views to other NOCC members or to the facilitators. If a news story misquotes or inaccurately represents an individual's views, then that individual should inform the NOCC of this occurrence as soon as possible.

Regular press conferences will not be held, but the facilitators may periodically produce draft press releases to keep the media informed about the NOCC's work. These draft releases will be reviewed, initially, by all members of the NOCC within seven days of their distribution. At a later time, a designated subcommittee of NOCC members may be granted authority to approve press releases. All draft meeting summaries can be distributed to the public without the approval of the NOCC.

Meeting Summaries

The facilitation team will prepare a summary of each meeting. The summary will include the key points covered in the discussion, as well as areas of agreement and disagreement described without attribution. A draft version will be sent to NOCC members and alternates after each NOCC meeting. Approval of the summary will occur at the following meeting, after the facilitators take note of any proposed additions, corrections, or clarifications. If substantial changes are made, a revised version will be sent to members and alternates, as well as any observers who wish to receive it.

Attendance will be kept at each meeting, and a roster of the those in attendance will be mailed out with each meeting summary.

Draft Ground Rules
December 20, 1996 Page 5

Revised Groundrules for the Northern Oxford County Coalition

(1) Listen when someone else is speaking in order to encourage respect among all members.

(2) Give others a chance to express their views. (3) Describe your own views rather than the views of others.

(4) Encourage discussion, not speeches.

(5) Speak to the point, not the person. (6) Stay on track with the agenda.

(7) Members should signal a "time out" if they think other members are not following the ,groundrules. When a timeout is signaled, the facilitators will ask the group if the groundrules have or haven't been followed.

(8) When necessary, the facilitators will use an egg timer to limit individual comments to a reasonable time period. (9) Facilitators will play an active role in enforcing the groundrules. (10) There will be a "disagreement list" to post outstanding issues and disagreements.

Draft Ground Rules for the Coastal Zone Act Regulation Negotiating Committee

Purpose

The purpose of the Coastal Zone consensus-based negotiation process is to build agreement among all the stakeholding groups regarding regulations for implementing the Coastal Zone Act, 7 Delaware Code, Chapter 7. The process shall provide the Secretary of the Department of Natural Resources and Environmental Control clear and detailed guidance to assist the Secretary in proposing effective and long-lasting regulations to the Coastal Zone industrial Control Board. While the process will be advisory, it is the stated intent of the Secretary to adhere to the intent of the guidance in proposing regulations if consensus is reached.

Representation

A. Selection

Members and alternates of the Coastal Zone Act Regulation Negotiating Committee are appointed by the Governor. The membership is as follows:

[to be determined]

Upon convening of the first full meeting of this Committee, the members will consider whether essential stakeholders are missing and if so, may nominate additional members.

B. Role of Members

Members are expected to fully participate in all meetings of the Committee and to articulate their views and the views of their constituencies. They are also expected to keep constituencies informed about the deliberations and to actively seek their input. To this end, members should make an effort to stay in contact with all relevant individuals and groups with regard to the subject and the results of each meeting.

C. Role of Alternates

If a member is unable to attend a Committee meeting, then the member's designated alternate will sit at the table and participate in the discussion.

To the extent that time permits, alternates may be able to address the group on a particular issue under discussion. If any working ~oups are formed, alternates may participate fully in the discussions.

Delaware Coastal Zone Act Conflict Assessment: Attachment B December 18, 1996 Page 57

Alternates will be on the mailing list and will receive copies of all meeting summaries, reports, handouts, and other documents necessary to keep informed of the process so that they will be ready at any time to participate. They are encouraged to attend all meetings in order to keep informed about the progress of the consensus group's deliberations.

D. Role of Advisors

Members and alternates may actively seek out the support and input of advisors who can aid them in expressing their concerns and interests and provide members the information necessary to make decisions. Advisors will not be allowed to speak for members or alternates at the table. However, they may confer with members by speaking to them away from the table during negotiations, at breaks, or when members call for caucuses with their advisors and/or constituents during the deliberations.

E. Role of Other Members of the Public

Meetings are open to the public, and interested citizens are invited and encouraged to attend for the purposes of observing and listening to the proceedings. Observers will be seated separately from the members, away from the negotiating table. They will not be permitted to interrupt the discussion taking place at the table.

At designated times during meetings, members of the public will be invited to address the committee.

Primary Responsibilities of Members and Alternates

Members and alternates agree to:

1)   Attend all of the regularly scheduled meetings;

2)   Arrive at each meeting fully prepared to discuss the issues on the agenda. Preparation will include reviewing meeting summaries, technical information, and drafts of single text draft documents distributed in advance of each meeting;

3)   Present their own views and the views of the members of their constituents on the issues being discussed and will be willing to engage in respectful constructive dialogue with other members of the group.;

4)   Strive throughout the process to bridge gaps in understanding, to seek creative resolution of differences, and to commit to the goal of achieving consensus on the contents of the regulations under discussion.

Delaware Coastal Zone Act Conflict Assessment: Attachment B December 18, 1996 Page 58

IV.   Decision Making

The purpose of the process is to share information, discuss concerns and viewpoints, and build consensus. The group will operate by consensus, and every effort will be made to meet the interests of all the participating stakeholder groups.

A. Definition of Consensus

Consensus means that there is no dissent by any member. There will be no formal votes taken during deliberations. No one member can be outvoted. Members should not block or withhold consensus unless they have serious reservations with the approach or solution that is proposed for consensus. If members disagree with the approach or solution selected by the rest of the group, they should make every effort to offer an alternative satisfactory to all stakeholders.

Members should remain at the table during deliberations to hear the full discussions in order to make informed judgments when decision-making occurs. Absence will be equivalent to not consenting. Any consensus achieved on a specific issue will be tentative pending an agreement on all the issues being considered by the group.

B. Interaction with the Secretary of DNREC

The goal of the process is to develop a written set of guidelines to clearly inform the the Secretary who must promulgate a set of regulations under the Coastal Zone Act. Upon receipt of a consensus set of guidelines, the Secretary will draft the regulations. The draft regulations will be circulated to committee members for a review for consistency with the guidance.

C. Dispute Resolution Mechanism

If any member, after conferring with their constituency, believes that any portion of the re~7ulations has not met the intent of the consensus guidelines, the member shall contact the facilitators. Subsequently, the facilitators will assist the Secretary and the committee members in an effort to resolve whatever differences have emerged. If a satisfactory solution cannot be achieved through informal discussion, then members may call for the reconvening of the process.

As needed, the facilitators will reconvene a single meeting of the consensus-based negotiation group within six weeks of the issuance of the draft regulations. All members will work with the Secretary at this meeting to resolve any and all outstanding issues.

Upon acceptance of the draft regulations, or upon completion of this dispute resolution meeting (if necessary), the Secretary will forward the draft regulations to the Coastal Zone Industrial Control Board to initiate formal promulgation process as required by law.

D. Support for the Consensual Agreement

If the process generates a consensus on the guidelines, members agree to support and advocate for the agreement within their own organisations and stakeholder groups as well as with the public. If consensus is reached, members agree to refrain from commenting negatively on the agreement.

To the extent that the process does not reach a final consensus on some or all issues, members shall retain the right to comment negatively on those aspects of the agreement that are not based on a final consensus.

Communication

Participation in discussions will be restricted to the members seated at the table, unless the facilitator sets aside time on the agenda for others to speak. In order to facilitate an open and collaborative discussion, all those seated at the table will seek to abide by the following rules:

Only one person will speak at a time and no one will interrupt when another person is speaking;

2)   Each person will express his or her own views rather than speaking for others at the table;

3)   No one will make personal attacks or issue statements blaming others for specific actions or outcomes;

4)   Each person will make every effort to stay on track with the agenda and avoid, grandstanding and digressions in order to move the deliberations forward.

5)   Each person will strive to maintain a sense of humor, listen well, and be open minded.

Members are expected to communicate concerns, interests and ideas openly and to make the reasons for their disagreements clear. In the event that a member is unable to speak about a concern directly to another member, he or she can contact the facilitators by phone (or in person). The facilitators will serve as a channel for such concerns. Upon request, all information or views shared during conversations with the facilitators will be kept confidential.

Role of Facilitators

Facilitation will be provided by the Consensus Building Institute under the lead of Gregory Sobel, Esq. The members of the facilitation team will:

Delaware Coastal Zone Act Conflict Assessment: Attachment B December 18, 1996 Page 60 formulate the agenda for all meetings and facilitate these proceedings;

2)   conduct or coordinate any joint fact-finding required;

3)   identify and synthesize points of agreement and disagreement and communicate these in the form, of written meeting summaries (see below for further detail);

4)   prepare single text drafts of proposals between meetings to serve as a basis for deliberations;

5)   assist in building consensus among members;

6)   ensure compliance with all the ground rules

7)   serve as a confidential communication channel for members, alternates or observers who wish to express views but do not feel comfortable addressing the full group;

8)   advocate for a fair , effective, and credible process, but remain utterly nonpartisan with respect to the outcome of the deliberations;

9)   communicate the results of the process to the Governor and the Secretary of the Department of Natural Resources and Environmental Control; and,

10)   facilitate discussions between members and the Secretary, and/or the full group, if necessary, to resolve disagreements over the Secretary's draft of the regulations.

The facilitation team will prepare a summary of each meeting. The summary will include the key points of discussion as well as items of agreement and disagreement described without attribution. A draft version will be sent to members and alternates after each meeting. Approval of the summary will occur at the following meeting, after the facilitators take note of any proposed additions, corrections, or clarifications. If substantial changes are made, a revised version will be sent to members and alternates, as well as any observers who wish to receive it. Attendance will be kept at each meeting, and a roster of the those in attendance will be mailed out with each meeting summary.

The facilitation team can be reached at the Consensus Building Institute, 1-800-4333043.

VIL Working Groups

Working groups may be established to undertake more in-depth discussion or carry out discrete tasks. These working groups will meet between meetings of the full group and would report back on the results of their discussions when asked to do so. The representation, roles, and responsibilities of the members of working groups will be determined by the full membership.

VIII. Media

All meetings will be open to the public and the media. Press conferences will not be held in conjunction with these meetings. However, the facilitators may periodically produce press releases, for approval by the members, to keep the media informed of the ongoing deliberations.

Members and alternates are free to make statements to the press regarding their own opinions, but agree to not attribute statements to others involved in the process. No member or alternate should presuppose to speak for the group as a whole. In order to facilitate productive deliberations, members and alternates will make every effort to abide by the ground rules under the section "Communication" listed above while interacting with the media.

If an article or report appears that misquotes or inaccurately represents an individual, that individual should inform the group of that occurrence as soon as possible.

MMR IRP Citizen Team Groundrules

I. Responsibilities of Team Members

Members agree to:

1)   Attend all of the regularly scheduled meetings. Members will notify the chair or facilitator if they cannot attend.

2)   Arrive at each meeting fully prepared to discuss the issues on the agenda. Preparation will include reviewing meeting summaries, technical information, and drafts of single text draft documents distributed in advance of each meeting;

3)   Present their own views and the views of the members of their constituents on the issues being discussed and be willing to engage in respectful, constructive dialogue with other members of the group and report back to their constituents;

4)   Strive throughout the process to bridge gaps in understanding, to seek creative resolution of differences, and to commit to the goal of achieving consensus on topics under discussion.

In order to assure that team members are meeting their responsibilities, the Installation Restoration Program's (IRP) meeting support contractor will track meeting attendance and the Senior Management Board will review these attendance lists annually.

IL   Communication among Team Members

In order to facilitate an open and collaborative discussion, team members will seek to abide by the following rules:

Only one person will speak at a time and no one will interrupt when another person is speaking;

2)   Each person will express his or her own views rather than speaking for others at the table;

No one will make personal attacks or issue statements blaming others for specific actions or outcomes;

4)   Each person will make every effort to stay on track with the agenda and avoid grandstanding and digressions in order to move the deliberations forward;

5)   Each person will strive to maintain a sense of humor, listen well, and be open minded; and,

Teams will provide opportunities for the general public's questions and comments; each team may decide where best to provide these opportunities for the public on the team's meeting agenda.

Members are expected to communicate concerns, interests and ideas openly and to make the reasons for their disagreements clear. In the event that a member is unable to speak about a concern directly to another member, he or she can contact the facilitators by phone (or in person). The facilitators will serve as a channel for such concerns. Upon request, all information or views shared during conversations with the facilitators will be kept confidential.

III. Team Decisionmaking

The purpose of each team is to share information, discuss concerns and viewpoints, and build consensus around advice and recommendations to the Installation Restoration Program's (IRP) Remedial Program Managers (RPMs). The team will operate by consensus, and every effort will be made to meet the interests of all team members.

A. Definition of Consensus

Consensus means that there is no dissent by any member. There will be no formal votes taken during deliberations. No one member can be outvoted. Members should not block or withhold consensus unless they have serious reservations with the approach or solution that is proposed for consensus. If members disagree with the approach or solution selected by the rest of the group, they should make every effort to offer an alternative satisfactory to all stakeholders.

Members should remain at the table during deliberations to hear the full discussions in order to make informed judgments when decision-making occurs. Absence will be equivalent to not dissenting.

If all efforts have been made to arrive at consensus, but it appears that the group will not be able to achieve it, the group may choose to vote in order to come to agreement, resolve the issue, and maintain progress in their deliberations, regarding their recommendations.

D. Support for Consensual Agreements

If a meeting or meetings generates a consensus on specific issues and/or recommendations, members agree to support and advocate for the agreement within their own organizations and stakeholder groups as well as with the Public. If consensus is reached, members agree to refrain from commenting negatively on the agreement.

To the extent that the process does not reach a final consensus on some or all issues, members shall retain the right to comment negatively on those aspects of the agreement that are not based on a final consensus.

Role of Chairs and Go-Chairs When the team uses Chairs or Go-Chairs, the Chair(s) will:
1) assist in formulating the agendas;
2) facilitate the meetings or assist the facilitator in facilitating meetings;
3) ensure compliance with all the ground rules;
4) identify and synthesize points of agreement and disagreement. The IRP's meeting support contractor will track action items and future agenda items;
5) assist in building consensus among members;
6) maintain a meeting schedule and ensure that meetings are held on an agreed upon frequency; and,
7) appoint a citizen chair or co-chair to represent the team to the SMB.

V. Role of Facilitators

When the team uses facilitation, the facilitator(s) will:
1) assist in formulating the agendas;
2) facilitate these meetings;
3) ensure compliance with all the ground rules;
4) identify and synthesize points of agreement and disagreement. The IRP's meeting support contractor will track action items and future agenda items;
5) assist in building consensus among members;
6) serve as a confidential communication channel for members or observers who wish to express views but do not feel comfortable addressing the full group; and,
7) advocate for a fair, effective, and credible process, but remain utterly nonpartisan with respect to the outcome of the deliberations.

VI. Media

All meetings will be open to the public and the media. Members are free to make statements to the press regarding their own opinions, but agree to not attribute statements to others involved in the process. No member should presuppose to speak for the group as a whole. In order to facilitate productive deliberations, members will make every effort to abide by the ground rules under the section "Communication" listed above while interacting with the media.

If an article or report appears that misquotes or inaccurately represents an individual, that individual should inform the group of that occurrence as soon as possible so that it may be discussed.

Annex 2 - Wiedner Chapter

LOCCUMER CODE FOR GOOD PRACTICE IN ENVIRONMENTAL CONFLICT RESOLUTION IN GERMANY

Initial Comments

We want approaches to solutions of environmental conflicts in Germany to be developed and implemented creatively. We believe that in addition to creativity, ethical principles must be at the basis of a good practice. We believe that for this purpose it is possible to find a common basis for the future. We wish that the attached draft prepared on the basis of a discussion in Loccum meets with the approval of a maximum number of mediators in Germany.

Preparation of Procedure

1.   A mediator ensures that a problem and conflict analysis is carried out highlighting positions, preferences and interests for all participants.
2.   On the basis of the conflict analysis the mediator endeavours to take into account all fundamental interests into the mediation process.
3.   The mediator commences the procedure only after considering his own expertise and possible limits to his neutrality.
4.   The mediator only initiates the procedure when, on the basis of the problem, there is opportunity for decision and the balancing out of interests is feasible.
5.   All participants take part in the process towards finding a consensus and achieving the goals set by the mediation. They decide what alternatives are available.
6.   The participants agree at the beginning common ground rules to help them in achieving their goals. The ground rules are laid dawn in writing.
7.   At the beginning the participants prepare a list of issues or tasks to be dealt with. In addition, it can also be sensible to set limits to the mediation process (for example time limits, irrevocable decisions and conditions).

When the participants agree derogations to these guidelines and the mediator assumes responsibility for such derogations he is under a duty to disclose the particular reasons for such derogation.

The Mediator

9.   The participants expressly select the person to take the role of mediator for the team.

10.   The mediator has no interests in the final result apart from the mediation itself. He discloses his own values.

11.   The mediator respects the participants and their emotions.

Completion of Process

12.   The mediator is responsible for ensuring that all participants have the opportunity to have a say in the agenda and the issues to be discussed.

13.   The mediator is responsible for ensuring that all participants have the opportunity to express their position, preferences and interests.

14.   The mediator is responsible for ensuring that participants have access to the necessary information. He ensures that information is distributed evenly.

15.   The mediator is responsible for ensuring that the procedure and results are transparent to the outside and that consensus, disagreements and recommendations are identified. The results of the procedure to be documented.

Dealings after the Procedure

16.   The participants discuss responsibilities, steps and a time plan to put into effect the results. The result is to be documented in writing.

17.   At the end of the procedure the participants are asked about their views on the procedure and the results. The responses are part of the documentation dealing with the results of mediation.

Loccum, 12 December 1995

Loccumer Kodex f ür eine gute Praxis bei Verfahren zur alternativen L ösung von Umweltkonflikten

Vorbemerkung

Wir wollen, daß Verfahren zur Lösung von Umweltkonflikten in Deutschland kreativ entwickelt und umgesetzt werden können.

Wir meinen, daß einer guten Praxis neben aller Kreativität auch ethische Prinzipien zugrunde liegen müssen.

Wir glauben, daß es möglich ist ,dafür eine gemeinsame Grundlage für die Zukunft zu finden.

Wir wünschenr uns, daß der folgende Entwurf nach einer Diskussion in Loccum bei mölichst vielen aktiven Mittlern in Deutschland Zustimmung findet und unterzeichnet wird.

Vorbereitung von Verfahren

1. Der Mittler sorgt für eine Problem-und Konfliktanalyse, die Positionen , Präferenzen und Interessen für alle Beteiligte transparent macht.

2. Auf der Basis der Konfliktanalyse bemüht sich der Mittler um die Einbeziehung aller wesentlichen Interessen in das Verfahren.

3. Der Mittler beginnt das Verfahren nur nach einer Selbstreflexion seiner Fachkenntnisse und evetuellen Grenzen seiner Allparteilichkeit.

4. Der Mittler beginnt das Verfahren nur dann, wenn im Hinblick auf das zugrundeliegende Problem ein Entscheidungsspielraum besteht , und ein Ausgleich der Interessen möglich erscheint.

5. Der Konsensfindungsprozeß und die Ziele des Prozesses werden von allen Beteiligten mitgetragen. Sie klären, welche Alternativen zu diesem Prozeß bestehen.

6. Die Beteiigten vereinbaren zu Beginn gemeinsame Verfahrensregeln, die Ihnen bei der Erreichung der Ziele helfen. Die Regeln werden schriftlich fixiert.

7. Die Beteiligten des Verfahrens entwickeln zu Beginn einen Katalog der zu verhandelnden Themen oder Aufgaben. Dazu kann es sinnvoll sein, auch Grenzen

des Verfahrens (z.B zeitliche Grenzen ,unumstößliche Entscheidungen und Bedingungen) zu benennen.

8. Wenn die Beteiligten Abweichungen von diesen Grundsätzen vereinbaren und der Mittler dies mitträgt, hat er die Pflicht, die besonderen Beweggründe hierfür offenzulegen.

Zum Mittler

9. Die Beteiligten des Verfahrens stimmen ausdrücklich der als Mittler tätigen Person (oder dem Team) zu.

10. Der Mittler hat keine Interessen am Verfahrensausgang außer oder Mitteilung selbst.

11. Der Mittler respektiert die beteiligten Personen und ihre Gefühle.

Drchführung von Verfahren

12. Der Mittler trägt dafür Sorge, daß alle Beteiligten die Möglichkeit haben, Einfluß auf die Tagesordnung und die zu verhandelnden Themen auszuüben.

13. Der Mittler trägt dafür Sorge, daß alle Beteiligten die Möglilchkeit haben , ihre Positionen, Präferenzen und Interessen darzulegen.

14. Der Mittler trägt dafür Sorge,daß Beteiligten Zugang zu den notwendigen Informationen erhalten. Er bemüht sich um den Ausgleich von Informationsdefiziten.

15. Der Mittler trägt dafür Sorgen, daß Verlauf und Ergebnisse des Verfahrens auch nach außen transparent werden und daß Konsense, Dissense und Empfehlungen festgestellt werden. Die Ergebnisse des Verfahrens werden dokumentiert.

Nachbereitung von Verfahren

16. Die Beteiligten klären Verantwortlichkeiten, Maßnahmen und Zeitplan zur Umsetzung der Ergebnisse. Das Ergebnis wird schriftlich dokumentiert.

Annex 3

CENTRE FOR DISPUTE RESOLUTION
MODEL MEDIATION PROCEDURE

Mediation Procedure

1. The Parties to the Dispute or negotiation in question will attempt to settle it by mediation. Representatives of the Parties [and their Advisers] and the Mediator[s] will attend [a] Mediation meetings[s]. All communications relating to, and at, the Mediation will be without prejudice.

2. The Representatives must have the necessary authority to settle the Dispute. The procedure at the Mediation will be determined by the Mediator, after consultation with the Representatives.

Mediation Agreement

3. The Parties, the Mediator and CEDR will enter into an agreement ("Mediation Agreement") based on the CEDR Model Mediation Agreement ("the Model Agreement") in relation to the conduct of the Mediation.

The Mediator

4. The Mediator will:

• attend any meetings with any or all of the Parties preceding the Mediation, if requested or if the Mediator decides this is appropriate;

• read before the Mediation each Summary and all the Documents sent to him/her in accordance with paragraph 9;

• determine the procedure (see paragraph 2 above);

• assist the parties in drawing up any written settlement agreement;

• abide by the terms of the Model Procedure, the Mediation Agreement and CEDR's Code of Conduct.

5. The Mediator [and any member of the Mediator's firm or company] will not act for any of the Parties individually in connection with the Dispute in any capacity either during the currency of this agreement or at any time thereafter.

The Parties accept that in relation to the Dispute neither the Mediator nor CEDR is an agent of, or acting in any capacity for, any of the Parties. The Parties and the Mediator accept that the Mediator (unless an employee of CEDR) is acting as an independent contractor and not as agent or employee of CEDR.

CEDR

6. CEDR, in conjunction with the Mediator, will make the necessary arrangements for the Mediation including, as necessary:

• assisting the Parties in appointing the Mediator and in drawing up the Mediation Agreement;

• organising a suitable venue and dates;

• organising exchange of the Summaries and Documents;

• meeting with any or all of the Representatives (and the Mediator if he/she has been appointed) either together or separately, to discuss any matters or concerns relating to the Mediation;

• general administration in relation to the Mediation.

7. If a dispute is referred to CEDR as a result of a mediation (or other ADR) clause in a contract, and if there is any issue with regard to the conduct of the Mediation (including as to the appointment of the Mediator) upon which the Parties cannot agree within a reasonable time from the date of the notice initiating the Mediation ("the ADR notice") CEDR will, at the request of any Party, decide the issue for the Parties, having consulted with them.

Other participants

8.   Each Party will notify the other party[ies], through CEDR, of the names of those people (the Adviser[s], witnesses etc - in addition to the Representatives) that it intends will be present on its behalf at the Mediation. Each Party, in signing the Mediation Agreement, will be deemed to be agreeing on behalf of both itself and all such persons to be bound by the confidentiality provisions of this Model Procedure.

Exchange of information

9. Each Party will, simultaneously through CEDR, exchange with the other

and send to the Mediator at least two weeks before the Mediation or such other date as may be agreed between the Parties:

• a concise summary ("the Summary") stating its case in the Dispute;

• copies of all the documents to which it refers in the Summary and to which it may want to refer in the Mediation ("the Documents").

In addition, each Party may send to the Mediator (through CEDR) and/or bring to the Mediation further documentation which it wishes to disclose in confidence to the Mediator but not to any other Party, clearly stating in writing that such documentation is confidential to the Mediator and CEDR.

10. The Parties will, through CEDR, agree the maximum number of pages of each Summary and of the Documents and try to agree a joint set of documents from their respective Documents.

The Mediation

11. No formal record or transcript of the Mediation will be made.

12. If the Parties are unable to reach a settlement in the negotiations at the Mediation and only if all the Representatives so request and the Mediator agrees, the Mediator will produce for the Parties a non-binding written recommendation on terms of settlement. This will not attempt to anticipate what a court might order but will set out what the Mediator suggests are appropriate settlement terms in all of the circumstances.

Settlement agreement

13. Any settlement reached in the Mediation will not be legally binding until it has been reduced to writing and signed by, or on behalf of, the Parties.

Termination

14.   Any of the Parties may withdraw from the Mediation at any time and shall immediately inform the Mediator and the other Representatives in writing. The Mediation will terminate when:

• a Party withdraws from the Mediation; or

• a written settlement agreement is concluded; or

• the Mediator decides that continuing the Mediation is unlikely to result in a settlement; or

• the Mediator decides he should retire for any of the reasons in the Code of Conduct.

Stay of proceedings

15. Any litigation or arbitration in relation to the Dispute may be commenced or continued notwithstanding the Mediation unless the Parties agree otherwise.

Confidentiality etc

16. Every person involved in the Mediation will keep confidential and not use for any collateral or ulterior purpose:

• the fact that the Mediation is to take place or has taken place; and

• all information, (whether given orally, in writing or otherwise), produced for, or arising in relation to, the Mediation including the settlement agreement (if any) arising out of it

except insofar as is necessary to implement and enforce any such settlement agreement.

17. All documents (which includes anything upon which evidence is recorded including tapes and computer discs) or other information produced for, or arising in relation to, the Mediation will be privileged and not be admissible as evidence or discoverable in any litigation or arbitration connected with the Dispute except any documents or other information which would in any event have been admissible or discoverable in any such litigation or arbitration.

18. None of the parties to the Mediation Agreement will call the Mediator or CEDR (or any employee, consultant, officer or representative of CEDR) as a witness, consultant, arbitrator or expert in any litigation or arbitration in relation to the Dispute and the Mediator and CEDR will not voluntarily act in any such capacity without the written agreement of all the Parties.

Fees, expenses and costs

19. CEDR's fees (which include the Mediator's fees) and the other expenses of the Mediation will be borne equally by the Parties. Payment of these fees and expenses will be made to CEDR in accordance with its fee schedule and terms and conditions of business.

20. Each Party will bear its own costs and expenses of its participation in the Mediation.

Waiver of liability

21. Neither the Mediator nor CEDR shall be liable to the Parties for any act or omission in connection with the services provided by them in, or in relation to, the Mediation, unless the act or omission is fraudulent or involves wilful misconduct.

GUIDANCE NOTES

The paragraph numbers and headings in these notes refer to the paragraphs and headings in the Model Procedure

Text in the Model Procedure in square brackets may be inappropriate and therefore inapplicable in some cases.

Introduction

The essence of mediation (and many other ADR procedures) is that:

• it involves a neutral third party to facilitate negotiations;

• it is quick, inexpensive and confidential;

• it enables the parties to reach results which are not possible in an adjudicative process such as litigation or arbitration and may be to the benefit of both parties, particularly if there is a continuing business relationship;

• it involves representatives of the parties who have sufficient authority to settle. In some cases, there may be an advantage in the representatives being people who have not been directly involved in the events leading up to the dispute and in the subsequent dispute.

The procedure for the mediation is flexible and this model procedure can be adapted (with or without the assistance of CEDR) to suit the parties.

A mediation, can be used:

• in both domestic and international disputes;

• whether or not litigation or arbitration has been commenced; and

• in two party and multi-party disputes.

Rules or rigid procedures in the context of a consensual and process which is the essence of ADR are generally inappropriate. The Model Procedure and the Model Agreement and these guidance notes should be sufficient to enable parties to conduct a mediation.

In some cases the agreement to conduct a mediation will be as a result of an "ADR clause" (such as one of the CEDR Model ADR clauses) to that effect in an underlying commercial agreement between the Parties. Where that is the case the Model Procedure and Mediation Agreement may need to be adapted accordingly.

The Model Agreement, which has been kept as short and simple as possible, incorporates the Model Procedure (see para. 3). The Mediation Agreement can include amendments to the Model Procedure; the amendments can be set out in the body of the Mediation Agreement or the Mediation Agreement can state that amendments made in manuscript (or otherwise) to the Model Procedure and initialled by the Parties, are to be incorporated into the Mediation Agreement.

Mediation Procedure, paras 1 and 2

The Advisers can and usually do attend the Mediation. Although a lead role in the Mediation is often taken by the Representatives, the Advisers can play an important role in the exchange of information, in advising their clients on the legal implications of a settlement and in drawing up the settlement agreement. However, the commercial interests of the Parties will normally take the negotiations beyond strict legal issues, hence the importance of the role of the Representatives.

It is essential that the Representatives are sufficiently senior and have the authority of their respective Parties to settle the Dispute.

Mediation Agreement - para 3

If CEDR is asked to do so by a party wishing to initiate a mediation, it will approach the other party(ies) to a dispute to seek to persuade it/them to participate.

Ideally the Representatives, the Advisers (and the Mediator if he/she has been identified) and CEDR (or whatever other ADR body is involved, if any) should meet to discuss and finalise the terms of the Mediation Agreement.

Alternatively, the party who has taken the initiative in proposing the Mediation may wish to send a draft agreement based on the CEDR Model Mediation Agreement to the other party(ies).

The Mediator - paras 4-5

The success of the Mediation will, to a large extent, depend on the skill of the Mediator. CEDR believes it is very important for the Mediator to have had specific training and experience. CEDR has its own body of trained and experienced mediators and can assist the Parties in identifying a suitable mediator.

In some cases it may be useful to have more than one Mediator, or to have an independent expert who can advise the Mediator on technical issues ("the Mediator's Adviser"). All should sign the Mediation Agreement which should be amended as appropriate.

It is CEDR's practice, as part of its mediator training programme, to have a pupil mediator ("the Pupil Mediator") attend most mediations. The Pupil Mediator signs the Mediation Agreement and falls within the definition "the Mediator" in the Model Procedure and the Mediation Agreement.

It is advisable, but not essential, to involve the Mediator in any preliminary meeting between the Parties.

CEDR, paras 6-7

The Code of Conduct covers such points as the Mediator's duty of confidentiality, impartiality and avoiding conflicts of interest.

The Model Procedure envisages the involvement of CEDR because in most cases this is likely to benefit the Parties and generally to facilitate the setting up and conduct of the Mediation. Its involvement, however, is not essential and this Model Procedure can be amended if CEDR is not to be involved.

Exchange of information - paras 9 - 10

Documentation which a Party wants the Mediator to keep confidential from the other Party(ies) (e.g. a counsel's opinion, an expert report not yet exchanged) must be clearly marked as such. It can be disclosed by the Party before or during the Mediation. It will not be disclosed by the Mediator or CEDR without the express consent of the Party.

One of the advantages of ADR is that it can avoid the excessive discovery process (including witness statements) which often blights litigation and arbitration. The Documents should be kept to the minimum necessary to give the Mediator a good grasp of the issues. The Summaries should be similarly brief.

The Mediation - paras 11 - 12

The intention of paragraph 12 is that the Mediator will cease to play an entirely facilitative role only if the negotiations in the Mediation are deadlocked. Giving a settlement recommendation may be perceived by a Party as undermining the Mediator's neutrality and for this reason the Mediator may not agree to this course of action. Any recommendation will be without prejudice and will not be binding.

Settlement agreement - para 13

If no agreement is reached, it is nonetheless open to the Parties to adjourn the Mediation to another time and place. Experience shows that even where no agreement is reached during mediation itself, the Parties will often reach a settlement shortly after, as a result of progress made during that mediation.

Stay of proceedings - para 15

Although a stay may engender a better climate for settlement it is not however essential that any proceedings relating to the Dispute should be stayed. If they are stayed, the effect on limitation periods needs to be agreed. Although under English law the parties can agree to limitation periods not running the position may differ in other jurisdictions and the position on this should be checked.

Confidentiality - paras 16-18

The CEDR Code of Conduct provides that the Mediator is not to disclose to any other Party any information given to him by a Party in confidence without the express consent of that Party.

In any related litigation in England and Wales such documents (see paragraph 16) should in any event be inadmissible and privileged as "without prejudice" documents since they will have been produced in relation to negotiations to settle the dispute. Documents which pre-existed the Mediation and would in any event have been discoverable will, however, not become privileged by reason of having been referred to in the Mediation and will therefore still be discoverable. The position may differ in other jurisdictions and should be checked.

Fees, expenses and costs - paras 19-20

The usual arrangement is for the Parties to share equally the fees and expenses of the procedure, but other arrangements are possible. A party to a dispute which is reluctant to participate in a mediation may be persuaded to participate if the other party(ies) agree to bear that party's share of the mediation fees.

International disputes - Language and governing law/jurisdiction

The Model Agreement is designed for domestic disputes but can be easily adapted for international cross-border disputes by the addition of the following paragraphs:

"Language
The language of the Mediation will be... Any Party producing documents or participating in the Mediation in any other language will provide the necessary translations and interpretation facilities."

"Governing Law and Jurisdiction
The Mediation Agreement shall be governed by, construed and take effect in accordance with [English] law.

The courts Of [England] shall have exclusive jurisdiction to settle any claim, dispute or matter of difference which may arise out of or in connection with the Mediation."

Where the law is not English or the jurisdiction not England the Mediation Agreement may need to be amended to ensure the structure, rights and obligations necessary for a mediation are applicable.

Annex 4

MEDIATION

REVISION HISTORY

1987 CPR published Model ADR Procedures: Mediation of Business Disputes.
1994 Revised and published as Mediation Procedure for Business Disputes.
1995 Amendment of paragraph 2, p. I-17, requiring use of CPR Panels of Neutrals unless otherwise agreed.
1998 Revised and effective as of April 1, 1998.

CPR Advisory Committee
These individuals advised CPR on the 1998 revision of the CPR Mediation Procedure.

Tom Arnold
Arnold, White & Durkee, P.C.

John G. Bickerman
Bickerman Dispute Resolution Group

Frederick K. Conover II
Faegre & Benson

Prof. Dwight Golann
Suffolk University Law School

Prof. Stephen B. Goldberg
Northwestern University School of Law

J. MICHAEL KEATING, JR.
Little Bulman & Reardon

Hon. Thomas A. Masterson
Thomas A. Masterson & Associates, P.C.

Harry N. Mazadoorian
Assistant General Counsel
CIGNA Corporation

Hon. Frank J. McGarr
Foley & Lardner

PROF. CARRIE MENKEL-MEADOW
Georgetown University Law Center

David W. Plant
Fish & Neave

Margaret L. Shaw
Wittenberg, Shaw & Ross

Linda R. Singer
Lichtman, Trister, Singer & Ross

Hon. Sidney O. Smith Jr.
Alston & Bird

Hon. John J. Upchurch
Upchurch Watson White & Fraxedas

Hon. John L. Wagner
Irell & Manella

CPR Staff Director
Peter H. Kaskell
Vice President
Introduction

The most widely used ADR process, mediation is a process in which a third party neutral—a mediator—sits down with the disputing parties and actively assists them in reaching a settlement.

Mediation should not be confused with binding arbitration or private adjudication. The mediation process is non-binding, although a settlement agreement resulting from a mediation usually is binding. The mediator has no authority to make any binding decisions or impose a resolution. The role of the mediator—and the goal of the process—is to help parties achieve their own resolution.

Mediation is private and generally confidential. It is highly flexible and informal. Typically, it is concluded expeditiously at moderate cost. The subject matter can be complex or simple, the stakes large or small, the number of parties few or many. An exchange of information commonly occurs in a mediation, and limited discovery also is possible. All parties can participate in tailoring the ground rules. The process typically is far less adversarial than litigation or arbitration, and therefore less disruptive of business relationships. Since other options are not foreclosed if mediation should fail, entering into a mediation process presents few risks.

In fact, in voluntary mediation failure is the exception. Time and again, with the assistance of a skillful mediator, parties to a great variety of business disputes and other types of disputes have succeeded in bridging wide gaps in their positions and in developing creative, mutually-advantageous solutions. The principal pre-condition to successful mediation is that the parties share a genuine desire to resolve the dispute promptly in an equitable manner.

Not all cases lend themselves to creative solutions. However, even when the amount of money damages is the principal issue, the non-partisan perspective of a trusted mediator can prove very helpful in bringing about a settlement. When the client has unrealistic expectations, of which the lawyer is reluctant to disabuse him, the mediator's views can be critical in breaking an impasse in negotiations.

There are different styles of mediation, e.g., "facilitative mediation" and "evaluative mediation," that are discussed in this paper. With all styles, the dynamics of the negotiations usually change markedly with the addition of the neutral mediator. Mediation enables parties to communicate perceptions, feelings and information directly to one another in a safe, controlled environment managed by the mediator. The mediator helps to build a cooperative, problem solving atmosphere. This manner of communication often reduces hostility and facilitates rational discussion. Mediation gives the parties a sense of ownership both in the dispute and in its resolution.

Mediation also can be a highly efficient dispute resolution process. The mediation process can "telescope" into a few days factual and legal development likely to consume many months in litigation.

One of the important features of mediation is that each party can discuss with the mediator certain confidential information that it would not disclose to the other party. Equipped with such information, a skillful mediator often is able to identify hidden interests and settlement alternatives that would not have been considered in unassisted negotiations and that may help overcome barriers to settlement.

Another benefit is that principals on each side participate in the process. They deal directly with each other, unless the mediator sees fit to keep them apart due to extreme hostility or for other reasons.

Each party is given an opportunity to state its business goals and interests, as well as its legal position and its views regarding the conduct and issues in dispute. However, the primary focus is on solving problems and developing a tailor-made solution. Business disputes are often resolved on the basis of underlying business interests and concerns—not only on the basis of legal rules or fact differences. Mediation can be utilized to preserve, or even improve, long-term relationships, as well as to resolve a particular dispute.

Once parties to a dispute agree to engage in mediation, they often arrive at a resolution of their dispute even before the mediation process has begun. The imminence of a mediation, much like the imminence of a trial, can serve as a "settlement event" that induces parties and attorneys to focus on the case and to enter into serious negotiations. Negotiations aimed at establishing a fair procedure for resolving a dispute create an atmosphere of cooperative problem-solving that is conducive to resolving the dispute itself. CPR recommends that the parties first attempt to settle the dispute themselves, without the intervention of a mediator.

Frequently cited advantages of mediation include:
• substantial savings in legal fees and other litigation expenses
• promptness of resolution
• creative, business-driven solutions generally better for both parties than a solution available in court
• maintaining control over the outcome of the dispute
• preservation of business relationships
• privacy and essential confidentiality

The procedure and commentary set forth below reflect the experience of the CPR Mediation Advisory Committee, a group of the nation's leading mediators. The procedure can be incorporated by reference in the dispute resolution clause of a business agreement or in a submission agreement entered into after a dispute has arisen (see Section 1 of the Mediation Procedure and Form 1 annexed to the procedure). The procedure is suitable for transnational disputes as well as for disputes between U.S. parties.

There is no one right way to conduct a mediation. Parties may adapt the procedure to their own needs. There is also no one right time to conduct a mediation. The opportunities to reduce the costs and wear and tear of court proceedings are greatest before litigation has commenced, but mediation may be a sensible option at any point in the litigation process, even while an appeal from a trial court judgment is pending. Parties not ready for a mediation at the outset of litigation may be more receptive as litigation runs its course. Mediation also can be useful as an adjunct to litigation—it can be used for "parts" of disputes, as well as for the whole matter.

Many federal and state courts already have adopted procedures mandating the referral of a broad range of cases to mediation or to early neutral evaluation, a process different from mediation, but which shares some of its characteristics. Other courts are expected to follow suit. Litigants can expect that increasingly their cases will be referred to court-selected neutrals, frequently members of the bar who have volunteered for such service on a pro bono basis or are paid. However, most courts will accept the parties' agreement to mediate privately in lieu of the court's procedure, with the advantage that the parties may select an agreed upon mediator in whom they have confidence. Of course, even when mediation is mandated the process remains non-binding. The mediator is not a decisionmaker.

Despite its advantages, once a dispute has arisen the parties often are reluctant to propose mediation, and adversaries typically find it difficult to agree about anything. With this in mind, CPR urges parties entering into a business agreement to include clauses providing for unfacilitated negotiation and mediation of future disputes, possibly with binding arbitration as a fallback, should mediation fail. A sample pre-dispute mediation clause appears in the CPR Mediation Procedure, below. Sample multistep clauses appear in A Drafter's Guide to CPR Dispute Resolution Clauses (CPR, 1998).

The CPR Corporate Policy Statement on Alternatives to Litigation has been signed by more than 800 companies on behalf of themselves and their 3200 domestic operating subsidiaries. Signatories agree to explore negotiation or ADR when in a dispute with another signatory. This statement helps parties overcome hesitancy to propose or agree to ADR.

The CPR Mediation Procedure and commentary were prepared in 1987 with business disputes in mind. Since then there has been a rapid growth both in the volume of cases that are mediated and in the type of cases. As different types of cases were mediated successfully the CPR Mediation Procedure proved to be suitable for these cases as well. CPR has published an Employment Dispute Mediation Procedure that differs somewhat from the CPR Mediation Procedure.

In the Commentary, below, at page 16, we list the many types of disputes that have been mediated successfully, and we outline factors to be considered in analyzing suitability. The CPR ADR Suitability Screen readily enables a party to identify and analyze factors favoring and disfavoring mediation.

The CPR Panels of Distinguished Neutrals consist of eminent former judges, legal academics, other leaders of the bar and outstanding conflict resolution professionals, who are well qualified to serve as mediators of significant disputes. A brochure listing the members of the Panels and describing services they may perform is available. The panel roster appears at CPR's web site, www.cpradr.org. CPR will assist the parties in selecting a mediator well qualified for their needs. CPR can also, at the request of a party, contact the other party or parties to interest them in entering into a mediation or other form of private dispute resolution.

The CPR Mediation Procedure:
1. Agreement to Mediate
2. Selecting the Mediator
3. Ground Rules of Proceeding
4. Exchange of Information
5. Presentation to the Mediator
6. Negotiations
7. Settlement
8. Failure to Agree
9. Confidentiality
Form 1: Model Agreement for Parties and Mediator

The CPR Mediation Procedure
(Revised and effective as of April 1, 1998)

1. Agreement to Mediate
The CPR Mediation Procedure (the "Procedure") may be adopted by agreement of the parties, with or without modification, before or after a dispute has arisen. The following provisions are suggested:

A. Pre-dispute Clause
The parties shall attempt in good faith to resolve any dispute arising out of or relating to this Agreement promptly by confidential mediation under the [then current] CPR Mediation Procedure [in effect on the date of this Agreement], before resorting to arbitration or litigation.

B. Existing Dispute Submission Agreement
We hereby agree to submit to confidential mediation under the CPR Mediation Procedure the following controversy:
(Describe briefly)
2. Selecting the Mediator
Unless the parties agree otherwise, the mediator shall be selected from the CPR Panels of Neutrals. If the parties cannot agree promptly on a mediator,

they will notify CPR of their need for assistance in selecting a mediator, informing CPR of any preferences as to matters such as candidates' mediation style, subject matter expertise and geographic location. CPR will submit to the parties the names of not less than three candidates, with their resumes and hourly rates. If the parties are unable to agree on a candidate from the list within seven days following receipt of the list, each party will, within 15 days following receipt of the list, send to CPR the list of candidates ranked in descending order of preference. The candidate with the lowest combined score will be appointed as the mediator by CPR. CPR will break any tie.

Before proposing any mediator candidate, CPR will request the candidate to disclose any circumstances known to him or her that would cause reasonable doubt regarding the candidate's impartiality. If a clear conflict is disclosed, the individual will not be proposed. Other circumstances a candidate discloses to CPR will be disclosed to the parties. A party may challenge a mediator candidate if it knows of any circumstances giving rise to reasonable doubt regarding the candidate's impartiality.

The mediator's rate of compensation will be determined before appointment. Such compensation, and any other costs of the process, will be shared equally by the parties unless they otherwise agree. If a party withdraws from a multi-party mediation but the procedure continues, the withdrawing party will not be responsible for any costs incurred after it has notified the mediator and the other parties of its withdrawal.

Before appointment, the mediator will assure the parties of his or her availability to conduct the proceeding expeditiously. It is strongly advised that the parties and the mediator enter into a retention agreement. A model agreement is attached hereto as a Form.

3.   *Ground Rules of Proceeding*
The following ground rules will apply, subject to any changes on which the parties and the mediator agree.

(a) The process is non-binding.
(b) Each party may withdraw at any time after attending the first session, and before execution of a written settlement agreement, by written notice to the mediator and the other party or parties.
(c) The mediator shall be neutral and impartial.
(d) The mediator shall control the procedural aspects of the mediation. The parties will cooperate fully with the mediator.

i. The mediator is free to meet and communicate separately with each party.

ii. The mediator will decide when to hold joint meetings with the parties and when to hold separate meetings. The mediator will fix the time and place of each session and its agenda in consultation with the parties. There will be no stenographic record of any meeting. Formal rules of evidence or procedure will not apply.

(e) Each party will be represented at each mediation conference by a business executive or other person authorized to negotiate a resolution of the dispute, unless excused by the mediator as to a particular conference. Each party may be represented by more than one person, e.g. a business executive and an attorney. The mediator may limit the number of persons representing each party.

(f) Each party will be represented by counsel to advise it in the mediation, whether or not such counsel is present at mediation conferences.

(g) The process will be conducted expeditiously. Each representative will make every effort to be available for meetings.

(h) The mediator will not transmit information received in confidence from any party to any other party or any third party unless authorized to do so by the party transmitting the information, or unless ordered to do so by a court of competent jurisdiction.

(i) Unless the parties agree otherwise, they will refrain from pursuing litigation or any administrative or judicial remedies during the mediation process or for a set period of time, insofar as they can do so without prejudicing their legal rights.

(j) Unless all parties and the mediator otherwise agree in writing, the mediator and any persons assisting the mediator will be disqualified as a witness, consultant or expert in any pending or future investigation, action or proceeding relating to the subject matter of the mediation (including any investigation, action or proceeding which involves persons not party to this mediation).

(k) If the dispute goes into arbitration, the mediator shall not serve as an arbitrator, unless the parties and the mediator otherwise agree in writing.

(l) The mediator may obtain assistance and independent expert advice, with the prior agreement of and at the expense of the parties. Any person proposed as an independent expert also will be required to disclose any circumstances known to him or her that would cause reasonable doubt regarding the candidate's impartiality.

(m) Neither CPR nor the mediator shall be liable for any act or omission in connection with the mediation, except for its/his/her own willful misconduct.

(n) The mediator may withdraw at any time by written notice to the parties (i) for serious personal reasons, (ii) if the mediator believes that a party is not acting in good faith, or (iii) if the mediator concludes that further mediation efforts would not be useful. If the mediator withdraws pursuant to (i) or (ii), he or she need not state the reason for withdrawal.

4.   Exchange of Information

If any party has a substantial need for documents or other material in the possession of another party, or for other discovery that may facilitate a settlement, the parties shall attempt to agree thereon. Should they fail to agree, either party may request a joint consultation with the mediator who shall assist the parties in reaching agreement.

The parties shall exchange with each other, with a copy to the mediator, the names and job titles of all individuals who will attend the joint mediation session.

At the conclusion of the mediation process, upon the request of a party which provided documents or other material to one or more other parties, the recipients shall return the same to the originating party without retaining copies.

5.   Presentation to the Mediator

Before dealing with the substance of the dispute, the parties and the mediator will discuss preliminary matters, such as possible modification of the procedure, place and time of meetings, and each party's need for documents or other information in the possession of the other.

At least 10 business days before the first substantive mediation conference, unless otherwise agreed, each party will submit to the mediator a written statement summarizing the background and present status of the dispute, including any settlement efforts that have occurred, and such other material and information as the mediator requests or the party deems helpful to familiarize the mediator with the dispute. It is desirable for the submission to include an analysis of the party's real interests and needs and of its litigation risks. The parties may agree to submit jointly certain records and other materials. The mediator may request any party to provide clarification and additional information.

The parties are encouraged to discuss the exchange of all or certain materials they submit to the mediator to further each party's understanding of the other party's viewpoints. The mediator may request the parties to submit a joint statement of facts. Except as the parties otherwise agree, the mediator shall keep confidential any written materials or information that are submitted to him or her. The parties and their representatives are not entitled to receive or review any materials or information submitted to the mediator by another party or representative without the concurrence of the latter. At the conclusion of the mediation process, upon request of a party, the mediator will return to that party all written materials and information which that party had provided to the mediator without retaining copies thereof or certify as to the destruction of such materials.

At the first substantive mediation conference each party will make an opening statement.

6. Negotiations

The mediator may facilitate settlement in any manner the mediator believes is appropriate. The mediator will help the parties focus on their underlying interests and concerns, explore resolution alternatives and develop settlement options. The mediator will decide when to hold joint meetings, and when to confer separately with each party.

The parties are expected to initiate and convey to the mediator proposals for settlement. Each party shall provide a rationale for any settlement terms proposed.

Finally, if the parties fail to develop mutually acceptable settlement terms, before terminating the procedure, and only with the consent of the parties, (a) the mediator may submit to the parties a final settlement proposal; and (b) if the mediator believes he/she is qualified to do so, the mediator may give the parties an evaluation (which if all parties choose, and the mediator agrees, may be in writing) of the likely outcome of the case if it were tried to final judgment, subject to any limitations under any applicable mediation statutes/rules, court rules or ethical codes. Thereupon, the mediator may suggest further discussions to explore whether the mediator's evaluation or proposal may lead to a resolution.

Efforts to reach a settlement will continue until (a) a written settlement is reached, or (b) the mediator concludes and informs the parties that further efforts would not be useful, or (c) one of the parties or the mediator withdraws from the process. However, if there are more than two parties, the remaining parties may elect to continue following the withdrawal of a party.

7. Settlement

If a settlement is reached, a preliminary memorandum of understanding or term sheet normally will be prepared and signed or initialed before the parties separate. Thereafter, unless the mediator undertakes to do so, representatives of the parties will promptly draft a written settlement document incorporating all settlement terms. This draft will be circulated, amended as necessary, and formally executed. If litigation is pending, the settlement may provide that the parties will request dismissal of the case. The parties also may request the court to enter the settlement agreement as a consent judgment.

8. Failure to Agree

If a resolution is not reached, the mediator will discuss with the parties the possibility of their agreeing on advisory or binding arbitration, "last offer" arbitration or another form of ADR. If the parties agree in principle, the mediator may offer to assist them in structuring a procedure designed to result in a prompt, economical process. The mediator will not serve as arbitrator, unless all parties agree.

9. Confidentiality

The entire mediation process is confidential. Unless agreed among all the parties or required to do so by law, the parties and the mediator shall not disclose to any person who is not associated with participants in the process, including any judicial officer, any information regarding the process (including pre-process exchanges and agreements), contents (including written and oral information), settlement terms or outcome of the proceeding. If litigation is pending, the participants may, however, advise the court of the schedule and overall status of the mediation for purposes of litigation management. Any written settlement agreement resulting from the mediation may be disclosed for purposes of enforcement.

Under this procedure, the entire process is a compromise negotiation subject to Federal Rule of Evidence 408 and all state counterparts, together with any applicable statute protecting the confidentiality of mediation. All offers, promises, conduct and statements, whether oral or written, made in the course of the proceeding by any of the parties, their agents, employees, experts and attorneys, and by the mediator are confidential. Such offers, promises, conduct and statements are privileged under any applicable mediation privilege and are inadmissible and not discoverable for any purpose, including impeachment, in litigation between the parties. However, evidence that is otherwise admissible or discoverable shall not be rendered inadmissible or non-discoverable solely as a result of its presentation or use during the mediation.

The exchange of any tangible material shall be without prejudice to any claim that such material is privileged or protected as work-product within the meaning of Federal Rule of Civil Procedure 26 and all state and local counterparts.

The mediator and any documents and information in the mediator's possession will not be subpoenaed in any such investigation, action or proceeding, and all parties will oppose any effort to have the mediator or documents subpoenaed. The mediator will promptly advise the parties of any attempt to compel him/her to divulge information received in mediation.

FORM
CPR Model Agreement for Parties and Mediator*

Agreement made _____, _____
                              (date)
between_____
represented by_____
and_____
represented by_____
and_____
                          (the Mediator)

   A dispute has arisen between the parties (the "Dispute"). The parties have agreed to participate in a mediation proceeding (the "Proceeding") under the CPR Mediation Procedure [, as modified by mutual agreement] (the "Procedure"). The parties have chosen the Mediator for the Proceeding. The parties and the Mediator agree as follows:

A. Duties and Obligations

1. The Mediator and each of the parties agree to be bound by and to comply faithfully with the Procedure, including without limitation the provisions regarding confidentiality.
2. The Mediator has no previous commitments that may significantly delay the expeditious conduct of the proceeding and will not make any such commitments.
3. The Mediator, the CPR Institute for Dispute Resolution (CPR) and their employees, agents and partners shall not be liable for any act or omission in connection with the Proceeding, other than as a result of its/his/her own willful misconduct.

B. Disclosure of Prior Relationships

1. The Mediator has made a reasonable effort to learn and has disclosed to the parties in writing (a) all business or professional relationships the Mediator and/or the Mediator's firm have had with the parties or their law firms within the past five years, including all instances in which the Mediator or the Mediator's firm served as an attorney for any party or adverse to any party; (b) any financial interest the Mediator has in any party; (c) any significant social, business or professional relationship the Mediator has had with an officer or employee of a party or with an individual representing a party in the Proceeding; and (d) any other circumstances that may create doubt regarding the Mediator's impartiality in the Proceeding.
2. Each party and its law firm has made a reasonable effort to learn and has disclosed to every other party and the Mediator in writing any relationships of a nature described in paragraph B.1. not previously identified and disclosed by the Mediator.

3. The parties and the Mediator are satisfied that any relationships disclosed pursuant to paragraphs B.1. and B.2. will not affect the Mediator's independence or impartiality. Notwithstanding such relationships or others the Mediator and the parties did not discover despite good faith efforts, the parties wish the Mediator to serve in the Proceeding, waiving any claim based on said relationships, and the Mediator agrees to so serve.

4. The disclosure obligations in paragraphs B.1. and B.2. are continuing until the Proceeding is concluded. The ability of the Mediator to continue serving in this capacity shall be explored with each such disclosure.

C. Future Relationships

1. Neither the Mediator nor the Mediator's firm shall undertake any work for or against a party regarding the Dispute.

2. Neither the Mediator nor any person assisting the Mediator with this Proceeding shall personally work on any matter for or against a party, regardless of specific subject matter, prior to six months following cessation of the Mediator's services in the Proceeding.

3. The Mediator's firm may work on matters for or against a party during the pendency of the Proceeding if such matters are unrelated to the Dispute. The Mediator shall establish appropriate safeguards to insure that other members and employees of the firm working on such matters unrelated to the Dispute do not have access to any confidential information obtained by the Mediator during the course of the Proceeding.

D. Compensation

1. The Mediator shall be compensated for time expended in connection with the Proceeding at the rate of $_____, plus reasonable travel and other out-of-pocket expenses. The Mediator's fee shall be shared equally by the parties. No part of such fee shall accrue to CPR.

2. The Mediator may utilize members and employees of the firm to assist in connection with the Proceeding and may bill the parties for the time expended by any such persons, to the extent and at a rate agreed upon in advance by the parties.

_____   _____
Party   Party

by _____   by _____
    Party's Attorney   Party's Attorney

_____
Mediator

COMMENTARY

Suitability for Mediation

Most bona fide disputes are amenable to settlement by negotiation. Mediation is a facilitated form of negotiation. Virtually every case in which negotiation is appropriate but difficult is suitable for mediation, whether direct negotiations have taken place or litigation is pending. Mediation can be particularly helpful if there is an opportunity to structure a creative business solution. When a dispute involves several or many parties it may not be essential for all to be at the table, but any party crucial to a settlement must be represented.

The following is a partial list of the many types of domestic and international business disputes that have been successfully mediated:

- bankruptcy and creditor/debtor issues
- commercial, financial and real estate transactions
- construction
- copyright
- dealerships and franchises
- defamation
- eminent domain
- employment
- environmental
- insurance coverage
- mineral extraction
- partnerships or joint ventures
- patents, trade secret, technology
- personal injury
- private antitrust
- product liability
- professional malpractice
- regulatory matters
- securities
- trademarks and unfair competition

Mediation has become the most popular choice of parties seeking a non-binding form of dispute resolution. However, other forms of non-binding ADR do exist, and there are cases for which non-binding procedures may not be appropriate.

The minitrial is another effective form of collaborative dispute resolution. It is a more formal and structured proceeding than mediation, with the roles of counsel and business executive more precisely defined. The neutral is often expected to evaluate the parties' chances of success in litigation. The CPR

Minitrial Procedure provides ground rules and a commentary. Features of mediation and the minitrial can be combined. A mediator conducting a mediation proceeding may stage a meeting resembling the minitrial "information exchange." A minitrial neutral adviser frequently plays a mediating role in the negotiation phase, whether or not such a role was contemplated at the outset.

Professors Stephen B. Goldberg and Frank E.A. Sander have developed an analytical method that encourages each party to articulate its objectives in the dispute and to appraise the likelihood that any of five ADR procedures— mediation, minitrial, summary jury trial, neutral evaluation or arbitration/ private judging—will overcome the impediments to settlement. Two charts the practitioner may use in applying the Goldberg-Sander analysis and a commentary appear at 12 Alternatives 49 (April 1994). Goldberg and Sander refer to mediation as the "presumptive" choice, recognizing that in most cases the analysis will lead to the conclusion that mediation is indeed the most appropriate procedure.

Outlined below are factors to be considered in deciding whether mediation is appropriate.

The Parties

The factors favoring mediation are likely to be particularly strong when, but for the dispute, the parties would or could be in a business relationship. The settlement then may well take the form of a renegotiated contract or some other business deal.

Where the parties are unevenly matched with respect to business sophistication, economic resources, or information concerning the underlying facts, the "stronger" party may be able to impose lopsided settlement terms. However, this imbalance is not necessarily a reason to reject mediation. The imbalance may well be offset by the caliber of the person(s) representing the "weaker" party, and a settlement through mediation may be more desirable for even a "weak" party than the alternatives of direct negotiation or litigation with its "win-lose" outcome, high costs and other burdens. Mediators may be effective in counteracting "power imbalances" to facilitate an equitable solution.

Personal and emotional factors cannot be ignored. Animosity is likely to get in the way of unaided negotiation and to underscore the need for skillful mediation. A key function of a mediator is to defuse hostility and distrust and to encourage cooperation.

Bringing about a settlement may be more difficult if there are numerous parties with dissimilar interests; however, mediations involving many parties are becoming commonplace and are frequently successful.

The Case

Fact Issues Predominate

Cases involving predominantly fact issues or mixed questions of fact and law tend to be well suited for mediation. In mediation, the parties need not resolve fact issues to agree on a resolution of their dispute.

Stakes

Even when a party believes that a vital interest rides on the outcome of a case, it may well favor mediation over the uncertain decision of a judge, jury or arbitrator. The parties remain in control of the outcome; if the mediation is unsuccessful, other options remain. If the stakes are moderate, mediation may also be appealing; for one thing, the cost and burdens of litigation may be disproportionate even for the winner of a lawsuit.

Opportunities for Joint Gains

Many business disputes are not zero-sum games; the issue is not, or need not be solely, whether X owes Y money, and if so, how much. Frequently, there are opportunities for non-cash settlements which a court or arbitrator generally cannot impose. Even if the subject matter is limited to money, there may be differences in the availability and cost of credit to the parties, or in the value of delayed payments, which can be exploited to add to the value of a settlement to each side. Development of such "value-creating" solutions requires cooperation between the parties. This is easier to foster with the help of a mediator.

Costs

The direct and indirect costs and burdens of full-scale litigation are likely to be of a different order of magnitude from those of mediation. Even parties with ample resources are likely to welcome the potential savings in transaction costs.

Confidentiality

Parties to a business dispute frequently are anxious to avoid placing the details of their transactions in public court records and exposing them to media publicity. The privacy and confidentiality of mediation is likely to be seen as a significant advantage.

Barriers to Settlement

Only 5%-10% of all civil lawsuits are tried. Most cases settle. The primary aim of mediation is to facilitate faster, less costly and more productive settlements. Common barriers to settlement are outlined below. These barriers should be identified and addressed in a mediation proceeding, and often they can be overcome.

Differing Perceptions

Perceptions can differ about a number of issues relevant to settlement. Do the parties have different views regarding what the facts are? Do they disagree about what proposition the facts prove? Is this disagreement based on each side having access to limited information? Is disagreement primarily the result of each side's partisan assessments of the evidence and its implications? Do the parties have different views as to how the law will be applied or as to the likelihood of success at trial? Do the parties have different views of what is at stake? Do they make different assessments concerning the value of those stakes? It is very common for each party to be unduly optimistic about its chances of success at trial, particularly during the early stages of litigation. A mediation proceeding is likely to lead to a much more realistic appraisal and thereby greatly enhance prospects for settlement.

Extrinsic Pressures, Linkage

Are there pressures working on one or more parties that cut against prompt settlement? Do time constraints operate differently on the parties? Is resolution of this dispute linked to other similar disputes, pending or contemplated? Does either side have constituencies that would criticize a settlement? Are there "strategic" considerations to avoid settlement, e.g., to discourage other suits?

Process Failures

Communication problems between the parties or their lawyers are a common barrier. Does the negotiation process afford sufficient opportunities to devise and explore settlement options? Do the lawyers have different incentives than the parties in interest?

Need for Discovery

An attorney determined to "leave no stone unturned" in discovery will not readily agree to mediation before discovery is completed; however, limited discovery can be conducted within the mediation framework, and the submission agreement can define the scope of discovery each party may conduct and establish a time schedule therefor.

Delay Considered Advantageous

A party may believe, rightly or wrongly, that it will benefit from delay; but, when a dispute arises while a business relationship is ongoing, both parties have an incentive to put the matter behind them. Even when there is no continuing relationship, there are likely to be advantages to all parties in having the matter resolved.

Parties

Are all of the parties with a stake in the dispute available for negotiation? Should non-disputants with a stake (e.g., insurers) be invited to participate? Mediation is more successful when all individuals or entities with an interest are included, either by participating or by being kept informed. Even such inactive inclusion reduces the prospect of their later opposing the mediated settlement.

Many attorneys remain concerned that a proposal to mediate will be seen by the adversary, however incorrectly, as leading from weakness. When the dispute is in litigation a judge's suggestion to try mediation often is welcomed by both sides. The CPR Corporate Policy Statement on Alternatives to Litigation serves the purpose of overcoming hesitancy to take the initiative on the part of a signatory. Contractual commitments to mediate future disputes greatly increase the likelihood that mediation will take place, and at an early juncture of any dispute.

The CPR ADR Suitability Screen (CPR, 1996) poses 30 questions, which provide a disciplined, analytical process for appraising a dispute's suitability for mediation. The screen will identify many of the factors that bear on suitability. The weight to be given to each factor must then be assessed. In certain cases the answer to a single question may be dispositive.

The Mediation Process

There is a continuum of approaches to mediation, going from "facilitative mediation" to "evaluative mediation." The mediator, meeting jointly or separately with each party, usually first explores with the parties their underlying interests. Having identified these interests, the mediator and the parties explore opportunities for a creative solution, such as a mutually-advantageous new business arrangement. This approach is likely to be most effective when a business relationship already exists between the parties. In facilitative mediation the mediator ordinarily will not offer opinions on the merits of the case or the positions of the parties.

Frequently, parties harbor vastly differing estimates of litigation risk and the likely outcome of trial. In evaluative mediation, the mediator, through careful questioning, usually in private caucuses, may focus more on the strengths and weaknesses of the parties' legal rights to assist them in assessing more objectively the likely outcome if their case were tried in court. In this way, parties may be better able to weigh the advantages of settlement against the benefits and risks of trial. This approach is likely to be used if the case does not present opportunities for interest mediation or if the interest mediation approach has been unsuccessful.

Many cases call for both approaches. The two approaches can be combined or alternated, with the mediator developing an evaluation during the later phase of the mediation on one or more remaining issues after interest-based mediation has been partially successful in moving the parties toward settlement. The mediator should address an evaluation only on an issue on which he or she has expertise.

There are different ways for mediators to be evaluative, reflecting various levels of intrusiveness on the parties' own decision-making. Timing may determine when one or another of those approaches is appropriate. The earlier in the mediation, the more restraint the mediator should exercise, given the mediator's need both to build trust and to understand (and be perceived as understanding) the parties' case. Mediator approaches may range from questions about the parties' case and elements of proof and asking a party to respond to the other side's arguments, to offering opinions about elements of a party's case, opinions about the strengths and weaknesses of a party's entire case, or to expressing opinions about how the court is likely to decide the case (subject to any limitations under any applicable mediation statutes/rules, court rules or ethical codes) or proposing a settlement. A preferable approach is to draw an evaluation out of the party representatives and counsel, aided by the mediator, but not solely delivered by the mediator. An evaluation of the likely court outcome or a settlement proposal should only be given with the prior consent of all parties as a final step to avoid impasse and stimulate a settlement. Once having given an evaluation, the mediator's influence is likely to be impaired in the view of a party whose position is weakened by the evaluation.

There is no one right way to conduct a mediation. The CPR Mediation Procedure represents a process that appears logical and has proven effective in numerous cases. It can be modified to fit the circumstances of the case and the wishes of the parties.

Initial Consultation with Mediator
The initial consultation of the parties with the mediator serves several purposes:

• The parties are given an opportunity to size up the mediator. If one or more parties do not gain a favorable impression, a substitution may be proposed, to which the mediator should freely agree.
• The mediator will discuss the entire mediation process, including the ground rules, with the parties. They may agree on modifications.
• If they have not done so previously, they should develop a retention agreement with the mediator (see Model Agreement Form, above).
• A meeting schedule may be discussed.

• The mediator and the parties will discuss the role(s) the mediator will play.
• If appropriate, the parties will begin to familiarize the mediator with the dispute.
• The mediator can confirm that the parties have a genuine interest in resolving their dispute through the mediation process, and that they have the persistence to stick with the process.
• The parties' representatives will begin to talk to each other in a manner appropriate to their joint goal of reaching an accommodation.
• There will be discussion of who will represent the parties at future sessions, and the extent of their authority. If the stakes are large, it may not be possible for the negotiators to have complete authority to sign a settlement agreement, but each should have authority to negotiate a settlement, and the authority of the negotiators should be comparable.
• The exchange of certain documents may be discussed, as well as a form and schedule of mini-discovery, if necessary.
• If litigation is pending between the parties regarding the subject matter of the mediation, the parties and the mediator may discuss the suspension or curtailment of discovery and other pre-trial activities. They also may discuss whether the court should be informed of the mediation, and whether court approval of curtailment of pre-trial activities is required.

In a relatively simple case, a discussion of the preliminary matters listed above may be followed immediately by a joint session such as described below.

Familiarizing the Mediator with the Case

The mediator must be familiarized with the dispute, and the parties must be given an opportunity to state their case. The mediator usually will ask the parties to submit on an agreed time schedule such written materials as the mediator or the parties consider necessary or advisable. A statement summarizing the background and status of the dispute is likely to be the principal document.

It will be helpful to the mediator and the submitting party if its submission includes a confidential analysis of the party's underlying interests and needs and a realistic evaluation of its litigation risks. The mediator may request the parties to jointly prepare a written statement of facts. Their doing so would clarify areas of agreement and disagreement and perhaps would help narrow the latter. The joint preparation also would help foster a cooperative spirit between the two sides at an early stage in the process. If litigation is pending, court documents such as pleadings and briefs may be submitted. If an exchange of certain documents between the parties has been agreed upon, that exchange also should occur during this phase of the proceeding.

Joint Sessions and Caucuses

Following submission of written materials, a joint session is likely to be scheduled at which the parties' representatives and/or their counsel will state their views orally in an informal manner and will address the conflicting views of the other party or parties. Each party will present its views in what it considers the most effective manner. Usually there will be opportunities for rebuttal and for discussion and clarification of issues. Rules of evidence will not apply and the presentations will not be transcribed. The mediator will prescribe the sequence of presentations, may impose time limits and is likely to ask clarifying questions.

Opening statements are of great importance. They represent the first opportunity each side will have to hear uninterrupted what the other side considers to be its best case, and, if the client speaks, to hear what is important to him or her. Each side will also have the opportunity to assess the other side's representative as a witness. All participants should be prepared to listen with an open mind. They may learn things that lead them to reevaluate their case, or to identify new possibilities for settlement.

Following the joint session, the mediator may caucus with each party. The parties tend to be more candid in such a private meeting. The mediator may well elicit in confidence information not disclosed at the joint session. The mediator may explore certain aspects of the party's presentation and may request additional materials. The mediator will explore with each business executive his or her company's underlying interests and aims, will identify barriers to settlement and will help the parties address those barriers.

When strong hostility exists between opposing party representatives or their attorneys a joint session may be counterproductive. Under those circumstances the mediator may decide to meet with the parties separately from the beginning.

The mediator must understand the case fully from each side's perspective; the mediator should then assure that each side better understands how the case looks from the other side's viewpoint. The mediator, to be effective, must keep fully informed of all developments and must be able to control dialogue between the parties.

Developing Information

Even when there are no issues of credibility, the "facts" relevant to a dispute can be elusive. The party submissions to the mediator or statements made in meetings may well indicate that the parties see the facts differently, or draw different conclusions from them. At times, it will be useful for the mediator to address any such differences and seek to bring about agreement on the most salient facts and the issues of the dispute. At other times, focusing on the facts may be counterproductive if it will encourage the parties to focus on past disputes rather than on reaching an arrangement that will enable them to better deal with each other in the future. An "agreement to disagree" on past facts may still be used productively to reach a forward-looking solution. This is a case-by-case decision for the mediator.

Some controversies hinge on key factual issues which can be resolved by an independent expert operating under ground rules on which the parties have agreed. Does the machine perform in accordance with contractual specifications? Is the former executive using information proprietary to the former employer? Were the soil conditions as represented to the contractor, and if not, how much additional expense was incurred? Once such critical questions have been answered by a neutral expert, the controversy may, as a practical matter, resolve itself. Independent expert appraisals are a key part of dispute resolution.

Negotiation of Settlement Terms

Negotiation is most productive when the parties focus on their underlying interests and concerns, avoiding fixed positions which often obscure what a party really wants. The mediator can help the parties crystallize their own interests and understand each other's interests, defuse adversarial stances and develop a more cooperative approach. The mediator can narrow or expand the range of issues as appropriate for effective resolution of a particular dispute.

Settlement proposals are likely to be generated through discussion in caucus. The mediator can help each party to generate ideas, to develop options and alternative proposals that will lead to a mutually acceptable solution, and to try out unusual solutions in a relatively safe and confidential setting. The mediator can help parties frame proposals and responses in such a way as to further the settlement effort. The mediator may advance as his own a proposal made by a party in caucus to avoid the skepticism with which an adversary's proposal is sometimes greeted.

The first settlement proposal, by whomever made, is seldom the last. Usually, it will provide a basis for negotiation. At this juncture, some experienced mediators will usually engage in "shuttle diplomacy," i.e., meet with the parties individually to try to bridge a gap or develop a more acceptable solution; other mediators are likely to conduct joint sessions to bring the parties together. When conveying one party's position to the other, the mediator must take care to state that position accurately. On some occasions, the mediator may consider it advisable to meet with the principals of the parties, separately or together, outside the presence of counsel. Any such meetings should occur only if the principals and attorneys agree to them.

Some mediators favor a "one-text" approach. Late in the process they will prepare a first draft of a settlement agreement, seek the parties' comments, and prepare successive drafts until all parties are in agreement.

Section 6 of the Procedure contemplates that if the parties do not develop mutually acceptable settlement terms the mediator, only with the parties' consent, (a) may submit a settlement proposal, and (b) if the mediator feels qualified to do so, may give the parties an evaluation of the likely outcome of the case in court, subject to any limitations under any applicable mediation statutes/rules, court rules or ethical codes. When submitting a settlement proposal it is advisable for the mediator to assure the parties that acceptance of the proposal by either party will not be communicated to the other, unless and until the other also accepts.

If agreement is reached on settlement terms, by whatever technique, a preliminary memorandum of understanding or term sheet normally should be prepared and signed immediately. Thereupon, a settlement agreement is drafted, circulated, edited as necessary and executed.

When it is clear that no agreement can be reached through mediation, other alternatives to litigation remain. The mediator may discuss with the parties whether arbitration or another form of ADR may be preferable to a lawsuit. In particular, a "last offer" arbitration would require each side to submit an offer to an arbitrator who would be required to select the offer he or she considers the more reasonable. If the parties agree in principle, the mediator may be able to help them structure appropriate ground rules. Moreover, if the parties so agree after the mediation, the mediator, if willing, could serve as the arbitrator. It is not desirable for parties to agree before the mediation that the mediator will become an adjudicator, as that may well inhibit discussions in caucus between each party and the mediator. It is also doubtful whether the mediator should serve as the adjudicator if either party, or both, have given the mediator significant confidential information that will not be placed in evidence in the arbitration but may influence the arbitrator's decision.

Why Mediation Works

A high percentage of mediations of business disputes result in a resolution. Even when agreement does not occur during the proceeding, the greatly enhanced mutual understanding substantially improves the prospects for a later agreement. Satisfaction with the process on the part of users is high.

What are the reasons for the success of the process? Each case has unique aspects, but the following factors are common:

• Disputes ostensibly between dispassionate corporate entities involve human beings endowed with emotions. The mediator can help the parties deal with emotional issues. Discussions in the presence of a mediator tend to reduce misunderstandings and antagonism frequently subsides. Concerns beyond legal issues are discussed. The process itself presents a joint challenge to all participants to devise solutions. The momentum of mediation leads to accommodation. Settlement represents success for all involved.

• Just as an impending trial often induces litigants to stop posturing and seriously seek a settlement, commitment of the parties to a mediation is likely to motivate them to "bite the bullet" rather than to postpone unpleasant decisions. The mediator will reinforce this motivation.

• The mediator can establish ground rules designed to maximize the chances of success. For instance, the mediator may first urge discussion of non-controversial subjects or those for which agreement is readily achieved and postpone consideration of difficult issues. These early agreements help build a spirit of cooperation.

• Mediation provides the parties with an opportunity—at little or no risk—to crystalize issues and learn more about the other party's perceptions of the pertinent facts.

• In caucusing with each party, the mediator can diplomatically urge that party to face facts and dispel unrealistic expectations such as over-optimism regarding chances of prevailing in court. The mediator also can point to the costs and burdens of prolonged litigation.

• Once the mediator understands the true interests of each party, he or she can recommend opportunities for common gains. Many business disputes are resolved through innovative business arrangements not previously contemplated.

The Mediator

Mediator Characteristics

The selection of a highly capable mediator is absolutely vital. A mediator is not vested with the legal authority of a judge or arbitrator, but must rely on his or her own resources. To effectively mediate a complex business dispute, a mediator must possess a combination of qualifications. The ideal mediator:

• is absolutely impartial and fair and so perceived
• inspires trust and motivates people to confide in him or her
• has experience as a mediator
• is able to size up people, understand their motivations and relate easily to them
• sets a tone of civility and consideration in dealings with others
• is a good listener
• is capable of understanding the law and facts of a dispute, including surrounding circumstances
• is able to analyze complex problems and get to the core

• is creative, imaginative and ingenious in developing proposals and knows when to make them
• is a problem solver
• is articulate and persuasive
• possesses a thorough understanding of the negotiating process
• is flexible, patient, persistent, indefatigable, and "upbeat" in the face of difficulties
• has a personal stature that commands respect
• is an energetic leader, a person who can stimulate others and make things happen

The size and complexity of the case will influence the selection of the mediator. In a major case, the mediator might be a former judge, a leading attorney, the dean or a professor of a law school or business school, a senior executive, or a skilled conflict resolution professional. An evident flair for dispute resolution is as important as long experience.

The styles, personalities and orientations of mediators vary significantly. Some mediators are facilitative and focus predominantly on party interests and insist on party-generated solutions, while evaluative mediators focus centrally on the positions of the parties and the merits of the legal claims. Strict facilitators will not offer opinions about legal claims or court outcomes. Other facilitators will not offer such opinions unless party interests have been fully explored and parties directly request the opinions. Evaluative mediators tend to be more aggressive in forcing the parties to make frank assessments of their interests and the legal merits of their positions. Through pointed questioning and direct observations, they may force a party to re-evaluate the likely outcome of a trial. They may bypass interest exploration. A mediator's orientation will affect the mediator's techniques throughout the process, but many experienced mediators will adapt their style to the particular situation.

These differences should be borne in mind in selecting a mediator. However, in advance of a mediation parties and their attorneys may not perceive opportunities for interest exploration that a skilled facilitative mediator can uncover. CPR believes that unless it is certain that such opportunities do not exist, the parties will be best served by a mediator who can play both roles. When CPR is asked to assist in the selection process, the parties' preferences should be discussed.

An insightful analysis by Prof. Leonard L. Riskin of the roles mediators can play, "Mediator Orientations, Strategies and Techniques," appears at 12 Alternatives 111 (September 1994).

When legal issues are critical, there may be significant advantages to select-ing as the mediator a lawyer or legal academic with expertise in the field (e.g., patent, trademark, construction). Similarly, when the subject matter is technical, it may well be desirable to select a person who has an understanding of the technology. Some experienced mediation practitioners and parties, however, believe that even in legally or technically complex disputes, the key to resolution does not lie in adding yet another expert to the process. Instead, they prefer a mediator who is a skilled deal-maker and who can shift the parties' focus from resolving the legal or technical dispute to reaching a mutually satisfactory agreement.

In most cases a single mediator will be used; however, in complex cases the mediator may need assistance, and it is helpful for the mediator to be able to discuss issues or possible solutions with another neutral person familiar with the case. On rare occasions, using two mediators may be considered. They can represent different disciplines relevant to the dispute, e.g., science and law. One can possess relevant technical expertise and the other can be a deal-maker. By conferring with each other they may develop additional settlement options. In a multiparty case they can deal with a number of parties and interests. There is a risk that the two mediators may not be in sync, in which case using both actually can be counterproductive. It is advisable to confer with the potential mediators, preferably jointly, before selecting them.

The mediator may well need administrative assistance, legal research, or other forms of assistance. It is desirable for the mediator and the parties to discuss early the types of assistance likely to be needed and the mediator's resources for obtaining such assistance.

Selection of the Mediator

The parties may select any mediator of their choice. It is advisable for the parties to jointly interview one or more candidates before making a selection, and to question candidates regarding matters such as their mediation style, their training and their experience. Unless they agree otherwise, the mediator will be selected from the CPR Panels of Distinguished Neutrals. These panels consist of nationally and internationally prominent attorneys, former judges, academ-ics and legally-trained executives available to resolve business and public dis-putes. The CPR Panels include: the National Panel, U.S. Regional Panels, the International Panel, and Specialized Panels in Banking/Financial Services, Con-struction, Employment, Environmental, Franchise, Insurance, Taxation, Tech-nology and Trademarks. The CPR rosters and brief biographical data may be found on the CPR Web site, www.cpradr.org (click on Neutrals).

Parties may contact CPR panelists directly, or may request CPR's assistance in selecting a mediator. Section 2 of the Mediation Procedure requires the parties to request CPR's assistance if they do not promptly agree on a mediator. Upon receiving such a request, CPR will promptly pre-screen candidates for their availability and absence of conflicts of interest. CPR then will submit jointly to the parties in writing the names of candidates who are available, together with each candidate's qualifications and current hourly rate.

It is critical that the mediator be totally impartial and be so perceived by all parties. CPR will not propose any individual who has disclosed a clear conflict. As to candidates CPR proposes, it will disclose to the parties any circumstances made known to CPR that could cause doubt but that the parties probably will not regard as disbarring. Broad disclosure by the mediator of past, current or foreseeable future conflicts is encouraged. Because mediator conflicts of interest is an unsettled area of law and practice, full disclosure—with the possibility of party consent and waiver—is the most prudent approach for both mediators and parties.

CPR will urge parties to agree on one of the candidates. If the parties do not so agree, each party will number the candidates in order of preference, and CPR thereupon will designate as the mediator the candidate for whom the parties jointly have expressed the highest preference.

The Roles of Executives and Lawyers

In a business mediation, the business executive and counsel function as a team. Business executives have the best understanding of their company's interests and are the most likely to embrace creative, business-oriented solutions. The executive should participate actively in every phase of the mediation process. It is preferable for a company to be represented by an executive who does not feel a need to defend past actions, who can be relatively objective and unemotional, but who has a thorough knowledge of the facts. It will be helpful for the executives representing the parties to relate well to each other and to be experienced negotiators. Each executive should be a decision maker authorized to negotiate a settlement, if need be subject to board of directors approval.

An executive who has had prior experience in mediation is likely to function more effectively than one new to mediation. Efforts must be made to educate the novice about the process. CPR's videotape, "Mediation in Action: Resolving a Complex Business Dispute" will be particularly useful in giving the executive a feel for the dynamics of the process.

Success in negotiation, as at trial, depends on thorough preparation on the part of each participant. As a rule, the attorney will prepare the client for the mediation. Normally, the attorney will make the opening statement, presenting the company's views in joint session, but persuasive opening statements also can be made by executives. In any event, when it comes to discussing business interests and exploring options for settlement, the executive should take the leading role. All participants should be encouraged to speak freely.

Counsel to the company, who may be a senior in-house or outside attorney, has a critical role to play:

Counseling and Preparation
- Counsel on the advisability of settlement and mediation
- Persuade parties to agree to the process
- Design or adapt the procedure
- Select the mediator
- Select a suitable executive
- Educate the executive about the process and the legal issues
- Help the executive think through goals for the process
- Assure that the executive thoroughly evaluates his and the adversary's BATNA and WATNA**
- Draft statements for submission to the mediator
- Prepare for effective presentations by counsel and client
- Counsel on management or suspension of litigation
- Assure the confidentiality of the process

Participation in Proceeding
- Advocate in a non-confrontational manner designed to impress the mediator and other side with the reasonableness of your position
- Listen carefully to the other side's statements, so as to understand their interests
- Ask questions
- Answer questions about legal claims and issues
- Serve as a sounding board for the client, brainstorming and discussing settlement options as the mediation progresses
- Help the client articulate business concerns and formulate proposals
- Avoid compromise of the client's litigation position should the mediation fail
- Be aware of legal ramifications of possible solutions and options
- Re-evaluate BATNAs and WATNAs in light of new information
- Draft the settlement agreement and assure its enforceability

The skills required for effective mediation advocacy differ substantially from trial advocacy skills. Exaggeration or making what lawyers call "a jury appeal" is counterproductive in mediation. Arguments that are likely to offend or fail to impress the mediator or the adversary should be soft pedaled. Some trial lawyers may have difficulty adjusting to the mediation environment.

Role of Neutral Organization
Mediation services are being offered by an increasing number of national, regional and local organizations. Essentially, three types of services may be provided:

(a) Help bring parties to the table, i.e. secure their agreement to participate in the process.
(b) Identify candidates well qualified to serve as mediator in the particular dispute, secure the agreement of all parties to the retention of one of the candidates, recruit that person and make compensation arrangements.
(c) Administer the proceeding.

Once an adversarial relationship has developed, a party who wishes to engage in mediation may be reluctant to take the lead in "selling" mediation to its adversaries or may have difficulty persuading them to mediate. A neutral organization can play a useful role in explaining the mediation process and its advantages to parties whose agreement to participate is being sought. CPR has successfully played that role in numerous cases involving both few and very large numbers of parties.

Selection of a well qualified mediator in whom all parties have confidence is the most critical step in assuring the success of the mediation. Parties often need the assistance of a neutral organization in the selection process. CPR's Panels of Distinguished Neutrals have the highest qualifications, and CPR regularly assists parties in selecting the "right" mediator.

Given the highly informal and voluntary nature of mediation, CPR believes that once the mediator is in place, the parties and the mediator do not need a neutral organization as an "administrator" of the process; indeed, the involvement of such an organization can be counter-productive. However, a number of organizations offer that service.

Role of Insurers
In certain cases one or more insurers are direct parties to the dispute, as in a coverage dispute with a policyholder or in an allocation dispute among insurers. Obviously, these insurers must be at the table.

In other cases, the immediate parties are not insurers, but one or more insurers are expected to bear all or part of the liability of a party, and any settlement therefore will be subject to their approval. Under these circumstances, it is essential for the policyholder to assure in advance that the insurers do not object to the insured's participation in the mediation. It will be desirable for the insurers to agree informally in advance to the parameters of a settlement, and for the insured to keep the insurers informed as the mediation progresses. Representation of the insurers in the mediation, or in certain phases, is common. Before agreeing to a settlement the policyholder should ascertain whether the terms are acceptable to the insurers. Reaching an agreement with the other side, subject to uncertain insurer approval, is not a desirable solution.

If insurers are denying coverage to which a policyholder believes it is entitled, or if differences exist among two or more insurers as to allocation of coverage among them, a second mediation may be in order, entirely separate from mediation of the underlying dispute or meshed with it. Sometimes it is productive to involve insurers in the primary mediation process, as well as to conduct a "secondary" insurance mediation.

"Selling" Mediation to the Other Party

The other party may well have to be "sold" on mediation, especially if it lacks prior experience. A suggestion or offer to mediate may not suffice. The advantages of mediation to both sides should be carefully explained. The proposer should emphasize that:

- The procedure is non-binding unless and until a settlement agreement is signed.
- The procedure is confidential.
- The parties retain control over the outcome.
- This particular dispute is well suited to mediation and mediation has worked in comparable situations.
- There is a likelihood of substantial savings in legal fees and other litigation costs and of a much quicker and more satisfactory outcome.
- The risk for each party is minimal.
- Mediation is much less adversarial and disruptive of business relationships than litigation or arbitration.
- The mediator must be acceptable to both parties.
- The ground rules must be acceptable to both parties.
- Either party may withdraw at any time after the first session.
- The parties may agree on limited discovery, if needed.
- The cost of the procedure is likely to be relatively modest.
- Experience shows that the chances of success are high. An 85% success rate is the commonly accepted average.
- The proposer will negotiate in good faith and trusts the other party will do likewise.
- Even if the procedure should not succeed, much will be gained through better mutual understanding, and the cost of the legal proceedings that follow is likely to be reduced substantially.

If the parties have a contractual relationship and the contract calls for ADR, the relevant clause should be invoked. If the initiating party has subscribed to a CPR policy on ADR, the policy may be invoked even if the other party is not a subscriber.

Special inducements to use ADR sometimes can persuade the adversary into the process, such as:

- Monetary Incentives: Offers to pay for the initial meeting with a me diator to determine if the process can be helpful to the parties, with shared costs beyond the first meeting; offers to pay the entire mediator fee unless the mediation is successful.
- Allowing the Opponent to Select the Neutral so long as significant con flicts of interest are not present. This technique has been used so the opponent feels confident in the neutral and may accept any recommenda tions more readily.

When litigation is pending, a judge can be very persuasive in convincing a reluctant party to participate in ADR. Indeed, the court may have a mandatory ADR program.

When the opponent cannot be convinced to use ADR for the entire matter, isolating a key issue or factual dispute, or even the damage portion for submission to ADR, might result in partial ADR use.

Consideration should be given to who should approach whom. Who is most likely to be receptive to early settlement and ADR? Who has had prior ADR experience? Who appears to be the principal decision-maker on the issue? Success will depend in part on the persuasiveness of the proposer.

If the persons to be induced to mediate are not familiar with the process, it may help to provide them with a copy of this paper or with other reading material (see the Selected Bibliography at page 38). Moreover, a neutral organization, such as CPR, may play a useful role in persuading parties of the advantages of mediation.

Timing of Mediation

The timing of a mediation is a major issue. The opportunities for savings in legal fees and other costs are greatest if mediation takes place early on—and is successful. In many cases the type of information exchange that can readily occur within the mediation framework will provide each side with the information it needs to evaluate its case and to responsibly negotiate a settlement. If either party believes firmly that it must engage in more extensive discovery, meaningful negotiations may have to be deferred until sufficient discovery has taken place, which still should fall far short of discovery required for a court trial. The desire to await the judge's decision on a dispositive motion is another reason sometimes given for deferring mediation.

It is not uncommon for a mediation process to be commenced, and for the parties and the mediator to agree to suspend the process until certain events have taken place.

Psychological factors can work for or against early productive mediation. The animosity often encountered at the outset of a dispute may diminish or become further exacerbated as litigation unfolds. Some persons simply are not prepared to "bite the bullet" until they have suffered the costs and burdens of full-scale pre-trial activity for awhile, but if mediation is delayed until pre-trial activity is substantially completed, the potential benefits will be greatly reduced.

Length of Procedure
The length of a mediation depends on factors such as the complexity of the case, the number and availability of the parties, the urgency, and the difficulty of reaching agreement on settlement terms. In any event, length usually will be measured in weeks, not in years. Most mediations are concluded in two to four sessions. The mediator may give the parties an estimate of the length of time required for each phase of the proceeding. Moreover, even during the early phases of the procedure the party representatives will develop a sense of the likelihood of success and of the approximate length of time that will be required. Note that under the Procedure any party may withdraw from the mediation at any time after the first session.

It is not uncommon for parties to agree to mediation on the express condition that a party will be permitted to commence litigation or arbitration if the mediation is not concluded within a specified period. Presumably that option will not be exercised if, when the deadline is reached, the prospective plaintiff is optimistic as to the outcome of the mediation.

The Cost
CPR panelists normally charge by the hour. Rates vary by location and by individual and are determined in advance of appointment. In 1998, most will charge in the range of $250-$350. The number of hours spent by the mediator might be in the range of 15-25 hours, exclusive of any required travel time. In 1998 CPR's standard fee for its assistance in selection of a mediator is $2,500.

The mediator's fee and other mediation expenses are normally shared equally. However, sometimes a party proposing mediation will offer to bear the expense of the early phase of the procedure in order to induce the other party or parties to try the process. Each party typically bears its own legal fees and other expenses.

The Site

If possible, the mediation should occur at a convenient neutral, congenial site—typically the mediator's office. There should be sufficient space for both joint sessions and separate caucuses. Refreshments should be available. Normally the mediator will attempt to reach agreement with the parties on the site, which need not be the same for all meetings. A site specified in a contract may be changed by agreement.

Confidentiality

[This section is adapted from CPR's Videotape Study Guide, Mediation in Action: Resolving A Complex Business Dispute, 1994.]

Among dispute resolution processes, mediation offers a maximum degree of confidentiality and privacy. Contractual and legal protections provide additional assurances against use or disclosure of mediation statements or documents. These confidentiality protections contrast sharply with the public nature of the litigation process and its procedures that encourage public disclosure.

Contractual Protections

Parties can increase the chances that mediation participants will maintain the confidentiality of the process by entering into various confidentiality agreements.

- Parties can execute a written confidentiality agreement reciting the pro tections of existing federal and state laws and privileges and agreeing not to reveal any information about the process. Adoption of the CPR Mediation Procedure provides these assurances of confidentiality, pro scribes transcription of meetings and requires the mediator to return docu ments to the originating party upon request without retention of copies.
- Mediators can execute confidentiality agreements as part of their re tainer provisions. (See Form of Model Agreement for Parties and Me diator Proceeding, annexed to the Mediation Procedure.)
- In the event of witness or expert attendance at mediation, some parties and mediators take the precaution of having them sign a confidentiality agreement as well.

Confidentiality contracts are well advised in view of limitations, gaps and variations in existing statutory confidentiality protections. Some courts may intrude into mediation confidentiality since the law is still developing in this area. There is also uncertainty whether federal courts will apply the confidentiality statutes of states in which a mediation is held. Nonetheless, confidentiality agreements may support party damage claims in the face of party breach. Some mediators may require indemnification from the parties for expenses they incurred in defending the confidentiality of the process and the documents it produces.

Statutory Protections

Various statutory principles protect the confidentiality of mediation. They vary significantly, however, in the extent of coverage afforded.

Federal Protections. Mediation, a form of negotiation facilitated by a third party neutral, enjoys the traditional protections associated with negotiation incorporated in the following rules. However, these rules have significant limitations.

Federal Rule of Evidence 408 protects against admissibility into evidence in subsequent proceedings in which the Federal Rules of Evidence apply of settlement offers and compromises made in negotiations over a disputed claim if the evidence is offered to prove liability or invalidity of the claim or the amount. Evidence of conduct or statements made in compromise negotiations are also inadmissible.

The Rule does not bar discovery of such information or admission into evidence for purposes other than validity of the claim (e.g., impeachment). Courts will frequently weigh Section 408 and Federal Rule of Civil Procedure 26(b) in analyzing discovery requests.

Federal Rule of Civil Procedure 68 prohibits later admissibility, for any purposes, of unaccepted offers of judgment (as defined in the rule) made in negotiations conducted during litigation.

State Statutory Protections: Varied Coverage. While ADR evidentiary or procedural codes of most states protect mediation confidentiality, the extent of such protection covers a wide spectrum. Often the statute is tied to a particular type of mediation or program.

Some statutes have broad coverage. For example, California Evidence Code, § 1152.2 prohibits admission or discovery of mediation statements and documents where there is a written confidentiality agreement, while § 703.5 prohibits mediators from testifying about mediation in related proceedings. In Massachusetts, mediation is confidential only if the mediator satisfies particular training, experience or affiliation criteria in the statute and if the agreement to mediate is in writing (Massachusetts Annotated Laws, Chapter 233, § 23C). The Texas Civil Practice and Remedies Code, § 154.073, protects all private or court-related mediation participants from compulsory process and makes all ADR records confidential.

Common Law

While privileges often are created by statute, case law is developing at the state and federal levels applying privileges to mediation and other facilitative ADR processes. Privileges may be applied wholly outside any specific ADR statutory provisions.

Court Rules

Special confidentiality rules applicable to court-related mediation may apply. Such rules need to be reviewed to determine their scope and protections.

CONTRACT CLAUSES

The best time to agree on a sensible way to resolve a business dispute is before any dispute has arisen. Once one has erupted, it can be much more difficult for parties to agree about anything. CPR strongly encourages the inclusion of multistep ADR clauses in business agreements, calling for the following steps, with appropriate time limits on steps 1 and 2.

1. Negotiation between Executives
2. Mediation
3. Arbitration or Litigation

A Drafter's Guide to CPR Dispute Resolution Clauses (CPR, 1998) offers a variety of sample clauses and commentary.

A clause providing for mediation of future disputes appears in Section 1 of the Mediation Procedure.

Whether or not the parties' business agreement provides for mediation, they may enter into a submission agreement such as that set forth in Section 1 of the Mediation Procedure once a dispute has arisen and they have agreed to engage in mediation.

adr readings and training

Persons who expect to participate in a mediation proceeding as an attorney or executive may improve their understanding of the process and their skill and their comfort level as "players" in a number of ways.

The literature of mediation has exploded apace with its use. In the Selected Bibliography, below, we list but a few works that we believe will be particularly helpful to persons contemplating participation in a mediation. CPR's 35-minute videotape, Mediation in Action: Resolving a Complex Business Dispute, demonstrates dramatically the dynamics of the mediation process. The tape and accompanying Videotape Study Guide will greatly deepen understanding of how mediation works in practice.

For skill development, interactive training in mediation has a value well beyond reading about the process or even watching a videotape. The CPR Training Program to Assure ADR Proficiency and CPR's trainers regularly are given highest marks by their "students." CPR's standard program for mediators is a two-day program; that for advocates and executives is of one-day's duration. Other organizations also offer sound training.

Selected Bibliography

Aaron, Marjorie Corman. "The Value of Decision Analysis in Mediation Practice." 11:2 Negotiation Journal 123 (April 1995).

Baruch-Bush, Robert. "Mediation and Adjudication: Dispute Resolution & Ideology: An Imaginary Conversation." 2 Journal of Contemporary Legal Issues (1990).

Brett, Jeanne M., Zoe I. Barsness and Stephen B. Goldberg. "The Effectiveness of Mediation: An Independent Analysis of Cases Handled by Four Major Service Providers." The Negotiation Journal (July 1996).

Buhring-Uhle, Christian. Arbitration and Mediation in International Business (Kluwer Law International, 1996).

Cooley, John. Mediation Advocacy, National Institute for Trial Advocacy (1996).

Dauer, Edward R. "Manual of Dispute Resolution: ADR Law and Practice." (Shepard's McGraw-Hill, 1994).

Feinberg, Kenneth R. "Mediation - A Preferred Method of Dispute Resolution." 16 Pepperdine Law Review 54 (1989).

Fisher, Roger, and William L. Ury, Getting to Yes. New York: Houghton Mifflin Co. (1981).

Folberg, Jay and Alison Taylor. "Mediation: A Comprehensive Guide to Resolving Conflicts Without Litigation." (Jossey-Bass Inc. 1984).

Freund, James C. "The Neutral Negotiator - Why and How Mediation Can Work to Resolve Dollar Disputes." Prentice Hall Law & Business (1994).

Galton, Eric. "Mediation: A Texas Practice Guide." (Texas Lawyer Press, 1993).

Golann, Dwight. Mediating Legal Disputes, Little Brown and Co. (1996).

Goldberg, Stephen B. and Frank E.A. Sander "Fitting the Fuss to the Forum: A

User Friendly Guide to Selecting an ADR Process." The Negotiation Journal (January 1994).

Goldberg, Stephen B., Frank E.A. Sander and Nancy Rogers. "Dispute Resolution: Negotiation, Mediation, and Other Processes." (Little Brown & Co. Second Edition, 1992).

Holz, Sara and Stephanie E. Smith. "Bad Reasons Good Lawyers Give for Not Using Mediation." ACCA Docket (November/December 1995).

Menkel-Meadow, Carrie. "Toward Another View of Legal Negotiation: The Structure of Problem Solving." 31 UCLA Law Review 754 (April 1984).

Mendel-Meadow, Carrie. "Ethics in Alternative Dispute Resolution: New Issues, No Answers from to Adversary Conception of Lawyers' Responsiblities." 38 South Texas Law Review 407 (May 1997).

Kovach, Kim. "Mediation." (West Publishing, 1994).

Moore, Christopher W. "The Mediation Process: Practical Strategies for Resolving Conflict." (Jossey-Bass, 1987).

Plapinger, Elizabeth, ed. "ADR Ethics: Selected Readings." (CPR, 1997).

Plapinger, Elizabeth and Donna Stienstra. "ADR and Settlement in the Federal District Courts: A Sourcebook for Judges and Lawyers." (Federal Judicial Center and CPR, 1996).

Riskin, Leonard L. "Understanding Mediator Orientations, Strategies and Techniques: A Grid for the Perplexed." 1 Harvard Negotiation L. Rev. 7 (Spring 1996).

Rogers, Nancy and Craig A. McEwen. "Mediation: Law, Policy, Practice." (Lawyer's Cooperative Publishing, 1989).

Singer, Linda R. "Settling Disputes: Conflict Resolution in Business, Families and the Legal System." (Westview Press, 2d Edition, 1990).

Ury, William, Jeanne Brett and Stephen B. Goldberg. "Getting Disputes Resolved: Defining Systems to Cut the Costs of Conflict." (Jossey-Bass Management Series and Jossey-Bass Social and Behavioral Science Series, 1988).

Ury, William. "Getting Past No; Negotiating Your Way From Confrontation To Cooperation." Rev Ed. (Bantam Publishing, Feb 1993).

SELECTED ARTICLES FROM ALTERNATIVES

Alternatives is a national ADR newsletter published by the CPR Institute for Dispute Resolution. It focuses on cutting-edge trends and information and acts as a practice guide for companies, firms and the courts. The articles listed below are available on WESTLAW® and LEXIS-NEXIS®. From the WESTLAW directory screen, enter <db ALTHCL>. On LEXIS, select the <ADR> library, then enter <altern>. Contact CPR for subscription information at (212) 949-6490 or by E-mail at Alternatives@cpradr.org.

A Style Index for Mediators, 15 Alternatives 157 (December 1997)

How Structure Helps Mediation, 15 Alternatives 110 (September 1997)

Federal Courts on Mediation: A Settlement Agreement is Upheld, a Firm is Disqualified, 15 Alternatives 111 (September 1997)

Mediation Without Administration, 15 Alternatives 65 (May 1997)

Planning for Mediation Evaluation, 15 Alternatives 49 (April 1997)

Benefits and Dangers of Mediation Evaluation, 15 Alternatives 35 (March 1997)

Mediating in Cyberspace, 14 Alternatives 128 (November 1996)

Evaluating Mediation for Coverage Cases, 14 Alternatives 107 (October 1996)

Mediating in the Dance for Dollars, 14 Alternatives 102 (September 1996)

Handling Potential Conflicts in Mediation, 14 Alternatives 83 (July/August 1996)

In Mediation, Caucus Can Be a Powerful Tool, 14 Alternatives 62 (May 1996)

ADR Toolbox: The Highwire Art of Evaluation, 14 Alternatives 62 (May 1996)

Laying Foundation for Successful Mediation: Questions Neutrals and Parties Need to Ask, 13 Alternatives 132 (October 1995)

ADR Resolves $1 Billion Suit, 13 Alternatives 85 (July 1995)

20 Common Errors in Mediation, Advocacy 13 Alternatives 48 (April 1995)

Getting Reluctant Parties To Mediate: A Guide for Advocates, 13 Alternatives 9 (January 1995)

Mediator Orientations, Strategies and Techniques, 13 Alternatives 109 (September 1994)

Mediation Preparation and Advocacy, 12 Alternatives 8 (August 1994)

What Makes an Effective Mediator? 12 Alternatives 101 (August 1994)

Index

Advisory Committee on Business
and the Environment   131, 160, 161

Agreement   29, 30, 80, 123, 131, 211, 212, 216, 218

Associations-

SPIDR	12, 21, 22, 26, 37, 49, 53, 55, 58
NIDR	21, 22, 26, 46, 47, 48, 53
CEDR	122, 161, 212, 218
ENDISPUTE	
Mediation Institute	22
FMCS	35
AAA	35,51
National Family Mediation	122

Campaigns - non-violent   188

Case studies -

Munchehagen	74
Neuss	74, 86, 87, 88, 89, 90, 91, 92, 93, 94, 95, 97, 98, 99, 108, 112, 113
Snoqualmie River Dam	18, 20, 21, 50, 53
Greyrocks Dam	19
National Coal Project	19, 20, 47
Storm King Mountain	20,51
Brent Spar	121, 131, 132, 133
Twyford Down	121
Blackdown Hills	126, 127, 128, 161
Highways Agency	129,130
Eastern Group PLC	139

Consensus building-   9, 17, 22, 23, 24, 25, 26, 33,34, 35, 40,119, 120, 121,123, 124,125, 126 127, 133, 134, 135, 136, 140, 141, 142, 143, 145, 147, 149, 150, 151, 152, 153, 154, 156, 159, 160, 164, 190, 209

CONSENSUS newsletter   23, 26
Conferences   23, 46, 127, 128, 189, 190, 196
Contaminated Land   13, 60, 208
Cooperation principle   73, 111
Corruption   188, 199
Decision making-   collaborative 24
                       command   171, 172, 175, 176,178, 200
                       consultative   172, 173
                       co-operative   173

Environmental mediation - theory 27, 43
                         ADR   17, 28, 38, 46, 48, 49, 53, 56, 85, 119, 121, 122, 124, 163

                       EDR   16, 21, 22, 27, 28, 39, 40, 41, 42, 43, 45, 57, 60, 61, 66, 68, 70, 74, 77, 78, 79, 82, 168, 186

   particular difficulties-
                       costs   31, 40, 93, 104
                       definition of terms/disputes   30, 170
                       ecological systems - unique features   30
                       geographic boundaries   31
                       government involvement   181
                       implementation of agreement   32
                       issues - multiplicity/ complexity   30, 197
                       public interest -   claims 32
                                          definition   33
                       social/cultural factors   32, 189, 197
                       evaluation of environmental benefits   11, 38,39, 87, 98, 100, 133
Energy -   from waste   76

policy		78
renewable		134, 162

Enforcement -

	deficits	80
	inefficiencies	72

EPA	13, 24, 38, 55, 56

ETSU	134, 135, 160, 162

Experts-	choice	87, 129, 195, 211, 212
	neutrality	44

Finance -

	European life fund	127
	foundations-	
	Ford Foundation	21, 51, 52, 182
	Hewlett	
	Foundation	21, 52, 182
	universities	180
	other sources	22, 56, 94, 104, 112, 154, 182, 201

Government- local-

	Agenda 21	70, 119, 123, 126, 136, 153, 154, 155, 163, 164
	national- involvement	38
	mediators	
	data providers	
	trainers	
	control 146	

Growth management	
Hazardous substances	56, 78, 88
Highway siting	147
Industry - sectoral agreements 73	
industrial relations	17, 58
influence on EDR	65, 71

Information - scientific and technical	34

Local Agenda 21	70, 119, 123, 126, 136, 153, 154, 155, 163, 164

Mediation- application to constitutional/
legal rights or basic values   105
         family-   divorce/separation   122
         neighbourhood disputes   13, 17, 25, 50, 119,
                                             120, 121, 122, 153,
                                             170
         pre-public enquiry   144
         pre-litigation   215, 218
         procedures-   culture specific   190, 197
                   flexibility   35, 61, 63, 64, 69, 80,
                                         103, 142, 152, 157
                  ground rules 33, 213, 215
                  institutionalisation 17
                  safeguards   104, 105
         small claims   123
         strengths and benefits   39

Mediators - accountability   35
         administrative   188, 193
         appointment   212
         benevolent   193
         certification   36, 55
         code of behaviour   36, 37, 41, 42
         commercialisation   104, 106
         elders / community
         leaders as   43, 175, 192, 193
         government /
         court appointed   37, 38, 55
         independence   153
         in-house   153
         licensing   36
         neutrality / impartiality   21, 44, 55, 213
         numbers of
         professional and firms of   104, 107, 180, 181, 195
         professionalisation   37, 195, 196
         registration   37
         responsibilities   39, 94
         selection of   33, 35, 37, 41, 43, 54, 122,
                                             186, 193, 195, 196

         skills and techniques -
                  Metaplan   157
                  Carousel   158

                                                   c o m m o n

grounding1   158
             management of
             uncertainty   158
             social network   193
             specialist knowledge 37, 58, 94, 106
             training   104, 193, 195
             volunteer   25, 26, 37, 186

Meetings-   freedom of information   34
             public/private   56, 120, 127, 147
             transparency   44

Nature conservation   78
Planning/siting   13, 51, 58, 64, 66, 70, 76, 78, 82, 86,
                               107, 124, 129, 130, 144, 147, 160
Press   92, 188
Remediation - cost   56
             liability
Rulemaking - negotiated   23, 24, 50, 147
Settlements-   tailored   18, 19
             precedential value 40
             quality   19
Stakeholders- assistance to
             equal treatment
             finance
             identification of 28, 29, 33
             inequality   43
             joint fact finding 34
             NGOs   148, 168, 169, 180, 181
             numerous   28, 29
             participation by   24, 34, 41, 43, 87, 129, 151
             splinter groups   29
Sustainable development   13, 139
Transport   78
Waste Disposal   76, 86, 89, 97, 114
Water quality   13, 26, 168
Woolf -   Access to Justice   122, 161, 163